徳島県の教員採用試験過去問シリーズ ⑤

2025年度版

徳島県の英語科

過去問

協同教育研究会 編

協同出版

本書には，徳島県の教員採用試験の過去問題を収録しています。各問題ごとに，以下のように5段階表記で，難易度，頻出度を示しています。

難　易　度

非常に難しい	☆☆☆☆☆
やや難しい	☆☆☆☆
普通の難易度	☆☆☆
やや易しい	☆☆
非常に易しい	☆

頻　出　度

◎	ほとんど出題されない
◎◎	あまり出題されない
◎◎◎	普通の頻出度
◎◎◎◎	よく出題される
◎◎◎◎◎	非常によく出題される

※本書の過去問題における資料，法令文等の取り扱いについて

本書の過去問題で使用されている資料や法令文の表記や基準は，出題された当時の内容に準拠しているため，解答・解説も当時のものを使用しています。ご了承ください。

はじめに～「過去問」シリーズ利用に際して～

教育を取り巻く環境は変化しつつあり，日本の公教育そのものも，教員免許更新制の廃止やGIGAスクール構想の実現などの改革が進められています。また，現行の学習指導要領では「主体的・対話的で深い学び」を実現するため，指導方法や指導体制の工夫改善により，「個に応じた指導」の充実を図るとともに，コンピュータや情報通信ネットワーク等の情報手段を活用するために必要な環境を整えることが示されています。

一方で，いじめや体罰，不登校，暴力行為など，教育現場の問題もあいかわらず取り沙汰されており，教員に求められるスキルは，今後さらに高いものになっていくことが予想されます。

本書の基本構成としては，出題傾向と対策，過去5年間の出題傾向分析表，過去問題，解答および解説を掲載しています。各自治体や教科によって掲載年数をはじめ，「チェックテスト」や「問題演習」を掲載するなど，内容が異なります。

また原則的には一般受験を対象としております。特別選考等については対応していない場合があります。なお，実際に配布された問題の順番や構成を，編集の都合上，変更している場合があります。あらかじめご了承ください。

最後に，この「過去問」シリーズは，「参考書」シリーズとの併用を前提に編集されております。参考書で要点整理を行い，過去問で実力試しを行う，セットでの活用をおすすめいたします。

みなさまが，この書籍を徹底的に活用し，教員採用試験の合格を勝ち取って，教壇に立っていただければ，それはわたくしたちにとって最上の喜びです。

協同教育研究会

C O N T E N T S

第1部 徳島県の英語科 出題傾向分析 ……………3

第2部 徳島県の 教員採用試験実施問題 ……………7

▼2024年度教員採用試験実施問題 ……………8
▼2023年度教員採用試験実施問題 ……………22
▼2022年度教員採用試験実施問題 ……………37
▼2021年度教員採用試験実施問題 ……………53
▼2020年度教員採用試験実施問題 ……………74
▼2019年度教員採用試験実施問題 ……………94
▼2018年度教員採用試験実施問題 ……………112
▼2017年度教員採用試験実施問題 ……………130
▼2016年度教員採用試験実施問題 ……………147
▼2015年度教員採用試験実施問題 ……………165
▼2014年度教員採用試験実施問題 ……………183
▼2013年度教員採用試験実施問題 ……………201
▼2012年度教員採用試験実施問題 ……………218
▼2011年度教員採用試験実施問題 ……………231
▼2010年度教員採用試験実施問題 ……………247
▼2009年度教員採用試験実施問題 ……………260
▼2008年度教員採用試験実施問題 ……………276
▼2007年度教員採用試験実施問題 ……………289
▼2006年度教員採用試験実施問題 ……………301
▼2005年度教員採用試験実施問題 ……………316

第１部

徳島県の
英語科
出題傾向分析

徳島県の英語科　傾向と対策

2024年度に出題されたのは，会話1問，読解3問，英作文1問そして学習指導要領関連1問の合計6題であり，2023年度と問題構成は同様であった。配点は，大問1から順に，20点。16点，24点，36点，18点，36点の150点満点である。記述解答が約半数を占める。

会話問題は，中程度の長さの会話文の空所を適切な文で補充する形式である。会話のつながりが比較的つかみやすく，特に難しい点はない。選択肢それぞれの文頭の語に注意することと，会話の流れをつかむことが必要である。相手の言葉を受け止めた返事なのか，関連する話題や問題を持ち出しているのかを判断しながら解答することが重要である。

読解問題は依然として様々なトピックの英文について，多様な問題形式で出題されている。英文量としては，100語，350語，700語程度である。大問2は和訳問題である。特に難しい語句や文法事項は含まれていない。意味を違えることなく，こなれた日本語を心掛けよう。過去には，要約問題も出題されている。「重なっている内容部分を削り最も本質的な内容を残す」「一般的表現や例示は除き，抽象的表現でまとめられている部分を生かす」「論調が途中で変わっている場合は対比や列挙が明確に伝わるように表現する」などの点に注意してまとめるとよいだろう。大問3は小説からの出題である。小説は複数の登場人物と代名詞に注意し，主語の混同が起きないよう注意する。小説内では，登場人物が急に回想をし始める場面があるので時制の把握にも注意が必要である。また，会話の羅列だけで物語が展開することもある。慣れるという意味で，洋書の小説を読むことを勧める。

英作文問題については，「東京オリンピックの延期の原因と延期されたことによる課題」，「グローバル人材を育てるための英語の授業について」，「子供に親の家事を手伝わせるべきか」等，年度によっては書きにくいトピックもある。今後はどのような傾向になるかは読めないため，時事的な話題を含めた様々なトピックについて，自分の考えを英語でまとめる練習をしておくとよい。公開解答は，7文で書きあげている。1文15～20語程度を目安にしよう。ライティングは，テーマに関して時間内に正確に書くことが大切である。そのためには，まずゆっくりでもよいので制限文字数の英作文を何度もこなし，文法や語彙の正確さ，流暢さを徐々に上げていく訓練を意識的に行いたい。

学習指導要領に関する問題は，中学校と高等学校の別問題である。空欄にあてはまる語句を記述する問題である。配点も高く，かなり対策が必要である。これまでも，空所補充形式の形式が多かったが，ある項目について内容をそのまま記述せよとの出題がされたこともある。そのため，学習指導要領の概要をつかむだけでなく，正確に文言を記憶しておく必要がある。その際，英作文問題への対策として，実際の指導場面を思い浮かべながら理解をするとよいだろう。また，志望する校種の学習指導要領だけでなく，全校種の学習指導要領に目を通しておくことをおすすめしたい。学習指導要領が改訂される背景は共通しているため，小中高の学習指導要領で類似した記述が用いられる傾向にある。また，目標や内容については，小学校から中学校そして高校に上がっていくにつれて，段階を踏んで高度化していく。そのため，該当する記述の内容を思い出すことができなかった場合でも，他校種の学習指導要領の記述を参考にして推測できる。過去に英語で解答する問題も出題されており，また特に高校では学習指導要領の英訳からの出題もあるので，英文の学習指導要領も読んでおくことが必要である。

過去には，リスニング問題と文法・語法問題(空所補充問題と正誤問題)も出題されたことがある。特に，文法・語法力は英文読解を下支えする。これらの問題が再び出題される可能性は未知数であるが，ここ数年は軽微ながらも継続的に出題傾向が変わっていることを踏まえると，余裕があれば，他の自治体の過去問を含めた様々な問題形式に慣れておくと安心であろう。

過去5年間の出題傾向分析

◎：中高共通　●：中学　▲：高校

分類	設問形式	2020年度	2021年度	2022年度	2023年度	2024年度
リスニング	内容把握	◎	◎			
発音・アクセント	発音					
	アクセント					
	文強勢					
文法・語法	空所補充	◎	◎			
	正誤判断	◎	◎			
	一致語句					
	連立完成					
	その他					
会話文	短文会話					
	長文会話	◎	◎	◎	◎	◎
文章読解	空所補充	◎	◎	◎	◎	◎
	内容一致文		◎	◎	◎	
	内容一致語句					◎
	内容記述					
	英文和訳	◎	◎			◎
	英問英答		◎			
	その他	◎	◎	◎	◎	◎
英作文	整序					
	和文英訳					
	自由英作	◎	◎	◎	◎	◎
	その他					
学習指導要領		●▲	●▲	●▲	●▲	●▲

第2部

徳島県の
教員採用試験
実施問題

2024年度　実施問題

【中高共通】

【１】次の対話文を読んで，[(1)]～[(5)]にあてはまる最も適切な英文を，ア～キから選び，記号で答えなさい。ただし，同じ選択肢を2度使わないこと。

A : Is everything OK? You look nervous.

B : [(1)]

A : Take it easy. Students are really excited for your first lesson.

B : Me too. I want them to feel relaxed and have fun in my class.

A : You practiced your introduction many times. [(2)]

B : Thanks, but can we go to the classroom during the recess? I want to check that my presentation works correctly.

A : Of course. [(3)]

(After the class)

A : Did you enjoy your first class?

B : Yes, very much, but I spoke too fast. Could you give me some feedback?

A : Sure. I think your smile and eye contact created a warm atmosphere. [(4)]

B : Thank you. I was very happy that they were interested in me and asked many questions.

A : [(5)] But as you said, your English was too fast. Try to speak in simple English and talk slowly with big gestures.

B : Thank you for your advice. I can't wait for the next lesson.

ア　That made our students relaxed.

イ　You had a good interaction with them.

ウ　Better luck next time.

エ　I have butterflies in my stomach.

オ　You can never be too prepared.

カ　You just made my day.

キ　You only have to enjoy yourself.

(☆☆◎◎◎◎)

【2】次の英文の下線部(1)・(2)を日本語にしなさい。

Thanks to karaoke, more people are getting up the nerve to sing, and as research has shown, singing has definite physiological and psychological benefits. Like exercise, singing is an aerobic activity that increases our oxygen intake and boosts the cardiovascular system. When we sing, we breathe more deeply, and this helps us relax and reduces stress. (1)Research shows that singing releases endorphins — "feel good" chemicals — into the bloodstream, elevating our mood. Provided we can overcome our shyness, getting up and singing can bolster confidence. (2)Since most songs are about love, singing allows us to express our feelings and to reach out to others, which is why we feel such a personal connection to our favorite singers. In a nutshell, singing is good for our bodies, our hearts, and our souls.

(☆☆☆☆◎◎◎)

【3】次の英文を読んで，(1)～(4)の問いに答えなさい。

One day I was listening to the AM radio. I heard a song: "Oh, I Long to See My Mother in the Doorway." By God! I said, I understand that song. I have often longed to see my mother in the doorway. As a matter of fact, she did stand frequently in various doorways looking at me. She stood one day, just so, at the front door, the darkness of the hallway behind her. It was New Year's Day. She said sadly, If you come home at 4 A.M. when you're seventeen, what time will you come home when you're twenty? She asked this question without humor or meanness. She had begun her worried preparations for death. She would not be present, she thought, when I was twenty. So she wondered.

(a)

At the door of the kitchen she said, You never finish your lunch. You run around senselessly. What will become of you?

(b)

Naturally for the rest of my life I longed to see her, not only in doorways, in a great number of places — in the dining room with my aunts, at the window looking up and down the block, in the country garden among zinnias and marigolds, in the living room with my father.

①<u>They</u> sat in comfortable leather chairs. They were listening to Mozart. They looked at one another amazed. It seemed to them that they'd just come over on the boat. They'd just learned the first English words. It seemed to them that he had just proudly handed in a 100 percent correct exam to the American anatomy professor. It seemed as though she'd just quit the shop for the kitchen.

I (　②　) I could see her in the doorway of the living room.

(c)

She stood there a minute. Then she sat beside him. They owned an expensive record player. They were listening to Bach. She said to him, (　③　) to me a little. We don't (　③　) so much anymore.

(d)

I'm tired, he said. Can't you see? I saw maybe thirty people today. All sick, and all talk talk talk talk. Listen to the music, he said. I believe you once had perfect pitch. I'm tired, he said.

④<u>Then she died.</u>

(GLACE PALEY, MOTHER　設問の都合上，表記を改めた箇所がある。)

(1)　下線部①は誰のことを指すか，日本語で書きなさい。

(2)　(　②　)にあてはまる最も適切な語を，1語で書きなさい。

(3) (③)には同じ語が入る。(③)にあてはまる最も適切な語を本文中から選び，1語で書きなさい。ただし，小文字で書き始めること。

(4) 下線部④は[(a)]～[(d)]のいずれかにも入る。最も適切な位置を[(a)]～[(d)]から1つ選び記号で答えなさい。

(☆☆☆◎◎◎)

【4】次の英文を読んで，(1)～(3)の問いに答えなさい。

Love of play is the most obvious distinguishing mark of young animals, whether human or otherwise. [(a)] Play and pretence are a vital need of childhood, for which opportunity must be provided if the child is to be happy and healthy quite independently of any further utility in these activities. There are two questions which concern education in this connection: first, what should parents and schools do in the way of providing opportunity? and secondly, should they do anything more, with a view to increasing the educational usefulness of games?

Let us begin with a few words about the psychology of games. There are two separate questions in this matter: the first is as to the impulses which produce play, the second is as to its biological utility. The second is the easier question. There seems no reason to doubt the most widely accepted theory, that in play the young of any species rehearse and practise the activities which they will have to perform in earnest later on. The play of puppies is exactly like a dog-fight, except that they do not actually bite each other. The play of kittens resembles the behaviour of cats with mice. [(b)] And they enjoy anything that gives them new muscular facilities, such as jumping, climbing, or walking up a narrow plank — always provided the task is not too difficult. But although this accounts, in a general way, for the usefulness of the play-impulse, it does not by any means cover all its manifestations, and must not for a moment be regarded as giving a psychological analysis.

Some psycho-analysts have tried to see a sexual symbolism in children's play. This, I am convinced, is utter moonshine. The main instinctive urge of childhood is not sex, but the desire to become adult, or, perhaps more correctly, the will to power. The child is impressed by his own weakness in comparison with older people, and he wishes to become their equal. I remember my boy's profound delight when he realized that he would one day be a man and that I had once been a child; one could see effort being stimulated by the realization that success was possible. From a very earl yage, the child wishes to do what older people do, as is shown by the practice of imitation. [(c)] The feeling of inferiority is very strong in children; when they are normal and rightly educated, it is a stimulus to effort, but if they are repressed it may become a source of unhappiness.

In play, we have two forms of the will to power: the form which consists in learning to do things, and the form which consists in fantasy. Just as the balked adult may indulge in day-dreams that have a sexual significance, so the normal child indulges in pretences that have a power-significance. [(d)] When I told my boy the story of Jack the Giant-Killer, I tried to make him identify himself with Jack, but he firmly chose the giant. When his mother told him the story of Bluebeard, he insisted on being Bluebeard, and regarded the wife as justly punished for insubordination. In his play, there was a sanguinary outbreak of cutting off ladies' heads. Sadism, Freudians would say; but he enjoyed just as much being a giant who ate little boys, or an engine that could pull a heavy load. Power, not sex, was the common element in these (　　). One day, when we were returning from a walk, I told him, as an obvious joke, that perhaps we should find a certain Mr. Tiddliewinks in possession of our house, and he might refuse to let us in. After that, for a long time, he would stand on the porch being Mr. Tiddliewinks, and telling me to go to another house. [(e)]

(Bertrand Russell, 'Play and Fancy' from *On Education*　設問の都合上，表記を改めた箇所がある。)

(1)　[(a)]～[(e)]にあてはまる最も適切な英文を，ア～オから選び，記号で答えなさい。ただし，同じ選択肢を2度使わないこと。

ア　Children love to imitate any work they have been watching, such as building or digging; the more important the work seems to them, the more they like to play at it.

イ　He likes to be a giant, or a lion, or a train; in his make-believe, he inspires terror.

ウ　His delight in this game was unbounded, and obviously the pretence of power was what he enjoyed.

エ　In human children, this is accompanied by an inexhaustible pleasure in pretence.

オ　Older brothers and sisters are useful, because their purposes can be understood and their capacities are not so far out of reach as those of grown-up people.

(2)　下線部の語の本文中での意味として最も適切なものをア～エから選び，記号で答えなさい。

ア　darkness　　イ　pleasure　　ウ　purity　　エ　nonsense

(3)　(　　)にあてはまる最も適切な語を本文中から選び，1語で書きなさい。

(☆☆☆☆◎◎◎)

【5】AIが私たちの生活で使われている例を示し，その長所と短所を述べたうえで，あなた自身の考えを90語～110語の英語で書きなさい。ただし，符号は語数に含めず，(　　)内に使用語数を書き入れること。

(☆☆☆☆◎◎◎)

【中学校】

【1】中学校学習指導要領「第2章　各教科」「第9節　外国語」について，次の(1)～(3)の問いに答えなさい。

(1)　次の文は「第2　各言語の目標及び内容等」「英語」「1　目標」「(3)　話すこと[やり取り]」である。(　a　)～(　c　)にあてはまる語句を書きなさい。

ア　関心のある事柄について，簡単な語句や文を用いて(　a　)で伝え合うことができるようにする。

イ　日常的な話題について，事実や(　b　)，気持ちなどを整理し，簡単な語句や文を用いて伝えたり，相手からの質問に答えたりすることができるようにする。

ウ　社会的な話題に関して(　c　)したことについて，考えたことや感じたこと，その理由などを，簡単な語句や文を用いて述べ合うことができるようにする。

(2)　次の文は「第2　各言語の目標及び内容等」「英語」「2　内容」「(3)　言語活動及び言語の働きに関する事項」の一部である。(　a　)～(　f　)にあてはまる語句を書きなさい。

> ①　言語活動に関する事項
>
> ウ　読むこと
>
> (ア)　書かれた内容や文章の構成を考えながら黙読したり，その内容を表現するよう(　a　)したりする活動。
>
> (イ)　日常的な話題について，簡単な表現が用いられている広告やパンフレット，予定表，(　b　)，電子メール，短い文章などから，自分が必要とする情報を読み取る活動。
>
> (ウ)　簡単な語句や文で書かれた日常的な話題に関する短い説明やエッセイ，物語などを読んで(　c　)を把握する活動。

> ②　言語の働きに関する事項
>
> イ　言語の働きの例
>
> (ア)　コミュニケーションを円滑にする
>
> ・話し掛ける　・(　d　)　・聞き直す
>
> ・繰り返す　など

(ウ)　事実・情報を伝える
・説明する　・報告する　・発表する
・(　e　)する　など
(オ)　相手の行動を促す
・質問する　・(　f　)する　・招待する
・命令する　など

(3)　次の文は「第2　各言語の目標及び内容等」「英語」「3　指導計画の作成と内容の取扱い」の(2)の一部である。(　a　)～(　c　)にあてはまる語句を書きなさい。

ク　各単元や各時間の指導に当たっては，コミュニケーションを行う(　a　)などを明確に設定し，言語活動を通して育成すべき(　b　)を明確に示すことにより，生徒が学習の(　c　)を立てたり，振り返ったりすることができるようにすること。

(☆☆☆☆◎◎◎◎)

【高等学校】

【1】高等学校学習指導要領「第2章　各学科に共通する各教科」「第8節　外国語」について，次の(1)～(3)の問いに答えなさい。

(1)　次は「第2款　各科目」「第1　英語コミュニケーションⅠ」「1　目標」「(5)　書くこと」の一部である。(　①　)～(　④　)にあてはまる語句を書きなさい。

イ　社会的な話題について，使用する語句や文，事前の準備などにおいて，多くの支援を活用すれば，(　①　)したことを基に，(　②　)な語句や文を用いて，情報や考え，気持ちなどを(　③　)に注意して(　④　)を書いて伝えることができるようにする。

(2)　次は「第2款　各科目」「第4　論理・表現Ⅰ」「2　内容」「(3)　言語活動及び言語の働きに関する事項」「①　言語活動に関する事項」「イ　話すこと[発表]」の一部である。(　①　)～(　④　)にあてはまる語句を書きなさい。

(ア)　関心のある事柄や(　①　)などの日常的な話題について，使用する語句や文，(　②　)が十分に示されたり，準備のための多くの時間が確保されたりする状況で，情報や考え，気持ちなどを適切な理由や(　③　)とともに話して伝える活動。また，発表した内容について，(　④　)をしたり，意見や感想を伝え合ったりする活動。

(3)　次は「第3款　英語に関する各科目にわたる指導計画の作成と内容の取扱い」の一部である。(　①　)～(　④　)にあてはまる語句を書きなさい。

2　内容の取扱いに当たっては，次の事項に配慮するものとする。 (8)　生徒が身に付けるべき資質・能力や生徒の実態，教材の内容などに応じて，視聴覚教材や(　①　)，情報通信ネットワーク，教育機器などを有効活用し，生徒の(　②　)をより高めるとともに，英語による情報の(　③　)に慣れさせるために，キーボードを使って英文を入力するなどの活動を効果的に取り入れることにより，指導の効率化や(　④　)の更なる充実を図るようにすること。

(☆☆☆☆◎◎◎◎)

解答・解説

【中高共通】

【1】(1) エ　(2) キ　(3) オ　(4) ア　(5) イ

〈解説〉(1) 「緊張しているようですね」に対して，エ「私はドキドキしています」。have butterflies in one's stomachは「緊張する，ドキドキする」の意味。　(2) AがBを励ます場面。「あなたは何度も導入を練習しました」に続いて，キ「あなたが楽しめばいい」が入る。　(3) 休み時間に教室に行って，プレゼンテーションが正しく機能するかチェックしたいと言うBに，オ「備えあれば憂いなし(準備しすぎることはない)」。　(4) AがBに授業のフィードバックをしている場面。「あなたの笑顔とアイコンタクトがあたたかい雰囲気をつくっていた」に続き，ア「それが生徒たちをリラックスさせました」。　(5) さらなるフィードバックとして，イ「彼らと良いやりとりができていました」。

【2】(1) 研究によると，歌うことで「気分を良くする」化学物質であるエンドルフィンが血流に放出され，気分が高揚することがわかっています。恥ずかしさを克服できれば，立ち上がって歌うことで自信を高めることができます。　(2) 歌は愛に関するものが多いので，歌うことによって自分の気持ちを表現したり，人と心を通わせたりすることができます。だから，私たちは好きな歌手に個人的なつながりを感じるのです。つまり，歌うことは私たちの体，心，そして魂に良い影響を与えるのです。

〈解説〉(1) release～「～を放つ」。elevate～「～を高める」。Provided(that)～「～という条件で，～であれば」。bolster～「～を支える，～を強める」。　(2) allow O to～「Oに～することを許す，Oに～することを可能にさせる」。reach out to～「～に手を伸ばす，～とつながる」。"which is why～"のwhichは前文の内容を受ける関係詞。「それが～である理由だ，だから～だ」と訳すことができる。in a nutshell

「簡潔に言えば，要するに」。

【３】(1)　筆者(作者)の父と母(両親)　(2)　wish　(3)　talk
(4)　(b)

〈解説〉(1)　生前の母と父のことを思い出している。theyは筆者の両親を指す。　(2)　I wish I could see her in the doorway of the living room.「リビングルームの入り口に彼女が見えたらいいのに」と仮定法の文にする。　(3)　talkを挿入する。母が父に「少しは私に話をして。私たちはもうあまり話をしていないわ」と言うが，父はおしゃべりをしないで，音楽を聞くように言ってそれを拒む流れになる。　(4)　第1段落では，母が死への準備を始めていたこと，母は筆者が20歳になるころには自分はもういないだろうと思ったことが書かれている。第2段落の「あなたは昼食を食べ終わらない。意味もなく走り回る。あなたはどうなるの」と母が筆者を心配するせりふのあとに，「それから彼女は亡くなった」が入る。母の死後，筆者がいろいろな場所で彼女に会いたいと思ったことが書かれている第3段落に続く。

【４】(1)　(a)　エ　(b)　ア　(c)　オ　(d)　イ　(e)　ウ
(2)　エ　(3)　pretences

〈解説〉(1)　(a)　冒頭の文は「遊び好きであることは，人間であろうとなかろうと，幼い動物の最も明白な特徴である」。空所には，エ「人間の子どもの場合，これには無尽蔵のごっこ遊び(まねごと)の楽しさが伴う」が入り，「遊びやごっこ遊び(まねごと)は子ども時代に不可欠な欲求であり…」と続く。　(b)　子犬や子猫の遊びに言及後，人間の子どもの遊びについて具体的に述べている部分。空所には，ア「子どもは，彼らが見ている仕事，たとえば建物を建てたり，掘ったりする仕事を真似るのが大好きである。子どもにとって重要に思える仕事であればあるほど，その遊びが好きになる」が入る。　(c)　子どもの「大人になりたいという欲求」について述べている部分。空所直前「幼い頃から，子どもは年上の人がやっていることをやりたがる」に続いて，オ「年上の兄や姉は役に立つ。なぜなら，彼らの目的は理解できるし，彼らの能力は大人のそれほど手の届かないものではないからだ」が入る。 (d) 空所前の文は「挫折した大人が性的な意味合いを持つ白昼夢にふけることがあるように，正常な子どもは権力志向の意味合いを持つごっこ遊び(まねごと)にふけるものである」という意味。よって，イ「子どもは巨人やライオンや列車になりたがる；作り話の中で，子どもは恐怖をかき立てる」が入る。 (e) 空所前は，筆者と息子のエピソード。「…，私はまったくの冗談として，ひょっとするとMr. Tiddliewinksがわが家を占領して中に入れてくれないかもしれない」と息子に言った。それからというもの，長い間，息子は自分がTiddliewinksだと言って玄関の前に立ち，私に向かってよその家へ行くようにと言ったものである」。これに続いて，ウ「このゲーム(勝ち負けのある遊び)をするときの息子の喜びようは無限で，息子が楽しんでいたのは明らかに自分に権力があるかのようなまねをすることであった」が入る。 (2) 筆者は，子ども時代の本能的な衝動は性ではなく，大人になりたいという欲求だと考えている。よって「子どもの遊びの中に性的な意味を見出そうとする者もいる。これは全くの『戯言』であると私は確信している」となる。moonshineは「たわごと，たわけた考え」という意味で，nonsenseと同意。 (3) 空所の前の文には「筆者の息子は小さい男の子たちを食べてしまう巨人の話や，重い荷物をひっぱる機関車になることも楽しんでいた」と述べられている。これを受けて，「これらのpretences『ごっこ遊び(まねごと)』に見られる共通の要素は，性ではなく権力志向であった」となる。

【5】AI is useful for us in many situations in our lives. For example, AI robots can do things that humans cannot do, such as working in dangerous places or carrying heavy loads. If we don't have enough workers, we can substitute AI for them. However, we must also keep in mind that it may change us for the worse. If we rely too much on AI and stop learning new things, AI will take away our human jobs. This is serious because we may not be able to think and live on our own. To avoid this, we should coexist with AI while valuing thinking and learning by ourselves. (109 words)

〈解説〉解答例では，AIロボットが危険な場所での作業や重い荷物の運搬，労働者不足の代用などに役立つことを挙げている。一方で，AIに頼りすぎることで，人間が自分で考え，生きていくことができなくなるかもしれない危険性を指摘し，自分で考え学ぶことを大切にしながら，AIと共存していかなければならないとまとめている。他にも，生産性，コスト削減，業務の効率化などの利点やセキュリティリスクなどにも触れることができるだろう。

【中学校】

【1】(1)　a　即興　　b　自分の考え　　c　聞いたり読んだり
(2)　a　音読　　b　手紙　　c　概要　　d　相づちを打つ　　e　描写　　f　依頼　　(3)　a　目的，場面，状況　　b　資質・能力　　c　見通し

〈解説〉他の自治体でも頻出の問題ではあるが，全て記述式解答でありハードルが高い。中学校学習指導要領(2017(平成29)年3月告示)改訂の趣旨や要点を頭に入れ，英語教育が目指す方向性を理解することが最も大切ではあるが，本問では「聞いたり読んだり」，「目的，場面，状況」をはじめ，コミュニケーションを円滑にする働きとして「相づちを打つ」など，詳細なところまで完全解答が求められている。さらに，本試験では大問【1】～【6】で150点満点であるが，そのうち本問全問で36点という配点がなされている。配点の高さから考えると，中学校学習指導要領については，同解説外国語編を参照しながら時間をかけて完璧に覚えておくべきだろう。

【高等学校】

【1】(1)　①　聞いたり読んだり　　②　基本的　　③　論理性　　④　文章　　(2)　①　学校生活　　②　発話例　　③　根拠　　④　質疑応答　　(3)　①　コンピュータ　　②　興味・関心

③　発信　　④　言語活動

〈解説〉他の自治体でも頻出の問題ではあるが，全て記述式解答でありハードルが高い。高等学校学習指導要領(2018(平成30)年3月告示)改訂の趣旨や要点を頭に入れ，英語教育が目指す方向性を理解することが最も大切ではあるが，本問では詳細なところまで完全解答が求められている。さらに，本試験では大問【1】～【6】で150点満点であるが，そのうち本問全問で36点という配点がなされている。配点の高さから考えると，高等学校学習指導要領については，同解説外国語編・英語編を参照しながら，時間をかけて完璧に覚えておくべきだろう。中学校種に比べて高等学校種では，目標や言語活動例が科目段階別(英語コミュニケーションⅠ～Ⅲ，論理・表現Ⅰ～Ⅲ)になっているという点でも，膨大な量である。高等学校学習指導要領解説外国語編・英語編の巻末には，科目段階別の目標と言語活動を一覧表の形にまとめたものが収録されている。大変わかりやすい資料であるので，ぜひそれらを活用して，効率的に取り組もう。

2023年度　実施問題

【中高共通】

【1】次の対話文を読んで，(1)～(5)にあてはまる最も適切な英文を，ア～キから選び，記号で答えなさい。ただし，同じ選択肢を2度使わないこと。

A : I had a big fight with my daughter, Karen last night, and we did not speak to each other this morning.

B : (1)

A : She has been addicted to her smartphone recently. I'm worried that she has been wasting her time, but she doesn't listen to me. I was annoyed with her attitude yesterday.

B : Don't worry. (2) My son is busy responding to texts and catching up on social media. I understand it's important for him to socialize with friends, but he often uses his smartphone during meals and family time. (3)

A : I know that life without smartphones is almost impossible for us, especially teens, so I want my daughter to learn how to handle it well.

B : (4) Smartphones have made our lives easier and more convenient. I do shopping, reading, and even bank transferring on the smartphone.

A : Me, too. But we must be careful not to use the devices too much for our health.

B : Right. I hear sleep deprivation and eyesight deterioration are serious health problems.

A : I'll talk to Karen this evening and make sure she knows how to use the smartphone responsibly.

B : (5)

ア　I agree with you.

イ　I have no choices.
ウ　You deserve it.
エ　I hope you'll make up.
オ　I can't stand it.
カ　What's going on?
キ　It happens.

(☆☆☆◎◎◎)

【2】次の英文を日本語にしなさい。

We must change our mindset about war itself, to prevent conflict through diplomacy and strive to end conflicts after they've begun; to see our growing interdependence as a cause for peaceful cooperation and not violent competition; to define our nations not by our capacity to destroy but by what we build.

(from a speech by Barack Obama)

(☆☆☆☆◎◎◎◎)

【3】次の英文は，あるエッセイの一部である。(1)～(5)にあてはまる最も適切な英文を，ア～オから選び，記号で答えなさい。ただし，同じ選択肢を2度使わないこと。

(1)

I did not keep in touch.

(2)

(3)

(4)

It was the most helpless I have ever felt in my life.

(5)

He died a few weeks later.

(*Tuesdays with Morrie: Mitch Albom*)

ア　One night in May, my uncle and I sat on the balcony of his apartment. It was breezy and warm. He looked out toward the horizon and said, through gritted teeth, that he wouldn't be around to see his kids into the next school year. He asked if I would look after them. I told him not to talk that way. He stared at me sadly.

イ　At the same time, I had my first serious encounter with death. My favorite uncle, my mother's brother, the man who had taught me music, taught me to drive, teased me about girls, thrown me a football—that one adult whom I targeted as a child and said,'That's who I want to be when I grow up" —died of pancreatic cancer at the age of forty-four. He was a short, handsome man with a thick mustache, and I was with him for the last year of his life, living in an apartment just below his. I watched his strong body wither, then bloat, saw him suffer, night after night, doubled over at the dinner table, pressing on his stomach, his eyes shut, his mouth contorted in pain. "Ahhhhh, God," he would moan. "Ahhhhhh, Jesus!" The rest of us—my aunt, his two young sons, me—stood there, silently, cleaning the plates, averting our eyes.

ウ　At this point, I should explain what had happened to me since that summer day when I last hugged my dear and wise professor, and promised to keep in touch.

エ　The world, I discovered, was not all that interested. I wandered around my early twenties, paying rent and reading classifieds and wondering why the lights were not turning green for me. My dream was to be a famous musician (I played the piano), but after several years of dark, empty nightclubs, broken promises, bands that kept breaking up and producers who seemed excited about everyone but me, the dream soured. I was failing for the first time in my life.

オ　In fact, I lost contact with most of the people I knew in college, including my beer-drinking friends and the first woman I ever woke up with in the morning. The years after graduation hardened me into someone quite different from the strutting graduate who left campus that day headed for New York City, ready to offer the world his talent.

(☆☆☆◎◎◎)

【4】次の英文を読んで，(1)・(2)の問いに答えなさい。

To speak of 'English' without qualification can be misleading. Historical changes must be taken into account, and their implications for criticism will be discussed later. [(a)] It is worth giving a little time to understanding it better before returning to its particular use as the medium of English literature. If we look at it closely, it will be easier to see what the writer has to work on and to judge how well he is using the material at his disposal.

A language can conveniently be divided into ***vocabulary*** or ***lexis*** and ***grammar*** or ***syntax***. The division is not one that can effectively be sustained for long in using or learning the language. [(b)] What we call the English language is in fact a large number of words capable of expressing meaning through certain structures. There is a great potential store of utterances which a native user can recognize and accept. This power of communication makes it possible to say that English is a language, in a more specific and limited sense than that in which we use the word 'language' to describe the general human power of articulate speech.

In this sense, 'English' means a language which can be used for (①) and other shared purposes by people who are described as 'English-speaking' , even though none of them will actually use all its total resources in a lifetime. It is what is sometimes described by the French word *langue*, as distinct from the *langage* which is the human power of articulate speech. The American linguist Noam Chomsky uses the word ***competence*** of the potential from which we draw all utterances that can be called 'English'.

One notable feature of modern English has already been noted: its very large vocabulary, drawn from other languages as well as from its native Saxon base. For the moment there is no need to be precise about what exactly constitutes a word, when we say that there are many words in English. When a foreigner learns the word *teach*, how many words has he learned? Should it be assumed that knowledge of how English verbs work will automatically add *teacher* and *teaching*? Is the irregular past *taught* a separate acquisition, or just part of the package that comes with *teach* in the textbooks? How many words are there in *coffee machine* or in *newspaper seller*? [(c)]

Questions of this kind are important in any serious analysis of English. Later it will be necessary to look at some of them in connection with literary examples. In everyday usage, however, the native speaker simply puts together the words which he needs, from the total number which he knows. Everyone has a bigger passive than active vocabulary. [(d)]

Individual vocabulary increases throughout our lives. The rate of increase is not constant, being very rapid in the years of early childhood and less thereafter, though with bursts of activity at times of intensive learning in an academic situation or in developing a new skill or way of life. No one avoids some (②) growth in the modern world, when new inventions and ideas continually impinge on our lives. Apart from what we know and can produce without much effort, we are aware of a great deal more that is accessible. If we read or hear a new word we can 'look up' its meaning in a dictionary. [(e)] The sight of a big English dictionary is a tangible proof of the size of the English vocabulary. The status of the lexicographer has risen since Samuel Johnson defined him in his own dictionary as 'a harmless drudge'.

(Raymond Chapman, 'The Use of English' from *The Language of English Literature*)

(1) [(a)]～[(e)]にあてはまる最も適切な英文を，ア～オから選び，記号で答えなさい。ただし，同じ選択肢を2度使わないこと。

ア The writer makes fuller use than most people of the words which are stored in his memory.

イ Even present-day English is not as simple or definable as we may think.

ウ Words can be used only in grammatical structures and grammar can operate only through arrangements of words.

エ We probably think of these as single words when they are spoken but can see the parts which combine in them when they are written down.

オ It is not surprising that English-speaking people generally have respect for what the dictionary can tell them.

(2) (①)・(②)にあてはまる最も適切な語を本文中から選び，それぞれ1語で書きなさい。

(☆☆☆☆◎◎◎)

【5】次の英文の指示に従って90語～110語の英語で答えなさい。ただし，符号は語数に含めず，解答の最後に使用語数を書き入れること。

Do you think that children should help their parents with household chores when they are old enough? Please give two reasons based on your own experience to support your opinion.

(☆☆☆☆◎◎◎◎)

【中学校】

【1】中学校学習指導要領「第2章　各教科」「第9節　外国語」について，次の(1)～(4)の問いに答えなさい。

(1) 次の文は「第1　目標」である。(①)～(④)にあてはまる語句を書きなさい。(同じ番号には，同じ語句が入るものとする。)

> 外国語によるコミュニケーションにおける見方・考え方を働かせ，外国語による聞くこと，読むこと，話すこと，書くことの言語活動を通して，簡単な情報や考えなどを理解した

り表現したり(　①　)するコミュニケーションを図る資質・能力を次のとおり育成することを目指す。

(1)　外国語の音声や語彙，表現，文法，言語の働きなどを理解するとともに，これらの知識を，聞くこと，読むこと，話すこと，書くことによる実際のコミュニケーションにおいて活用できる(　②　)を身に付けるようにする。

(2)　コミュニケーションを行う(　③　)や場面，状況などに応じて，日常的な話題や社会的な話題について，外国語で簡単な情報や考えなどを理解したり，これらを活用して表現したり(　①　)することができる力を養う。

(3)　外国語の背景にある文化に対する理解を深め，聞き手，読み手，話し手，書き手に(　④　)しながら，主体的に外国語を用いてコミュニケーションを図ろうとする態度を養う。

(2)　次の文は「第2　各言語の目標及び内容等」「英語」「1　目標」「(2)　読むこと」である。(　①　)～(　③　)にあてはまる語句を書きなさい。

ア　日常的な話題について，簡単な語句や文で書かれたものから(　①　)を読み取ることができるようにする。

イ　日常的な話題について，簡単な語句や文で書かれた短い文章の(　②　)を捉えることができるようにする。

ウ　社会的な話題について，簡単な語句や文で書かれた短い文章の(　③　)を捉えることができるようにする。

(3)　次の文は「第2　各言語の目標及び内容等」「英語」「2　内容」の「(3)　言語活動及び言語の働きに関する事項」の一部である。(　①　)～(　③　)にあてはまる語句を書きなさい。

カ　書くこと
(ア)　趣味や好き嫌いなど，自分に関する基本的な情報を語句や文で書く活動。
(イ)　簡単な手紙や(　①　)の形で自分の近況などを伝える活動。
(ウ)　日常的な話題について，簡単な語句や文を用いて，出来事などを説明する(　②　)のある文章を書く活動。
(エ)　社会的な話題に関して聞いたり読んだりしたことから把握した内容に基づき，(　③　)や気持ち，その理由などを書く活動。

(4)　次の文は「第2　各言語の目標及び内容等」「英語」「3　指導計画の作成と内容の取扱い」の(1)の一部である。(　①　)・(　②　)にあてはまる語句を書きなさい。

ウ　実際に英語を使用して互いの考えや気持ちを伝え合うなどの言語活動を行う際は，2の(1)に示す(　①　)について理解したり(　②　)したりするための指導を必要に応じて行うこと。

(☆☆☆☆◎◎◎◎)

【高等学校】

【1】高等学校学習指導要領「第2章　各学科に共通する各教科」「第8節　外国語」について，次の(1)～(3)の問いに答えなさい。

(1)　次は「第2款　各科目」「第1　英語コミュニケーションⅠ」「2　内容」「(3)　言語活動及び言語の働きに関する事項」「①　言語活動に関する事項」「イ　聞くこと」の一部である。(　①　)～(　④　)にあてはまる語句を書きなさい。

(ア)　日常的な話題について，話される(　①　)が調整されたり，基本的な語句や文での(　②　)を十分に聞いたりしながら，対話や放送などから必要な情報を聞き取り，話し手の(　③　)を把握する活動。また，聞き取った内容を話したり書いたりして(　④　)活動。

(2)　次は「第2款　各科目」「第4　論理・表現Ⅰ」「1　目標」「(3)　書くこと」の一部である。(　①　)～(　④　)にあてはまる語句を書きなさい。

イ　日常的な話題や(　①　)な話題について，使用する語句や文，事前の準備などにおいて，(　②　)を活用すれば，聞いたり読んだりしたことを活用しながら，基本的な語句や文を用いて，意見や(　③　)などを論理の構成や(　④　)を工夫して文章を書いて伝えることができるようにする。

(3)　次は「第3款　英語に関する各科目にわたる指導計画の作成と内容の取扱い」の一部である。(　①　)～(　④　)にあてはまる語句を書きなさい。

1　指導計画の作成に当たっては，小学校や中学校における指導との接続に留意しながら，次の事項に配慮するものとする。

(1)　単元など内容や時間の(　①　)を見通して，その中で育む資質・能力の育成に向けて，生徒の主体的・対話的で深い学びの実現を図るようにすること。その際，具体的な課題等を設定し，生徒が外国語によるコミュニケーションにおける(　②　)・(　③　)を働かせながら，コミュニケーションの(　④　)や場面，状況などを意識して活動を行い，英語の音声や語彙，表現，文法などの知識を五つの領域(「論理・表現Ⅰ」，「論理・表現Ⅱ」及び「論理・表現Ⅲ」においては三つの領域。3において同じ。)における実際のコミュニケーションにおいて活用する学習の充実を図ること。

(☆☆☆☆◎◎◎◎)

解答・解説

【中高共通】

【1】(1) カ　(2) キ　(3) オ　(4) ア　(5) エ

〈解説〉(1) 空所直後にAが悩みを打ち明けていることから，Bは「どうしたの」と聞いていると判断して，カが適切。 (2) 空所直後にBが自分の息子の同じような問題を話していることから「そんなこともありますよ」の意味のキが適切。 (3) 空所前のbut以下で，Bは息子が食事中や家族の時間にもスマートフォンを使っていることをよく思っていないことが読み取れる。よって「それには我慢できない」のオが適切。 (4) 空所直前のAの発話と直後のBの発話は，スマートフォンを適切に使わなければいけないという同じ趣旨のため「あなたに同意します」のアが適切。 (5) 空所直前に，Aは最後の発話で，ケンカしてしまった娘と話し合ってみると言っているので，「仲直りできるのを祈っています」の意のエが適切。

【2】私たちは，戦争そのものについての考え方を変えなければなりません。外交を通じて争いを防ぎ，すでに始まってしまった争いを終わらせるように懸命に努力するために。そして，相互依存の高まりが暴力的な競争の動機になるのではなく，平和的な協力を生むものだと考えるために。また，私たちの国々を，破壊する能力によってではなく，何を築き上げるかによって定義づけるために。

〈解説〉出題は，2016年5月27日，広島を訪問したバラク・オバマ元大統領が行ったいわゆる「広島スピーチ」の一部である。現職の米国大統領が初めて被爆地である広島を訪れたという歴史的な出来事であり，大変有名なスピーチである。できれば全文を読んでおきたい。to prevent～, to see～, to define～はすべて目的を表すto不定詞が並列されていることに注意して訳したい。strive to doで「～しようと懸命に努力する」，see A as Bは「AをBとみなす，考える」，capacity to doで「～する能力」，not by～but by…で「～によってではなく，…によって」という意味になる。

【3】(1)　ウ　　(2)　オ　　(3)　エ　　(4)　イ　　(5)　ア

〈解説〉(1)　空所直後のI did not keep in touch.に着目する。この文につながるのはpromised to keep in touchで終わるウとなる。　(2)　残りの選択肢を検討すると，I did not keep in touch.「私は連絡を取らなかった」と同様な意味のIn fact, I lost contact with most of the people I knew in collegeで始まるオが適切と判断できる。　(3)　空所直前の選択肢オの内容を検討すると，将来の希望に満ちている卒業生とは違う人生だったと述べられている。それに続くのは，ミュージシャンになろうとしても芽が出ないという否定的な内容であるエが適切。　(4)　エに続くのは人の死に出合ったという悪い内容が同時に起こったイが適切。この段落では叔父が病気で弱っていく様が述べられている。　(5)　イや空所前文に続く内容として，叔父と最後の言葉を交わす場面のアが適切。

【4】(1)　(a)　イ　　(b)　ウ　　(c)　エ　　(d)　ア　　(e)　オ

(2)　①　communication　　②　vocabulary

〈解説〉(1)　(a)　冒頭の文「英語について無条件で話すということは誤解を招きかねない」から選択肢を検討すると，イの「現代の英語ですら私たちが思っているほど単純でも定義できるものでもない」が適切と判断する。　(b)　第2段落では言語は語彙と文法・構文に分けられるという内容から始まっている。それに続くのは，語と文法の説明をしているウとなる。 (c) 第3段落では1つの単語から変化する名詞形や過去形などの派生語について述べられている。それを踏まえるとエが適切と判断できる。エの文中にあるtheseは空所前文の各単語を表す。 (d) 空所の前文で「人はみな能動的な語彙より受動的な語彙を多く持っている」と述べられており，一般人と比較した作家の特性としてアの「作家はほとんどの人より記憶の中に保存されている語彙を最大限に使いこなす」が続く。 (e) 空所直前の文で辞書について触れている。これに続くのは，英語話者は辞書に対して敬意を払っていると述べられているオが適切と判断できる。 (2) ① 空所直後のand other shared purposesより空所には何か人と分かち合う目的が入ることがわかる。英語が用いられる目的で適切な単語を本文中から探すとcommunicationが適切だと判断できる。 ② 最終段落では人の生涯に渡る語彙増加について述べられている。よって空所にもvocabularyが入り，vocabulary growthで「語彙の成長・増加」を表す。

【5】I think that children should help parents with household chores. When I was younger, my parents would have me help out around the house with small chores, such as doing my own laundry, cleaning house, and cutting the grass. Learning these essential skills so early has helped me in adulthood by making them so natural. Furthermore, they also taught me how simple tasks can be both rewarding and relaxing. I remember, even as a child, the simple pleasure of seeing a clean bathroom or bedroom. Doing chores at an early age is a formative and important experience, and can make a big difference in life. (105 words)

〈解説〉「子どもたちに親の家事の手伝いをさせるべきか」という，非常に書きやすくよく出題されるテーマである。問題文の指示通り，解答例では両親から家事を手伝わされたという実体験を挙げている。そこから家事をするのが当たり前のことになったこと，小さな仕事はやりがいがあり気分を落ち着かせることを学んだことの2つが，家事をすべき理由として述べられている。最後に家事を幼少期からやることが人生に大きな影響を及ぼすと結論づけている。

【中学校】

【1】(1)　①　伝え合ったり　　②　技能　　③　目的　　④　配慮　(2)　①　必要な情報　　②　概要　　③　要点　　(3)　①　電子メール　　②　まとまり　　③　自分の考え　　(4)　①　言語材料　②　練習

〈解説〉(1)　①　「理解する」,「表現する」という単に受け手となったり送り手となったりする単方向のコミュニケーションだけでなく,「伝え合う」という双方向のコミュニケーションも重視していることに留意する。　②　本目標は,「外国語の音声や語彙,表現,文法,言語の働きなどを理解する」という「知識」の面と,その知識を「聞くこと,読むこと,話すこと,書くことによる実際のコミュニケーションにおいて活用できる」という「技能」の面とで構成されている。
③　コミュニケーションを行う際は,その「目的や場面,状況など」を意識する必要があり,その上で,「簡単な情報や考えなどを理解」したり,理解したことを活用して「表現したり伝え合ったりする」ことが重要になってくる。　④　「コミュニケーションを図ろうとする態度」を養う上では,「聞き手,読み手,話し手,書き手に配慮しながら」コミュニケーションを図ることが大切であり,相手の外国語の文化的背景によって「配慮」の仕方も異なってくることが考えられる。
(2)　①　「必要な情報」については,書かれていることの全てを読み取ろうとするのではなく,目的や自分の置かれた状況などから判断して,何が必要な情報かを把握することが大切である。　②　「概要を捉える」とは,物語などで,文章の一語一語や一文一文の意味など特定の部分にのみとらわれたりすることなく,人物の行動や心情の変化,全体のあらすじなど,書き手が述べていることの大まかな内容を捉えることである。　③　「要点を捉える」場合は,文章から複数の情報を取り出し,どの情報がその説明の中で最も重要であるかを判断する必要がある。　(3)　①　具体的には,家族や親戚,友達などに自分の

近況を伝える手紙，旅行先からの手紙や葉書，留守番電話などの伝言を聞いてその返事を電子メールで送る活動を示している。自分の考えや気持ちなどが伝わるように文章を書くためには，メールなどの操作・練習のためのICTを活用した活動の充実が必要である。 ② 出来事などを説明する「まとまり」のある文章を書くためには，キーワードを整理したり5W1Hを意識したりしながら全体の構成を考えて書くこと，文と文のつながりを示す語句を効果的に用いながら書くことができるように指導することが大切である。 ③ 話題となっている内容を聞いたり読んだりして理解し，それを基に思考・判断したことについて，「自分の考え」や気持ちなどを主体的に伝え合う言語活動を設け，その発話内容を整理しながら書くという，領域間の統合を図ることが重要である。 (4) このような言語活動を行う場合は，言語材料について理解したり練習したりすることが目的となって，単に繰り返し活動を行うのではなく，生徒が言語活動の目的や言語の使用場面を意識して行うことができるように留意しなければならない。

【高等学校】

【1】(1) ① 速さ　② 言い換え　③ 意図　④ 伝え合う
(2) ① 社会的　② 多くの支援　③ 主張　④ 展開
(3) ① まとまり　② 見方　③ 考え方　④ 目的

〈解説〉(1) この活動で聞き取るのは，対話や放送などである。速さの調整とは，話す速度だけではなく，文と文とのポーズの長さや，聞いた後の意味の処理に必要な時間を十分にとるなどの調整を行うことであり，また，基本的な語句や文での言い換えとは，生徒が理解することが難しいと思われる表現が聞く内容に含まれる場合，既習の簡単な表現に言い換えたりすることなどである。実際の活動においては，生徒がこれから聞く内容を推測できるように，写真や実物などを活用して聞き取る内容と関連のある話をしたり，聞き取る上でキーワードとなる表現を生徒に提示したりすることで，生徒の理解を助けるなどの支援が考えられる。 (2) 「意見や主張などを論理の構成や展開を工夫して文章を書いて伝える」とは，自分の意見や主張などを論理的に伝えるために，モデルなどを通じて論理の構成や展開の仕方を学んだ上で，自分の意見などにおける論理に矛盾や飛躍がないか，理由や根拠がより適切なものとなっているかなどについて留意しながら文章を書いて伝えることを示す。　(3)　主体的・対話的で深い学びの実現に向けた授業改善を進めるに当たっては，特に「深い学び」の視点に関して各教科等の学びの深まりの鍵となるのが，「見方・考え方」である。各教科等の特質に応じた物事を捉える視点や考え方である「見方・考え方」を，習得・活用・探究という学びの過程の中で働かせることを通して，より質の高い深い学びにつなげることが重要である。また，高等学校においては，中学校における五つの領域を有機的に関連させた活動を通した指導を踏まえ，複数の領域を結び付けた統合的な言語活動の一層の充実を図ることが重要である。

2022年度　実施問題

【中高共通】

【1】次の対話文を読んで，[(1)]～[(5)]にあてはまる最も適切な英文を，ア～キから1つ選び，記号で答えなさい。ただし，同じ選択肢を2度使わないこと。

A : Hey Jeff, how's it going?

B : [(1)] I got a low score on my math test again.

A : The one in Mr. Cooper's class? [(2)]

B : Yeah, I didn't study enough. I have to take a make-up test.

A : That's too bad. I wanted to invite you to my friend's concert this weekend.

B : Oh? [(3)]

A : It's Saturday at 7 o'clock, but it's in the next town over. To get there on time, we'd need to leave in the afternoon. My plan was to get a hotel room and come back on Sunday afternoon.

B : That would be fun, but I really need to study for the test. If I fail again, my parents will be very disappointed with me.

A : Why don't I drive and then you can study in the car on the way there and back?

B : No, I can't because I always get sick when I read in the car.

A : That's no good, then. What about taking the train? [(4)]

B : That could work, but the train takes more time, so we'd need to leave earlier on Saturday.

A : [(5)] If I'm not driving, I can help you study too! Also, the train will give us more study time.

B : OK, I'm really looking forward to going to the concert!

A : Me too!

ア　Not so good.

イ　When did it start?

ウ　Would that give you problems as well?

エ　He needs study.

オ　That's perfect.

カ　He's really strict.

キ　What day is it on?

(☆☆☆◎◎◎◎)

【2】次の英文の内容を，160字以内の日本語に要約しなさい。ただし，句読点も字数に入れること。

If teachers and parents and psychologists understand the mistakes that can be made in giving a meaning to life, and if they do not make the same mistakes themselves, we can be confident that children who have been lacking in social interest will come to have a better feeling for their own capacities and for the opportunities of life. When they meet problems, they will not stop their efforts, look for an easy way out, try to escape or throw the burden on the shoulders of others, make Claims for tender treatment and especial sympathy, feel humiliated and seek to revenge themselves, or ask, "What is the use of life? What do I get from it?" They will say, "We must make our own lives. It is our own task and we are capable of meeting it. We are masters of our own actions. If something new must be done or something old replaced, no one need do it but ourselves." If life is approached in this way, as a cooperation of independent human beings, we can see no limits to the progress of our human association.

(ALFRED ADLER, 5 BOOK COLLECTION)

(☆☆☆☆◎◎◎)

【3】次の英文は，あるエッセイの一部である。[(1)]～[(5)]の内容に合う英文を，ア～オから1つ選び，記号で答えなさい。ただし，同じ選択肢を2度使わないこと。

(1)

Imagine for a moment two objects in your hands. One is a piece of paper and the other a rubber band. If you squeeze your hands together hard and let go, the paper will remain crumpled, but the rubber band will return to its original shape.

Economists tend to think of the economy as the rubber band. After a shock, they expect it to go back to normal. When it doesn't, like the crumpled paper, they call the effect "hysteresis" — lasting changes caused by some large perturbation. The Covid-19 pandemic is a classic example. What permanent damage to the economy will it leave behind?

(2)

The first place to look is in classrooms, say Eric Hanushek and Margaret Raymond, economists and education researchers at Stanford University. Lost study time for children during the pandemic has the potential to do lasting harm not just to their own long-term prospects but to American prosperity in general, say the married couple.

(3)

Ms. Raymond studied 18 states and Washington, D.C. and concluded that, on average, children lost 116 days of reading time during the early stages of the pandemic last year and 215 days of math work — instruction that will be hard to regain and could leave a whole generation of children struggling to keep up in their studies and testing. If your child misses out on learning fractions now, how will she perform in algebra later?

And the shock has been distributed unevenly. Children in rural areas and areas with large Black and Hispanic populations were hit the hardest. Among the states suffering the most are South Carolina and Illinois, according to Ms. Raymond's study.

(4)

Economic output is a function of innovation, the skills that workers bring to their jobs and the machines that they use to create goods and services. Innovation and skills are shaped by education. Over the next century, the skill shock of 2020 will produce $25 trillion to $30 trillion of lost economic output in today's dollars, Mr. Hanushek estimates, and the lifetime household incomes of the affected students will be 6% to 9% lower.

He came to this conclusion in part by examining the experience of German students. In 1966 and 1967, the German government temporarily shortened the school year in a rejiggering of the school calendar. Longitudinal studies, he says, show that this lost class time reduced the incomes of that cohort of students by 5% over their lifetimes. Today's students "are going to feel the long-term effects of Covid even when they are back in school," Mr. Hanushek says.

(5)

Hysteresis may be acting on whole industries this time, an economist Olivier Blanchard said. Air travel, commercial real estate and bricks-and-mortar retailing, for example, might never be the same.

Like Mr. Hanushek and Ms. Raymond, Mr. Blanchard is most worried about the long-run effects of the Covid crisis on children and their future as workers. "I would do everything I can to allow children to go safely back to school in person," he said. Ms. Raymond said that it might be time to start thinking about sending children to summer school to make up for lost time. At the very least, she said, it is time for educators to start thinking about how to fix schooling once the pandemic ends.

(Jon Hilsenrath, The Long-Term Economic Costs of Lost Schooling "*THE WALL STREET JOURNAL*" *2021*　設問の都合上，表記を改めた箇所

がある。)

ア The learning losses are more deeply felt by disadvantaged children in some communities.

イ There is an urgent need to rebuild school education when things return to normal after the pandemic.

ウ The big impact of the Covid-19 pandemic could inflict permanent damage on the economy.

エ Education is essential to build some elements closely related to the productivity of a nation.

オ The learning losses could affect the success of individual children and the whole nation.

(☆☆☆◎◎◎)

【4】次の英文を読んで，(1)・(2)の問いに答えなさい。

Why is everything so darned complicated? And I really mean everything: our taxes, schedules, bureaucracies, machines, algorithms, org charts, our school and welfare and health care systems, you name it.

Even — and I say this as an oft culpable columnist — our diction. "If it is possible to cut a word out, always cut it out," George Orwell stipulated in one of his rules of writing. I'm tempted to edit him thus: If it is possible to cut a word [out], [always] cut it [out].

[(A)] It's an ideal a lot of us subscribe to in theory but keep violating in practice. A lamentable secret of the universe seems to be that it takes enormous effort to simplify, but no effort at all to do the opposite. Put differently, it's easier to add things, even unnecessary ones, than to subtract.

That's the insight of a new paper published in Nature and authored by Gabrielle Adams, Benjamin Converse, Andrew Hales and Leidy Klotz, who hail from various faculties at the University of Virginia. In eight observational studies and experiments, they found that people systematically overlook opportunities to improve things by subtracting and default instead to adding.

For example, look at this little storm trooper seeking shelter under a Lego roof. A heavy masonry brick is about to land on the platform right above the poor guy's head. [(B)] We can take away Legos or add them from a pile, but each extra brick costs 10 cents.

The simplest and most elegant solution — and by design also the most profitable, netting the whole dollar — is to remove the one brick supporting the roof, so that the platform sits flush on the remaining base. But 59% of participants chose instead to add Legos — placing supports in the three other corners of the base, for instance.

So it went in one experiment after another, whether people were asked to improve the design of a miniature golf hole, a travel itinerary or an essay (Orwell must be turning in his grave). By huge majorities, participants (①) and rarely (②). Asked to edit their own essay, for instance, 80% padded verbiage, only 16% cut. Told to make the image below on the left symmetrical, most people added three shapes rather than taking away one, as shown.

The good news is that the researchers were able to nudge more people in the control groups to consider subtractions by providing cues. In the Lego experiment, for example, they told some people not only that adding pieces costs 10 cents each but also that "removing pieces is free." This wasn't new information. But it appeared to prime the participants' brains to consider other options.

The more intriguing insight was that people became less likely to consider subtraction the more they felt "cognitive load." [(C)] (This is why we should never fiddle with our phones while driving.)

Spotting solutions that are simple and elegant, in other words, requires mental effort or what the Nobel Prize winner Daniel Kahneman calls slow as opposed to fast thinking. It's an idea physicists might recognize in the second law of thermodynamics. One form of it says that any system will go from order to disorder, unless you add energy. [(D)]

Think of how you taught your kids to ride a bike. In my childhood, parents added something clunky, training wheels. These days, we subtract things — pedals and chains — and call the result balance bikes. [(E)]

Then dare to dream what thoughtful subtraction could do for the real mother lodes of self-propagating complexity — the U.S. tax code springs to mind, or the European Union's fiscal rules. We can simplify our lives, but we have to put in the work. That's what the philosopher Blaise Pascal captured when he apologized, "I would have written a shorter letter, but I did not have the time."

(Andreas Kluth, Science shows why simplifying is hard and complicating is easy "*The Japan Times*" *2021*　設問の都合上，表記を改めた箇所がある。)

(1) [(A)]～[(E)]にあてはまる最も適切な英文を，ア～オから1つ選び，記号で答えなさい。ただし，同じ選択肢を2度使わないこと。

ア　Our job is to renovate the structure so that it doesn't cave in on him, for which we get $1.

イ　In the same way, we humans tend to complicate things unless we make an effort not to.

ウ　Our children learn faster, and have more fun.

エ　The simplicity Orwell yearned for is synonymous with clarity, elegance, efficiency and integrity.

オ　This is basically brain strain, as when we're distracted by other tasks.

(2) (　①　)・(　②　)にあてはまる最も適切な語を本文中から選び，必要があれば適切な形に変えて，それぞれ1語で書きなさい。

(☆☆☆◎◎◎◎)

【5】グローバル人材を育成するために，あなたが学校において英語の授業やその他の教育活動等を通してやってみたいことは何ですか。2つの具体例とそれぞれの効果について，100～120語の英語で書きなさい。ただし，符号は語数に含めず，最後に使用語数を書き入れること。

(☆☆☆☆◎◎◎◎)

【中学校】

【1】中学校学習指導要領「第2章　各教科」「第9節　外国語」について，次の(1)～(3)の問いに答えなさい。

(1) 次の文は「第2　各言語の目標及び内容等」「英語」「1　目標」「(1)　聞くこと」である。(　①　)～(　④　)にあてはまる語句を書きなさい。(同じ番号には同じ語句が入るものとする。)

ア　(　①　)と話されれば，日常的な話題について，必要な(　②　)を聞き取ることができるようにする。 イ　(　①　)と話されれば，日常的な話題について，話の(　③　)を捉えることができるようにする。 ウ　(　①　)と話されれば，社会的な話題について，短い説明の(　④　)を捉えることができるようにする。

(2) 次の文は「第2　各言語の目標及び内容等」「英語」「2　内容」の「(3)言語活動及び言語の働きに関する事項」の一部である。(　①　)～(　⑤　)にあてはまる語句を書きなさい。(同じ番号には同じ語句が入るものとする。)

エ　話すこと[やり取り] (ア)　関心のある事柄について，相手からの質問に対し，その場で(　①　)に応答したり，(　②　)する質問をしたりして，互いに会話を継続する活動。 (イ)　日常的な話題について，伝えようとする内容を(　③　)し，自分で作成したメモなどを活用しながら相手と(　④　)で伝え合う活動。 (ウ)　社会的な話題に関して聞いたり読んだりしたことから把握した内容に基づき，(　⑤　)や感じたこと，考えたことなどを伝えた上で，相手からの質問に対して(　①　)に応答したり自ら質問し返したりする活動。

(3) 次の文は「第2　各言語の目標及び内容等」「英語」「3　指導計画の作成と内容の取扱い」の(1)の一部である。(　①　)～(　③　)に

あてはまる語句を書きなさい。

オ　(　①　)で扱う題材は，生徒の興味・関心に合ったものとし，(　②　)や理科，音楽科など，他の教科等で学習したことを活用したり，(　③　)で扱う内容と関連付けたりするなどの工夫をすること。

(☆☆☆☆☆◎◎◎)

【高等学校】

【１】高等学校学習指導要領「第2章　各学科に共通する各教科」「第8節　外国語」について，次の(1)～(3)の問いに答えなさい。

(1)　次は「第2款　各科目」「第1　英語コミュニケーションⅠ」「2　内容」「(3)言語活動及び言語の働きに関する事項」「①　言語活動に関する事項」「ウ　読むこと」の一部である。(　①　)～(　④　)にあてはまる語句を書きなさい。

(イ)　社会的な話題について，基本的な語句や文での(　①　)や，書かれている文章の背景に関する説明などを十分に聞いたり読んだりしながら，説明文や論証文などから必要な(　②　)を読み取り，(　③　)や要点を把握する活動。また，読み取った(　④　)を話したり書いたりして伝え合う活動。

(2)　次は「第2款　各科目」「第4　論理・表現Ⅰ」「1　目標」「(1)話すこと[やり取り]」の一部である。(　①　)～(　④　)にあてはまる語句を書きなさい。

イ　日常的な話題や社会的な話題について，使用する語句や文，(　①　)の展開などにおいて，多くの支援を活用すれば，(　②　)やディスカッションなどの活動を通して，聞いたり読んだりしたことを活用しながら，基本的な語句や文を用いて，(　③　)や主張などを論理の(　④　)や展開を工夫して話して伝え合うことができるようにする。

(3)　次は「第3款　英語に関する各科目にわたる指導計画の作成と内容の取扱い」の一部である。(　①　)～(　④　)にあてはまる語句を書きなさい。

> 2　内容の取扱いに当たっては，次の事項に配慮するものとする。
> (7)　生徒が(　①　)する機会を増やすとともに，他者と(　②　)する力を育成するため，ペア・ワーク，(　③　)などの学習形態について適宜工夫すること。その際，他者とコミュニケーションを行うことに課題がある生徒については，個々の生徒の(　④　)に応じて指導内容や指導方法を工夫すること。

(☆☆☆☆☆◎◎◎)

解答・解説

【中高共通】

【1】(1)　ア　　(2)　カ　　(3)　キ　　(4)　ウ　　(5)　オ

〈解説〉(1)　AがBに対して最近の調子を尋ねたところ，Bは数学のテストでまた低い点数を取ったと答えている。そのため，「あまりよくない」を意味するアが正解。　(2)　Aがクーパー先生の授業のテストのことかと尋ねると，Bは同意した上で，自分がしっかり勉強しなかったと答えている。そのため，「彼は本当に厳しい」を意味するカが正解。　(3)　空欄の前で，Aが今週末の友人のコンサートに誘いたかったと言い，Bの発話を受けて，Aはコンサートの日程を伝えている。そのため，「それはいつですか」を意味するキが正解。イは紛らわしい選択肢ではあるが，過去形になっていることに注意したい。

(4)　AとBの5回目のやり取りで，Aがコンサート会場まで車を運転し，その間Bは車内で勉強することを提案したが，Bは車酔いするからできないと答えている。続く6回目のやり取りでは，Aが電車で行くことを提案し，Bはそれであれば問題ないが時間がかかると答えている。これらを踏まえると，空欄に入るのは「それでも問題がありますか」を意味するウが正解。　(5)　空欄の前で，Bは，電車なら大丈夫だがその分(車より)早く出発しなければならないと言っている。そのBの発話を受けて，Aは，自分が車を運転しないならBの勉強を手伝えるし，車で行くより勉強の時間を多く取れると言っている。そのため，「それなら完璧です」を意味するオが正解。

【2】社会に関心のない子供でも，大人たちから生きる意味を正しく教われば，自分の人生をより前向きに捉えられるようになる。そうなれば，壁にぶつかったとしても自暴自棄になることなく，自らの力で未来を切り拓いていくことに努力を惜しまないだろう。このように，何かを変えようと行動する自立した人間が力を合わせれば，共同体は進歩し続ける。(159字)

〈解説〉パラグラフの構造に留意しながら，パラグラフのメインアイデアを中心に重要な情報をまとめていくとよい。今回の英文においては，最初の文と最後の文の内容を簡潔に整理しつつ，その文脈を埋める形で，間にある文の内容を加えていけばよい。なお，最後の文についてはほぼ直訳でも問題ないが，最初の文については従属節の部分を言い換える必要がある。直訳すると「大人が生きる意味を与える際の誤りを理解して，同じような誤りを犯さない」という意味であるが，「大人が生きる意味を誤って教えない」のように言い換えるとよいだろう。

【3】(1)　ウ　　(2)　オ　　(3)　ア　　(4)　エ　　(5)　イ

〈解説〉(1)　第2パラグラフの2文目以降に着目する。新型コロナウイルス感染症は，過去に生じた変化が継続するヒステリシスの典型的な例であり，新型コロナウイルス感染症は経済にどのような後遺症をもたらすのか，とある。そのため，「新型コロナウイルス感染症の流行による大きな影響は経済に後遺症を与えるかもしれない」を意味するウが正解。　(2)　2文目に着目する。(スタンフォード大学の教育経済学者であるエリック・ハヌシェク氏とマーガレット・レイモンド氏)夫妻は，新型コロナウイルス感染症の流行中における子供たちの学習時間の減少は，子供たちの将来だけでなく，アメリカの将来に長期的な影響を与える可能性があると述べている，とある。そのため，「学習の損失は個々の子供たちと国全体の成功に影響するかもしれない」を意味するオが正解。　(3)　第2パラグラフの1～2文目に着目する。新型コロナウイルス感染症による学習時間の損失による影響は不均等であり，特に，地方や，黒人やヒスパニックが多い地域の子供たちは大きな打撃を受けた，とある。そのため，「学習の損失は一部のコミュニティにいる恵まれない子供たちにより深く感じられる」を意味するアが正解。　(4)　第1パラグラフの2～3文目に着目する。イノベーションやスキルは教育によって形づくられるものであり，ハヌシェク氏によれば，2020年のスキルに対する打撃は，25兆ドルから30兆ドルの経済的損失をもたらし，被害を受けた子供たちの生涯世帯年収は6～9%減少するだろう，とある。そのため，「教育は国の生産性と密接に関連する要素を構築するために不可欠である」を意味するエが正解。
(5)　第2パラグラフの4文目に着目する。レイモンド氏は，少なくとも，新型コロナウイルス感染症の流行が収束し次第，どのように元に戻すかを教育者が考え始めるときであると述べている，とある。そのため，「新型コロナウイルス感染症の流行が終わって物事が通常に戻ったら，学校教育の再建が急務である」を意味するイが正解。

【4】(1)　(A)　エ　(B)　ア　(C)　オ　(D)　イ　(E)　ウ
(2)　①　added　②　subtracted

〈解説〉(1)　(A)　空欄前にあるパラグラフに着目する。ジョージ・オーウェルの「もし言葉を削ることができるのであれば，いつでも削るべきである」が引用されている。そのため，「オーウェルが憧れた単純さは，明瞭さ，上品さ，効率性そして誠実性と同義である」を意味するエが正解。　(B)　空欄の前後の文に着目する。直前の文では，重い石積みのレンガが哀れな男のちょうど真上にある台の上に落ちようとしている，とあり，直後の文では，レゴの山から取り除いたり加えたりすることもできるが，追加のレンガは一つ10セントする，とある。そのため，「私たちの仕事は，そのレンガが彼を潰さないようにその構造物を直すことであり，それによって1ドル得ることができる」を意味するアが正解。　(C)　空欄の直前の文に着目すると，さらに興味深い洞察として，人々は認知的な負荷を感じるほど，引くという発想を考えなくなったということであった，とある。そのため，「これは，一般的に，私たちがほかの作業に気を取られているようなときの脳の緊張である」を意味するオが正解。　(D)　このパラグラフでは，単純で明解な解決策には精神的な努力が必要であり，これは，熱量を加えない限りどんなシステムも秩序から無秩序に変化するという，物理学の熱力学第2法則にも見られる考え方である，と述べられている。そのため，「同様に，私たち人類はそれを避ける努力をしない限り，物事を複雑にする傾向がある」を意味するイが正解。　(E)　このパラグラフでは，子供に自転車の乗り方を教えるときのことを考えると，筆者が子供の頃は親に不格好な補助輪を取り付けられたが，最近は，自転車からペダルとチェーンを取り去ったものを，バランスバイクと呼んでいる，と述べられている。そのため，「私たちの子供たちはより早く学び，より楽しめる」を意味するウが正解。　(2)　空欄のある前後の文に着目すると，レゴブロックの実験に加えて，ミニチュアのゴルフホール，旅程表やエッセイのデザインを改良するよう依頼する実験が行われ，エッセイを編集する場合は，80％の人が冗長にし，削除をしたのは16％の人だけだった，とある。この部分を言い換えると，空欄のある文を「圧倒的多数で，実験参加者は足し算を行って，引き算を行うことはほとんどなかった」の意味になるようにすればよい。行われた実験について書いてあることから，動詞の時制は過去形にする。

【５】I would like to try to have students exchange their ideas and opinions directly with people from other countries by using ICT devices. This will help them learn not only English but also about different cultures. In addition to this, they often come to appreciate how great Japanese culture is as well. In other activities, I want to get students interested in SDGs. They should choose one topic, research about how it is dealt with worldwide, and discuss problems that have occurred. Then they will think about what they can do to solve them. Thus, they can understand what's happening in the world and see from different angles. (108 words)

〈解説〉英語の授業を通してグローバル人材を育成するための具体的な方法と，想定される効果を英語で論じる問題である。グローバル人材についてはいくつかの定義が存在するが，その一例として，語学力を含めたコミュニケーション能力を駆使し，多様な価値観を有する他者と協働しながら新しい価値を創造できる人物などが挙げられる。そのため，英語によるコミュニケーションを通して，異なる価値観を有する他者を理解したり，他者と協力しながら国際的な問題の解決策を模索したり，さらには，既存の常識にとらわれずに新しい価値を生み出したりする経験をさせることが考えられる。これらの具体的な方法としては，解答例にあるICTの活用やSDGsの導入の他にも，生徒同士のペアワークやグループワークを含めた他者との協力が必要とされる言語活動などが挙げられるだろう。

【中学校】

【１】(1)　①　はっきり　②　情報　③　概要　④　要点　(2)　①　適切　②　関連　③　整理　④　口頭　⑤　読み取ったこと　(3)　①　言語活動　②　国語科　③　学校行事

〈解説〉(1)は「聞くこと」の目標，(2)は「話すこと[やり取り]」の内容，そして，(3)は指導計画作成に当たっての配慮事項から出題されている。学習指導要領については志望している校種だけでなく，小・中・高すべての学習指導要領をひと通り理解しておくと，校種が上がるに伴って高度化していくことをヒントに類推することができる。また，接続する校種では類似した記述も多く見られる。例えば，(1)の①に入る「はっきりと」について，小学校では「ゆっくりはっきりと」となっているが，高校ではそのような記述がなくなる。また，(3)は，小・中・高でほぼ類似した記述になっている。その一方で，小・中学校では「学校行事で扱う内容と関連付けたりするなどの工夫をすること」となっているが，高等学校では「英語を用いて課題解決を図る力を育成する工夫をすること」となっている。

【高等学校】

【1】(1) ① 言い換え　② 情報　③ 概要　④ 内容

(2) ① 対話　② ディベート　③ 意見　④ 構成

(3) ① 発話　② 協働　③ グループ・ワーク　④ 特性

〈解説〉(1) この活動で読み取る英語は，説明文や論証文などである。「読むこと」において，論理的で主張のある文章に十分触れることが，論理的な文章の構成や論理の組み立て方，説得力のある表現などを学ぶことにつながる。こうして「読むこと」を通して培われた論理性が，「話すこと[やり取り]」や「話すこと[発表]」，「書くこと」における論理的に表現する能力の土台となることに十分留意した上で指導をすることが重要である。 (2)「話すこと[やり取り]」は，コミュニケーション能力の育成の充実を図るため，平成30年3月告知の高等学校学習指導要領において新設された領域である。ディベートやディスカッションを実施するときは，やり取りの目的や話題，生徒の習熟の程度などに応じて，適切な方法や形式を設定する必要があることに注意する。ディベートでは，生徒に賛否両方の立場を経験させることも可能であり，当該の話題について多様な観点から考察する力を育成することにもつながる。ディスカッションでは，ペアで簡潔な意見をやり取りしたり，グループで司会などの役割を決めて行ったりするなど，様々な方法で行うことが可能である。 (3) 教室では，生徒の様々な個性や特性を把握した上で，指導に効果的と考えられる学習形態を柔軟に選択していくことが求められる。特にペア・ワークやグループ・ワークを行う際は，生徒が互いに興味・関心をもって話し合い，相互理解を深められるような題材や活動の在り方を工夫していくことが求められる。

2021年度　実施問題

【中高共通】

【1】[Listening Test 1]

The listening test is about to begin. Listen carefully to the directions.

Listening Test 1.
You will hear two passages, A and B. The passages and the questions will be given only once. Choose the best answer from among the four choices written below. From now on, you have some time to look at the choices. (20 seconds)
Now, let's begin.

[Passage A]

For centuries, the humble windmill has been used for pumping water and grinding grain. Its role grew when the wind turbine was created, designed specifically to generate power. So today, around 2.5 percent of the world's electricity is produced by wind. And the industry hopes its output will quadruple in five years. It's technology driving growth.

When you compare turbine to turbine over the last couple decades, we are 30 times more efficient than we were several decades ago, because of the use of information and computer technologies.

Squeezing more energy out of thin air involves equipping the turbines with lasers. That allows them to communicate with each other as operators keep a watchful eye in high-tech control centers.

Worldwide, there are now more than 200,000 turbines, on land and offshore. The future is to take wind energy to new heights.

Question

(1) What is the role of the wind turbine?

ア to pump water and to grind grain.

イ To generate power.

ウ To communicate with each other.

エ To take wind energy to new heights.

[Passage B]

The financially strapped U.S. Postal Service is looking to make a few changes, which could affect jobs in New York City.

First-class mail would be slowed down by postal service cuts aimed at saving the agency from financial ruin—an estimated $3 billion in reductions, including closing more than half of the nation's mail processing centers as early as next March. With a longer journey from collection box to processing center, delivery standards for first-class mail would be lowered from one-to-three days to two-to-three days, pretty much ending any chance of overnight delivery.

Three processing centers in the city would close with operations in Brooklyn, Queens and Staten Island absorbed into the Morgan Processing Center in Manhattan. The processing operation in the Bronx was moved to Morgan in August. While some people said they were aggravated that so-called "snail mail" could get even slower, others said they rarely use regular mail anymore.

The newest cuts are in addition to the planned closing of some 3,700 local post offices around the country. To add insult to injury, the price of a first-class stamp goes up a penny, to 45 cents, beginning January 22.

Question

(2) According to the passage, which of the following is true?

ア First-class mail would be slowed down because of the lack of labor force.

イ　Delivery standards for first-class mail would be changed from one-to-three days to overnight delivery.

ウ　More than 3,500 local post offices are planned to disappear.

エ　More people will use regular mail because the price of a first-class stamp goes up to 45 cents.

(☆☆☆☆◎◎◎)

【2】[Listening Test 2]

You will hear a passage. <u>The passage and the questions will be given only once</u>. Choose the best answer for Number (1) and Number (2) from among the four choices written below. Your answer for Number (3) must be in one complete sentence written in English. From now on, you have some time to look at the choices.

Now, let's begin.

In 1972, as a fourth-year medical student, I studied at the medical school in Bangalore. The first class I attended was on examining kidney X-rays. Looking at the first image, I realized this must be kidney cancer. I decided to wait awhile before telling the class, out of respect. I didn't want to show off. Several hands then went into the air and the Indian students one by one explained how best to diagnose this cancer, how and where it usually spreads, and how best to treat it. On and on they went for 30 minutes, answering questions I thought only chief physicians knew. I realized my embarrassing mistake. I must have come to the wrong room. These must not be fourth-year students, these must be specialists. I had nothing to add to their analysis.

On our way out, I told a fellow student I was supposed to be with the fourth-years. "That's us," he said. I was stunned. They had caste marks on their foreheads and lived where exotic palm trees grew. How could they know much more than me? Over the next few days I learned that they had a textbook three times as thick as mine, and they had read it three times as many times.

I remember this whole experience as the first time in my life that I suddenly had to change my worldview: my assumption that I was superior because of where I came from, the idea that the West was the best and the rest would never catch up. At that moment, 45 years ago, I understood that the West would not dominate the world for much longer.

Questions

(1) Why did he decide not to tell what he saw in the first image?

ア He wanted to give other students enough time to think.

イ He was not sure if it was really kidney cancer.

ウ He wanted to keep it secret.

エ He wanted to learn three times as much as other students.

(2) What was it that he thought of as an embarrassing mistake?

ア The first image was not kidney cancer.

イ He was not the first student to look at the image.

ウ He was in the lower level class.

エ He was in the higher level class.

(3) What did he learn from this experience?

This is the end of the listening test.

(☆☆☆☆◎◎◎)

【3】次の各文の(　　)にあてはまる最も適切なものを，ア～エから1つ選び，記号で答えなさい。

(1) We guarantee not to disclose your data to any third party and to treat them absolutely (　　).

ア confidential　イ inconsequential　ウ tedious

エ enlightened

(2) This coat has a special surface that ( ) moisture.

ア isolates イ impedes ウ imports エ repels

(3) Community leaders are working hard to attract new industry and ( ) the downtown area.

ア revoke イ revitalize ウ revolt エ reverberate

(4) The government gave money to the citizens to ( ) economic stress.

ア eradicate イ immunize ウ diagnose エ alleviate

(5) The police are keeping the suspects under constant ( ).

ア remittance イ surveillance ウ accomplice

エ subtraction

(☆☆☆☆◎◎◎)

【4】次の各文の下線部ア～エの中で，誤っている箇所を1つ選び，記号で答えなさい。

(1) ア<u>Although</u> thought and action イ<u>tend to be considered</u> ウ<u>by two separate things</u>, some researchers エ<u>have suggested</u> that it is not necessarily the case.

(2) We must ア<u>embark to</u> a bold new program for making the イ<u>benefits of</u> our scientific advances and industrial progress ウ<u>available for</u> the improvement and エ<u>growth of</u> underdeveloped areas.

(3) Trees are ア<u>useful to us</u>, because they イ<u>provide us with wood</u> and other products, ウ<u>give us shade</u>, and help エ<u>to prevent from</u> floods.

(4) There can be wide disagreement ア<u>over</u> what an idea or a thought イ<u>exactly</u> is. But most of us probably agree ウ<u>with</u> any rate that language is the most common form we use to express it エ<u>by</u>.

(5) Everyone who ア<u>saw them work</u> イ<u>was amazed by</u> their ウ<u>ability of using</u> so many different エ<u>kinds of machines</u> at the same time.

(☆☆☆◎◎◎◎)

【5】次の対話文を読んで，(1)・(2)の問いに答えなさい。

A : And speaking of history, can I show you something? It'll just take a minute.

B : Oooh, what is it?

A : (　①　)

B : Look at that! Oh! It's heavy.

A : I know! It's a family keepsake. My grandfather always said that he hated being in the army. And one day he said to me, "(　②　)" And he opened it up for me. Like this.

B : But there's no arrow. And the tip's broken.

A : (　③　) And he replied, "See? There's no point!" So, in other words, this is something I keep to remind me that war is pointless.

B : Wow. [　　　　　　]

A : Yeah, yeah. He was.

(1)　(　①　)～(　③　)にあてはまる最も適切な英文を，ア～キから選び，記号で答えなさい。ただし，同じ選択肢を2度使わないこと。

ア　You'll get back to you on it.

イ　Well that's exactly what I said.

ウ　It's the ring my grandfather used to wear in the army.

エ　Right, right, all evidence points to the fact that he is innocent.

オ　I'll show you the point of war!

カ　To tell the truth, I don't think it was such a great experience overall.

キ　It's my grandfather's old compass, from back when he was in the army.

(2)　会話の流れに合うように，[　　　　　　]にあてはまる10語程度の英文1文を書きなさい。

(☆☆☆◎◎◎◎)

【6】次の英文の内容を，160字以内の日本語に要約しなさい。ただし，句読点も字数に入れること。

All persons are more or less apt to learn through the eye rather than the ear; and, whatever is seen in fact, makes a far deeper impression than anything that is merely read or heard. This is especially the case in early youth, when the eye is the chief inlet of knowledge. Whatever children see they unconsciously imitate. They insensibly come to resemble those who are about them—as insects take the colour of the leaves they feed on. Hence the vast importance of domestic training. For whatever may be the efficiency of schools, the examples set in our homes must always be of vastly greater influence in forming the characters of our future men and women. The home is the crystal of society—the nucleus of national character; and from that source, be it pure or tainted, issue the habits, principles and maxims, which govern public as well as private life. The nation comes from the nursery. Public opinion itself is for the most part the outgrowth of the home; and the best philanthropy comes from the fireside. "To love the little platoon we belong to in society," says Burke, "is the germ of all public affections." From this little central spot, the human sympathies may extend in an ever widening circle, until the world is embraced; for, though true philanthropy, like charity, begins at home, assuredly it does not end there.

(☆☆☆◎◎◎)

【7】次の英文を読み，あとの(1)～(6)は，(ア)～(オ)のどの段落について書かれているか，最も適切な段落をそれぞれ1つずつ選び，記号で答えなさい。

(ア)Families huddle on a once picturesque beach as their homes burn behind them. Baby koalas, their fur singed, cling to their mothers as they face a fiery demise. And military helicopters whomp overhead, searching the charred landscape for stragglers looking for a last-minute escape. These bracing scenes illustrate a terrifying reality on the ground in Australia, where more than two dozen people and millions of animals have died in wildfires that have destroyed more than 25 million acres since December and that are not expected to be contained anytime soon. The blazes, so large that they've created their own weather systems, have sparked widespread panic, prompted a military deployment and caused billions of dollars in damage.

(イ)The infernos have also captured the world's attention. While climate-linked disasters aren't new—from the uptick in deadly heat waves to increasingly powerful hurricanes, floods and blizzards—images of such destruction often fail to resonate and are quickly forgotten in the next day's news cycle. But what's happening in Australia feels different. Haunting pictures of cute koalas, kangaroos and wallabies that have died en masse tear at our heartstrings. And as cynical as it may sound, the fact that the devastation is occurring in a wealthy, English-speaking country reminds even the most privileged observer that money alone cannot buy immunity from the wrath of nature.

(ウ)Most significantly, the Australian fires are burning at a time when the world is becoming increasingly attuned to the catastrophic dangers of unchecked climate change. Activists, a series of dire scientific reports and other recent extreme, climate-linked events—including wildfires more than 7,000 miles away in California—have perhaps succeeded in sharpening the mind. Whether global leaders are able to translate this newfound awareness into meaningful political action is the next test.

(エ)There's no question about the link between the Australian wildfires and climate change. The country's famed bush—the continent's vast, often dry expanse that is sparsely inhabited but filled with vegetation—has always been prone to wildfires. But a warming climate has heightened the risk: decades of worsening droughts have killed off plants, grasses and trees, creating tinder for fires, and warmer average temperatures have created furnace-like conditions in which fire can easily spread. Last year was Australia's hottest and driest on record, with temperatures in some parts of the country topping 120°F in December, according to government data. A 2019 report from the Australian government concluded that climate change had already "resulted in more dangerous weather conditions for bushfires in recent decades."

(オ)But Australia's current leadership remains largely in denial about the problem. Along with the U.S., Russia and Brazil, Australia—where coal mining is a significant industry and a powerful lobby—is one of just a handful of countries with national politicians who have steadfastly refused to consider bold action to reduce greenhouse-gas emissions. Australian Prime Minister Scott Morrison isn't contesting that climate change is real or that it has worsened the bushfires. Instead, he argues that his country can't do anything about it because Australia's greenhouse-gas emissions make up only a small share of the global total.

(1) Despite the catastrophic damage by climate change, some countries are hesitating to take actions.

(2) Whether natural disaster occurs or not has nothing to do with how developed the country is.

(3) Australia cannot single-handedly prevent climate change in the country's backyard.

(4) Too much land was on fire unexpectedly and it destroyed the normal lives in Australia.

(5) The land in Australia is naturally likely to catch fire, which has been accelerated by climate change.

(6) The wildfires in Australia can be a trigger for people in other countries to take political measures for climate change.

(☆☆☆◎◎◎)

【8】次の英文を読み，下線部を日本語にしなさい。

I wasn't caught up in the school culture, and being in graduate school, I was boiling over with enthusiasm. My goat was to impart that enthusiasm to my students, to help them see the beauty of the world all around them in a new way, to change them so that they would see the world of physics as beautiful, and would understand that physics is everywhere, that it permeates our lives. What counts, I found, is not what you *cover*, but what you *uncover*. <u>Covering subjects in a class can be a boring exercise, and students feel it. Uncovering</u>

the laws of physics and making them see through the equations, on the other hand, demonstrates the process of discovery, with all its newness and excitement, and students love being part of it.

(☆☆☆☆◎◎◎)

【9】次の英文を読んで，［(1)］～［(4)］にあてはまる最も適切な英文をア～オから選び，記号で答えなさい。ただし，同じ選択肢を2度使わないこと。

In the late 1980s, workers excavating a new subway line in downtown Mexico City stumbled upon a long-lost cemetery. Documents showed it had once been connected to a colonial hospital built between 1529 and 1531—only about 10 years after the Spanish conquest of Mexico—for indigenous patients. As archaeologists excavated the buried skeletons, three stood out. Their teeth were filed into shapes similar to those of enslaved Africans from Portugal and people living in parts of West Africa. ［(1)］

During the 16th and 17th centuries, tens of thousands of enslaved and free Africans lived in Mexico. Today, almost all Mexicans carry a small amount of African ancestry. Rodrigo Barquera, a graduate student in archaeogenetics at the Max Planck Institute for the Science of Human History, suspected the remains might offer a window into lives often left out of historical records. To confirm their origins, he and his adviser Johannes Krause extracted DNA and analyzed chemical isotopes, including strontium, carbon, and nitrogen, from their teeth. Their DNA revealed that all three were men with ancestry from West Africa. And the ratios of the chemicals in their teeth, which preserve a signature of the food and water they consumed as children, were consistent with West African ecosystems, the researchers report today in Current Biology. ［(2)］

All three skeletons, now at the National School of Anthropology and History in Mexico City, show signs of trauma and violence. The men were likely in their late 20s or early 30s when they died. Before that, one man survived several gunshot wounds, and he and another man showed a thinning of their skull bones associated with malnutrition and anemia. The third man's skeleton showed signatures of stress from grueling physical labor, including a poorly healed broken leg. These signs of abuse make it likely that the men were enslaved rather than free, Krause says.

The two men with malnutrition also carried pathogens linked to chronic diseases, according to a genetic analysis of the microbes preserved in their teeth. One had the hepatitis B virus, and the other carried the bacterium that causes yaws, a disease in the same family as syphilis. Both microbes were most closely related to African strains, making it likely the men caught these pathogens in Africa. Or perhaps they picked up the microbes on an overcrowded slave ship voyaging to the Americas, suggests Ayana Omilade Flewellen, an archaeologist at the University of California, Berkeley, who studies the experiences of enslaved Africans and wasn't involved in the study. Such journeys killed millions between the 16th and 19th centuries. [(3)]

The men's presence in a hospital for indigenous people highlights the largely forgotten diversity of early colonies in the Americas, Flewellen says. [(4)]

ア　Either way, this is direct evidence that the transatlantic slave trade introduced novel pathogens to the Americas, Krause says, just as European colonization did.

イ　But researchers didn't find DNA from deadly infectious diseases in their remains.

ウ　"It's really nice to see how well the different lines of evidence come together," says Anne Stone, an anthropological geneticist, who wasn't involved with the research.

エ　We need to break out of the binary of just Native American and European experiences and remember that Africans were part of the story as well.

オ　Now, chemical and genetic analyses confirm these individuals were among the first generation of Africans to arrive in the Americas, likely as early victims of the burgeoning transatlantic slave trade.

(☆☆☆☆◎◎◎◎)

【10】2020年東京オリンピック・パラリンピック競技大会の開催が延期された理由と，延期され たことによって生じると思われる課題を2つ取り上げ，80語～100語の英語で書きなさい。ただし，符号は語数に含めず，最後に使用語数を書き入れること。

(☆☆☆☆◎◎◎◎)

【中学校】

【1】中学校学習指導要領「第2章　各教科」「第9節　外国語」について，次の(1)～(3)の問いに答えなさい。

(1)　次の文は「第2　各言語の目標及び内容等」「英語」「1　目標」「(4)　話すこと[発表]」である。(　①　)～(　⑥　)にあてはまる語句を書きなさい。

ア　関心のある(　①　)について，簡単な語句や文を用いて即興で話すことができるようにする。 イ　(　②　)な話題について，(　③　)や自分の考え，(　④　)などを整理し，簡単な語句や文を用いてまとまりのある(　⑤　)を話すことができるようにする。 ウ　(　⑥　)な話題に関して聞いたり読んだりしたことについて，考えたことや感じたこと，その理由などを，簡単な語句や文を用いて話すことができるようにする。

(2)　次の文は「第2　各言語の目標及び内容等」「英語」「2　内容」の(3)の「②　言語の働きに関する事項」の一部である。(　①　)～(　③　)にあてはまる語句を書きなさい。

ア　言語の使用場面の例
(ア)　生徒の身近な(　①　)に関わる場面
・　家庭での生活　　・　学校での学習や活動
・　地域の行事　　など
(イ)　(　②　)の表現がよく使われる場面
・　自己紹介　　・　買物　　・　食事
・　道案内　　・　(　③　)　　・　電話での対応
・　手紙や電子メールのやり取り　　など

(3)　次の文は「第2　各言語の目標及び内容等」「英語」「3　指導計画の作成と内容の取扱い」の(1)の一部である。(　①　)～(　③　)にあてはまる語句を書きなさい。

エ　生徒が英語に(　①　)機会を充実するとともに，授業を実際の(　②　)の場面とするため，授業は英語で行うことを(　③　)とする。その際，生徒の理解の程度に応じた英語を用いるようにすること。

(☆☆☆◎◎◎◎)

【高等学校】

【1】高等学校学習指導要領「第2章　各学科に共通する各教科」「第8節　外国語」について，次の(1)～(3)の問いに答えなさい。

(1)　次は「第2款　各科目」「第1　英語コミュニケーションⅠ」「1　目標」「(4)　話すこと[発表]」の一部である。(　①　)～(　④　)にあてはまる語句を書きなさい。

ア　日常的な話題について，使用する語句や文，事前の準備などにおいて，多くの支援を活用すれば，(　①　)な語句や文を用いて，(　②　)や考え，(　③　)などを(　④　)に注意して話して伝えることができるようにする。

(2)　次は「第2款　各科目」「第4　論理・表現Ⅰ」「2　内容」「(3)　言語活動及び言語の働きに関する事項」「①　言語活動に関する事項」「ウ　書くこと」の一部である。(　①　)～(　⑤　)にあてはまる語句を書きなさい。

(イ)　日常的な話題や社会的な話題に関して聞いたり読んだりした内容について，使用する語句や文，(　①　)が十分に示されたり，準備のための多くの時間が確保されたりする状況で，(　②　)から推敲（こう）まで段階的な手順を踏みながら，意見や主張などを適切な理由や(　③　)とともに段落を書いて伝える活動。また，書いた内容を読み合い，(　④　)をしたり，意見や(　⑤　)を伝え合ったりする活動。

(3)　次は「第3款　英語に関する各科目にわたる指導計画の作成と内容の取扱い」の一部である。(　①　)～(　③　)にあてはまる語句を書きなさい。

3　教材については，次の事項に留意するものとする。 (2)　英語を使用している人々を中心とする世界の人々や日本人の日常生活，風俗習慣，物語，地理，歴史，伝統文化，自然科学などに関するものの中から，生徒の発達の段階や興味・関心に即して適切な題材を効果的に取り上げるものとし，次の観点に配慮すること。 (ア)　多様な考え方に対する理解を深めさせ，公正な(　①　)を養い豊かな心情を育てるのに役立つこと。 (イ)　我が国の文化や，英語の背景にある文化に対する関

心を高め，理解を深めようとする(　②　)を養うのに役立つこと。

(ウ)　社会が(　③　)化する中で，広い視野から国際理解を深め，国際社会と向き合うことが求められている我が国の一員としての自覚を高めるとともに，国際協調の精神を養うのに役立つこと。

(エ)　人間，社会，自然などについての考えを深めるのに役立つこと。

(☆☆☆◎◎◎◎)

解答・解説

【中高共通】

【1】(1)　イ　　(2)　ウ

〈解説〉短いパッセージ2本と，内容に関する質問が各1問，1度だけ放送される。質問の解答の選択肢は問題用紙に印刷されている。パッセージのトピックはAが風力発電，Bが郵便局の営業縮小についてである。(1)　質問は「風力タービンの役割は何か」。スクリプト第1パラグラフ2文目の内容から「発電すること」が適切。　(2)　パッセージの内容に合致するものを選ぶ問題。スクリプト第4パラグラフ1文目の内容から「3500以上の地方郵便局の閉鎖が予定されている」が適切。

【2】(1)　ア　　(2)　エ　　(3)　Where you are from has nothing to do with how intelligent you are.

〈解説〉パッセージは250語程度。(1)と(2)は，パッセージと質問文が放送され，問題用紙に印刷された選択肢から解答を選ぶ4択問題である。(3)は，問題用紙に印刷された質問文を読み，英文1文で答える記述式問題である。放送は1回のみなので，集中して聞き取らなければならない。　(1)　スクリプトの第1パラグラフ4文目と5文目に「筆者にはすぐに答えがわかったが，誇示したくなかったので，少しの間ほかの生徒の様子を見ることにした」と述べられている。　(2)　スクリプト第1パラグラフ後ろから2文目と，第2パラグラフ1文目と2文目に「授業が専門家しかわからないような高度な内容で，教室と間違えていたと思っていたが，実は間違っておらず自分が行くべき4年生の教室で合っていた」と述べられている。　(3)　スクリプト第3パラグラフの内容を的確にまとめる必要がある。このパラグラフでは筆者は自分の出身地から優越感を持っていて世界の他の地域は西洋に追いつけないと考えていたが，インド人の勤勉ぶりから出身地は関係ないということを学んだのである。

【3】(1)　ア　(2)　エ　(3)　イ　(4)　エ　(5)　イ

〈解説〉(1)　英文は「我々はあなたのデータを第三者に公開せず完全に秘密に扱うことを保証する」の意である。confidentialは「秘密の」。　(2)　英文は「このコートは水分をはじく特殊な表面を持つ」の意である。moistureは「水分，湿気」，repelは「はじく，寄せ付けない」。　(3)　英文は「地域社会の指導者は新しい産業を誘致し，その中心部地域を再び活性化させるべく懸命に働いている」の意である。revitalizeはre＋vitalizeで「再び活性化させる」。　(4)　英文は「政府は，経済的ストレスを緩和させるために市民に金を与えた」の意である。alleviateは「軽減する，緩和する」。　(5)　英文は「警察はその容疑者を常に監視下に置き続けている」の意である。under surveillanceで「監視下に」。

【4】(1)　ウ　(2)　ア　(3)　エ　(4)　ウ　(5)　ウ

〈解説〉(1)　英文は「思考と行動が2つの別の物だと考えられている傾向にあるが，必ずしもそうとは限らないことを示唆する研究者もいる」の意である。considerは第5文型を取るので受動態の場合にbyは不要。　(2)　英文は「発展途上地域の発展と成長に利用できる私たちの科学的な前進と産業の進歩という利益を得るため，私たちは大胆な新しい計画に乗り出さなければならない」の意である。embark onで「～に乗り出す」。　(3)　英文は「木は私たちにとって役立つものである。なぜなら木材や他の生産物を私たちに提供し，木陰を与えてくれ，我々が洪水から身を守るのに役立つからである」の意。prevent O from ～で「Oを～から防ぐ」となり，prevent us from floodsが正しい。　(4)　英文は「考えや思考が正確には何であるかについては広く意見の不一致がありうる。しかし，いずれにせよ，言語がそれを表現するのに最も一般的な形であるいうことは，私たちのほとんどで意見がおそらく一致するだろう」の意。ここではagreeは他動詞でthat節を伴っている。at any rateで「いずれにせよ，ともかく」。　(5)　英文は「彼らが働くのを見る人は誰でも，非常に多くの様々な種類の機械を同時に使えることに驚いた」の意。abilityは後ろにto不定詞を伴い，ability to useが適切。

【5】(1)　①　キ　　②　オ　　③　イ　　(2)　It sounds like your grandfather was a pretty interesting guy.

〈解説〉(1)　①　空所①の直後でIt's heavy.とあり，選択肢の中で重いものはキのold compassのみである。　②　直接話法で表す内容としてはオ「おまえに戦争の目的を教えてやろう!」が最適。　③　空所の前の「コンパスの針がなく，先端も壊れている」というBの発言を受けて，それに続くのはイ「それこそが，まさに私の言ったことなのです」が適切。　(2)　空所の後でAがYeah, yeah. He was.と述べていることから，空所にはHe was ～.という文が入ることがわかる。会話全体を通して，Aの祖父は，コンパスの針がないことを戦争に目的がないことに巧みに例えたことから，解答例のような返答が考えられる。

【6】人は聞いたり読んだりしたことよりも，見たものから物事を学ぶ。特に幼少期にその傾向が強く見られ，子どもはいつのまにか，周囲の人間と似かよってくる。家庭で示される手本が，子どもの性格形成に大きな影響を与えることから，家庭は社会の結晶であり，国民性の核

を形成していると言える。家族を愛することが，社会全体を愛する第一歩となる。(160字)

〈解説〉英文を160字以内の日本語に要約する問題である。英文の重要な情報に着目して，重複する情報を整理しながら作成すればよいだろう。最初に着目すべき点としては，第1パラグラフの1文目と2文目「人は見たものから物事を学び，特に幼少期にその傾向が強い」ということである。そして6文目と7文目「家庭で示される手本が子供の性格形成に大きな影響を与えることから，家庭は社会の結晶である」ことが続く。その上で，10文目の「家庭を愛することが，社会全体を愛する第一歩である」という結論に結びつければよいだろう。

【7】(1)　(オ)　　(2)　(イ)　　(3)　(オ)　　(4)　(ア)　　(5)　(エ)　　(6)　(ウ)

〈解説〉(1)　英文は「気候変動による壊滅的な損害にも関わらず，行動を起こすのを躊躇している国もある」の意。これは(オ)の2文目の内容と一致する。　(2)　英文は「自然災害が発生するかどうかは，その国がどれだけ発展しているかとは関係がない」の意。これは(イ)の最終文の内容と一致する。　(3)　英文は「オーストラリアは国の身近な気候変動を単独で防ぐことはできない」の意。これは(オ)の3文目と4文目の内容と一致する。　(4)　英文は「多くの土地が予期せぬ火事になり，オーストラリアの通常の生活を破壊した」の意。これは(ア)の内容全体をまとめたものとなる。　(5)　英文は「オーストラリアの土地はもともと出火しやすく，気候変動によってそれは加速している」の意。これは(エ)の内容全体をまとめたものとなる。　(6)　英文は「オーストラリアの山火事は他の国の人々が気候変動に対して政治的措置を取る契機となりうる」の意。これは(ウ)の最終文の内容と一致する。

【8】授業で教科をひととおり教えることは，ともすれば退屈な作業になってしまいますし，生徒も退屈だと感じてしまいます。一方，生徒に方程式を通して物理の法則を見つけさせるようにすると，発見の過程

を，とりわけ新鮮さやわくわくする気持ちとともに示すことができ，生徒もその過程に参加することをとても喜ぶのです。

〈解説〉動名詞Coveringが1文目の主語であり，Covering subjects in a classで「授業の教科でひととおり教えること」を指す。助動詞canは可能性「～こともありうる」を表す。on the other hand「一方」が2文目の中に入っていることを見逃さないようにしたい。2文目の主語は動名詞Uncoveringとmakingであり，動詞はdemonstratesとなる。無生物主語なので「生徒に方程式を通して物理の法則を見つけさせるようにすると～を示す」という訳にするとよい。目的語はthe process of discoveryでwith all its newness and excitementがこの目的語を修飾している。and以下はloveの目的語がbeing part of it「その一部となること」となり，文脈を考慮して「その過程に参加すること」などと訳すとよい。

【9】(1)　オ　(2)　ウ　(3)　ア　(4)　エ

〈解説〉(1)　オのthese individualsは空所(1)の前文の，ポルトガルから来たアフリカ人奴隷や西アフリカに住むアフリカ人に歯の形が似ている，buried skeletons(埋められていた骸骨)を指すと判断できる。　(2)　第2パラグラフでは，DNA分析や歯の調査から，メキシコで発見された3つの骸骨は，西アフリカに祖先をもつことがわかったと述べられているので，パラグラフの最終文である空所(2)では，まとめとして「異なる証拠がつながった」という内容のウが入ると判断できる。　(3)　第4パラグラフでは，病原菌がアメリカ大陸に渡ったことと，アフリカ人が病原菌を持ち込んだことが述べられていることから，ア「ヨーロッパによる植民地化と同様に，大西洋を渡った奴隷売買が，新規の病原菌をアメリカに持ち込んだ」が適切。　(4)　残りの選択肢イとエを検討すると，イはDNAの話題で前文と全くつながらない。本文全体からアフリカ人がアメリカに影響を及ぼしていることが読み取れる。よって，本文全体のまとめとして，エの「アメリカ先住民とヨーロッパという二元論から離れ，アフリカ人も関係していたことを思い出すべきだ」という記述が適切だと判断できる。

【10】The Tokyo Olympic Games were postponed to safeguard the health of the athletes and everybody involved in the Olympic Games because of the spread of corona virus all over the world. The Olympic Games organizers had prepared a variety of stadiums, hotels, and other venues for the Games in 2020. All of them will have to be renegotiated, canceled and rebooked. It will cost a large amount of money to solve the problem. In addition, the postponement is difficult for aging athletes. They have to keep training very hard as representatives of their countries. (94words)

〈解説〉東京オリンピックが延期された原因は，言うまでもなく新型コロナウイルスの世界的流行であると述べればよい。延期されたことによって生じる課題はいくつも考えられるが，解答例のように「再準備に多額の費用と手間がかかること」，「ベテランの出場選手が国の代表としてとても大変なトレーニングを続けなければならないことの困難さ」などが一例として挙げられる。それ以外には選手や観客の安全面をどう担保するかなども考えられるだろう。

【中学校】

【1】(1)　①　事柄　②　日常的　③　事実　④　気持ち　⑤　内容　⑥　社会的　(2)　①　暮らし　②　特有　③　旅行　(3)　①　触れる　②　コミュニケーション　③　基本

〈解説〉(1)「話すこと」の領域は，平成29年3月告示の中学校学習指導要領から，「話すこと[発表]」と「話すこと[やり取り]」の2つに分けられた。ここでは，「発表」であるので，聞き手に対して一方向で話して伝えることができるようにする。なお，話す事柄や話題は，ア「関心のある事柄」→イ「日常的な話題」→ウ「社会的な話題」へと発展し，社会的な話題に対する自分なりの意見や感想を，理由や自分が学んだこと，経験したことの例示などとともに表現することが求められることに留意したい。　(2)　小学校の外国語科においても，本問と同様の「場面」が取り上げられている。中学校における指導では，小学校高学年の児童が，これらの場面でどのような英語表現を使用しているかを把握することが大切である。同じ言語材料を繰り返し使用させることでその確実な定着を図ったり，異なる言語材料を使用させることで表現内容の広がりや深まりをもたせたりすることを可能にするからである。　(3)　この配慮事項は，生徒が授業の中で「英語に触れる機会」を最大限に確保することと，授業全体を，英語を使った「実際のコミュニケーションの場面」とすることをねらいとする。生徒が自信をもって自分の英語を使っていけるようになるためには，授業における教師の英語使用に対する態度と行動が大きな影響力をもつ。そのため，教師の積極的な英語使用が求められるのである。

【高等学校】

【1】(1)　①　基本的　②　情報　③　気持ち　④　論理性
(2)　①　文章例　②　発想　③　根拠　④　質疑応答
⑤　感想　(3)　①　判断力　②　態度　③　グローバル

〈解説〉(1)　本目標では，使用される語句や文，情報量などについて支援することを示している。また，常に情報の詳細を理解しようとするのではなく，必要な情報に焦点を絞って理解した上で，そこから書き手が全体として何を伝えようとしているのかを把握することができるようになることが求められる。　(2)　意見や主張などを，論理の構成や展開を工夫して，文章を書いて伝えることができるようにする言語活動について示している。論理の構成とは，例えば，意見や主張を述べる一つの段落の場合，その段落の主題を述べるトピック・センテンスを用いた導入，主題を支持するためのサポーティング・センテンスによる展開，主題と展開をまとめる結論という構成などが考えられる。(3)　教材の選定に当たっては，生徒の発達の段階，興味・関心について十分に配慮しながら，英語の目標に照らして適切であり，学習段階に応じた言語材料で構成されているような適切な題材を，変化をもたせて取り上げるように配慮する必要がある。本文中の(ア)～(エ)は，題材の選択に関する4つの観点を示したものである。

2020年度　実施問題

【中高共通】

【1】[Listening Test 1]

The listening test is about to begin. Listen carefully to the directions.

Listening Test 1 is multiple choice. You will hear two passages, (A) and (B). Each passage will be followed by two questions, (1) through (4). The passages and the questions will be given only once. You are permitted to take notes. For each question, you will have 10 seconds to choose the best answer from among the four choices written below. From now on, you have some time to look at the choices. (30 seconds)
Now, let's begin.

[Passage A]

Waterfalls are furious cascades of water, sometimes scoring the landscape as they obey gravity's demands. Powerful as they may appear, there is a longstanding assumption that they can form only when permitted by other natural forces. Tectonic movement, alterations in sea level or changes in rock quality are all ways in which external forces are believed to influence where waterfalls form.

But this paradigm may be about to change. By building a scaled-down river in a laboratory at the California Institute of Technology, a team of researchers showed that waterfalls could sometimes bring themselves into existence without outside help.

Using a riverbed made of foam rather than real rock, the team was able to watch millenniums of erosion play out quickly. Without external changes, the turbulent flow eventually formed a deep, irregular pocket of erosion with a lip from which water jetted off to splash down farther along. A waterfall had appeared, all by itself. The research, published in Nature, could increase understanding of landscapes.

Questions

(1) According to the passage, what has been assumed for a long time?

ア Waterfalls may not always require events like earthshaking movements to form.

イ Frequent changes in sea level is the most important factor to a waterfall formation.

ウ In most cases rock quality is irrelevant to the size or the power of a waterfall.

エ The existence of a waterfall is dependent on a certain complex of physical conditions.

(2) To make a waterfall in the laboratory, the researchers used one thing which didn't exist in the natural environment. Which is it?

ア A soft material.

イ A water pressure machine.

ウ A zero-gravity chamber.

エ A device to measure tectonic movements.

[Passage B]

In the 1960s it took five hours to fly from New York to Los Angeles, and just 45 minutes to hop from New York to Washington, D.C. Today, these same flights now take six-plus hours and 75 minutes respectively, although the airports haven't moved further apart.

It's called "schedule creep" , or padding. And it's a secret the airlines don't want you to know about, especially given the spillover effects for the environment. Padding is the extra time airlines allow themselves to fly from A to B. Because these flights were consistently late, airlines have now baked delays experienced for decades into their schedules instead of improving operations.

It might seem innocuous enough to the passenger — after all, what it can mean is that even though you take off late, you're pleasantly surprised to arrive on time at your destination. However, this global trend poses multiple problems: not only does your journey take longer but creating the illusion of punctuality means there's no pressure on airlines to become more efficient, meaning congestion and carbon emissions will keep rising.

Questions

(3) Which is true about the passage?

ア The flight time from New York to Washington, D.C. was 75 minutes in 1960.

イ The flight time from New York to Los Angeles is now longer than in 1960.

ウ The airlines need special permission to change flight duration.

エ The airlines have been changing flight duration to decrease the impact on the environment.

(4) What is a bad point of padding?

ア The airlines must tackle the problem of airport capacity.

イ It is one of the barriers to entry into an airline industry.

ウ It costs too much maintain good service standards.

エ The airlines don't make enough effort to improve their performance.

(☆☆☆☆◎◎◎)

【2】 [Listening Test 2]

Here are the directions for Listening Test 2. Look at the question on your test paper. You will hear a passage, which will be given only once. You are permitted to take notes. After the statement "this is the end of the recording," write down your answer on your answer sheet. Your answer must be given in one English sentence. Then, you can go on to the next questions. Now, lets begin.

Handsome Her, a vegan café in Australia, was accused of reverse sexism after opening in Melbourne in 2017. Its owners provoked debate by offering women priority seating and charging men an extra 18% one week a month. Although non-compulsory, the "man tax" reflected "the gender pay gap" , the owners said.

Two years on and the owners have announced they will cease trading on the 28th of April. They made the announcement in the description of a Facebook event created to advertise their last day of business. The reaction to the man tax "showed us how fragile masculinity is and solidified the necessity for us to confront and dismantle patriarchy" , they wrote.

"We were just one little tiny shop on Sydney Rd that was trying to carve out a swathe of space to prioritise women and women's issues, and suddenly we became the punching bag of Melbourne and the Internet," they added.

[Question] Why did the owners of the café become "the punching bag of Melbourne and the Internet" ?

This is the end of the recording.

(☆☆☆☆◎◎◎)

【3】次の各文の(　　)にあてはまる最も適切なものを，ア～エから1つ選び，記号で答えなさい。

(1) This discovery gave a new (　　) to prospecting in south-western Nevada, and it was soon discovered that the district was not an isolated mining region but was in the heart of a great mineral belt.

ア nepotism　イ commotion　ウ duress　エ impetus

(2) The mayor of our town always spoke (　　), like an actor repeating a

stale part.

ア　languidly　　イ　astutely　　ウ　sweepingly　　エ　bucolically

(3)　If waking up early isn't (　　) for you, then why did you take the morning shift?

ア　feasible　　イ　sleek　　ウ　resonant　　エ　elastic

(4)　Along with people from different ethnicities, the range of cuisines further (　　) the city's diversity.

ア　purloin　　イ　infringe　　ウ　exemplify　　エ　graze

(5)　The two countries met at the conference to (　　) their differences.

ア　pay back　　イ　iron out　　ウ　hit off　　エ　patch through

(☆☆☆☆◎◎◎◎◎)

【4】次の各文の下線部ア～エの中で，誤っている箇所を1つ選び，記号で答えなさい。

(1)　Art and culture flourished ア briefly, during the Prague Spring, イ short period ウ of relaxed censorship and エ looser Soviet control.

(2)　ア Violence pervades television イ and cinema, ウ and my grandfather doesn't エ like them at all.

(3)　ア Artists must often イ make a choice between teaching ウ or devoting their time to エ creating art.

(4)　ア Like his other cookbooks, in his new book Chef Louis offers lengthy explanations イ of what ウ he considers to be エ basic cooking.

(5)　The presence of strong feeling, the cause ア of which is not fully understood, always has the イ effect of making ウ we human エ beings uneasy.

(☆☆☆◎◎◎◎)

【5】次の対話文を読んで，(1)・(2)の問いに答えなさい。

A : Hi, Jessica. How are you?

B : Just fine. Wow, I haven't seen you in a long time. What are you doing today?

A : I'm going to Food Fair in the city center. Would you like to go?

B : I'd love to go, but I can't. (①)

A : Oh, really? (②)

B : I'm not sure. She just won't put her front right paw down at all. She looks like she's in pain.

A : I'm sorry to hear that. Where is your vet's office?

B : I go to Dr. Samuel. Her office is on Lincoln Road. Do you know it?

A : Yes, of course!

B : (③)

A : Yes, it does. I like Dr. Samuel. She has a really good way of explaining things. I like how her office treats my dog. [ ]

B : Exactly. If my cat has any problems, I always take her to Dr. Samuel.

(1) (①)~(③)にあてはまる最も適切な英文を，ア～キから選び，記号で答えなさい。ただし，同じ選択肢を2度使わないこと。

ア I'd like to book some tickets for the fair.

イ Is there anywhere else you suggest I should go?

ウ We think we'll go for that option.

エ I have to take Maria to my vet.

オ Her office has a good reputation, you know.

カ Maria has a lot of experience of life on the street.

キ What's wrong with her?

(2) 会話の流れに合うように，[ ]に適する英文1文を書きなさい。

(☆☆☆◎◎◎◎)

【6】次の日本社会について述べた英文を読んで，その趣旨を160字以内の日本語で書きなさい。ただし，句読点も字数に入れること。

In the interpersonal relationships we value in our daily lives, the feelings and affects of the communicating parties are regarded as just as important as communication through words. Rather than asserting one's individual self, we form a reciprocal relationship through trusting and relying upon that other person and making efforts to accept their thoughts and ideas. Through relationships of affective tolerance, we gain a tacit understanding of others. The feeling of dependency and sense of relying on the other person is located at the base of relationships of trust that do not necessarily rely upon words.

It is considered desirable that reciprocal relationships based upon maternal emotions such as dependency can be brought into relationships across the whole of everyday society. People's sense of 'self' is an emotion that is formed in the 'ties' made 'between' themselves and others. Therefore, interpersonal relationships can be formed based upon perceptions of the situation or feelings of others without explanation. In European and North American society, mutual understanding based upon words is a major premise. Intentions and demands are communicated taking into account the distinctions and points of potential conflict between people. In contrast, in communication based on Japanese emotions, the sharing of information and communication of people's intentions can be sufficiently achieved without efforts to convince one's interlocutor through logical words.

(☆☆☆☆◎◎◎)

【7】次のA～Eは，"Should the British Museum return the cultural treasures to the countries of origin?" というトピックについて5人の生徒が書いた意見である。これらを読み，後の(1)～(6)はA～Eのどの意見に最も近いか，それぞれ1つずつ選び，記号で答えなさい。ただし，同じ選択肢を2度使ってもかまわない。

A

At present, England keeps other countries' cultural treasures and it is benefiting from them instead of the country of origin and this is unfair. The main benefit is that the British people can easily access artifacts — for example, a school trip to the British Museum to see the Rosetta Stone — whereas an Egyptian child would have to be very rich to fly to

England to see it. The masses are therefore denied access to their cultural heritage.

B

Cultural treasures belong to the world. Great works of art, artifacts from ancient civilization or items of political significance are relevant and significant to all of humanity. The fact that it was sculpted on your doorstep does not make it most relevant to you — especially when the civilizations have changed. Ancient Greece and Rome set up all of Western civilization — the treasures are not more significant to modern-day Greece and Italy than they are to Britain or France.

C

Because cultural treasures belong to the world, we should have the best access for the world. Cities such as London are a huge draw for tourists, so many people from around the world can see and enjoy the treasures while on a visit. Such cities also have the infrastructure to support these tourists and their viewing, and London is safe in a way that countries like Egypt and Ethiopia are not.

D

The British Museum has been preserving these artifacts for centuries. Without this, they would have been ruined. When the marbles were taken, the Parthenon was in disarray. The British saved the artifacts and have spent a fortune on them over the years — why should they now be punished?

E

Artifacts in a case in the British Museum cannot be understood or appreciated as they could be if they were to be seen in context. For example, would it not be better to walk into Tutankhamen's tomb and

see the artifacts there, or to see the Parthenon Marbles in the Parthenon? Such a context would improve the experience for tourists and academics alike.

(1) The British Museum has been making a lot of efforts to save cultural treasures.

(2) Nice public transportation is important to enjoy cultural treasures.

(3) Students could learn more if they could see the cultural treasures in the very place where they were found.

(4) It is strange that people have to have the privilege to enjoy their own cultural treasures.

(5) A lot of tourists come to London anyway even if their main purpose may not be visiting the British Museum.

(6) Artifacts may not be as important for the country where they were created.

(☆☆☆◎◎◎)

【8】次の英文の下線部を日本語にしなさい。

Something can happen to people when they get in the driving seat of a car. <u>A normally easy-going, non-argumentative person may, at the slightest provocation from other road users and pedestrians, suddenly become a person, unable to consider anyone but himself or herself and be determined to get from A to B without "unnecessary" interruptions — and nothing will get in his or her way.</u>

(☆☆☆◎◎◎◎)

【9】次の英文を読んで，(1)・(2)の問いに答えなさい。

We have no idea what the job market will look like in 2050. It is generally agreed that machine learning and robotics will change almost every line of work — from producing yoghurt to teaching yoga. However, there are conflicting views about the nature of the change and its imminence. Some believe that within a mere decade or two, billions of people will become economically redundant. Others maintain that even in the long run automation will keep generating new jobs and greater prosperity for all.

So are we on a verge of a terrifying upheaval, or are such forecasts yet another example of ill-founded Luddite hysteria? It is hard to say. Fears that automation will create massive unemployment go back to the nineteenth century, and so far they have never materialized. Since the beginning of the Industrial Revolution, for every job lost to a machine at least one new job was created, and the average standard of living has increased dramatically. (A)

Humans have two types of abilities — physical and cognitive. In the past, machines competed with humans mainly in raw physical abilities, while humans retained an immense edge over machines in cognition. Hence as manual jobs in agriculture and industry were automated, new service jobs emerged that required the kind of cognitive skills only humans possessed: learning, analyzing, communicating and above all understanding human emotions. However, AI is now beginning to outperform humans in more and more of these skills, including in the understanding of human emotions. (B)

It is crucial to realize that the AI revolution is not just about computers getting faster and smarter. It is fueled by breakthroughs in the life sciences and the social sciences as well. The better we understand the biochemical mechanisms that underpin human emotions, desires and choices, the better computers can become in analyzing human behavior, predicting human decisions, and replacing human drivers, bankers and lawyers.

In the last few decades research in areas such as neuroscience and behavioral economics allowed scientists to hack humans, and in particular to gain a much better understanding of how humans make decisions. It turned out that our choices of everything from food to mates result not from some mysterious free will, but rather from billions of neurons calculating probabilities within a split second. Vaunted ‘human intuition’ is in reality ‘pattern recognition’. Good drivers, bankers and lawyers don’t have magical intuitions about traffic, investment or negotiation — rather, by recognizing recurring patterns, they spot and try to avoid careless pedestrians, inept borrowers and dishonest crooks. It also turned out that the biochemical algorithms of the human brain are far from perfect. They rely on heuristics, shortcuts and outdated circuits adapted to the African savannah rather than to the urban jungle. (　C　)

Luddite　ラッダイト主義の(1811年から1817年頃イギリス中・北部織物工業地帯に起こった機械破壊運動)

(1) (　A　)～(　C　)にあてはまる最も適切な英文を，ア～オから選び，記号で答えなさい。ただし，同じ選択肢を2度使わないこと。

ア　For how can a computer understand the divinely created human spirit?

イ　No wonder that even good drivers, bankers and lawyers sometimes make stupid mistakes.

ウ　You might object that by switching from individual humans to a computer network we will lose the advantages of individuality.

エ　We don’t know of any third field of activity — beyond the physical and the cognitive — where humans will always retain a secure edge.

オ　Yet there are good reasons to think that this time it is different, and that machine learning will be a real game changer.

(2) 次の英文の指示に従って英語で答えなさい。

(a) Imagine what the job market will be like in 2050, and give good advice to students. You have to write in around 30 words in English and write the total number of words used inside 〈　〉 on the answer sheet.

(b) Among the school subjects written below, which one would YOU like to learn in 2050? Choose one and give some reasons why that subject would be important for you in 2050. You have to write in around 80 words in English and write the total number of words used inside 〈　〉

on the answer sheet.

[History　Geography　Music　Math　Art]

(☆☆☆☆◎◎◎◎)

【中学校】

【1】中学校学習指導要領「第2章　各教科」「第9節　外国語」について，次の(1)～(3)の問いに答えなさい。

(1) 次の文は「第1　目標」である。(　①　)～(　⑤　)にあてはまる語句を書きなさい。

> 外国語によるコミュニケーションにおける(　①　)・考え方を働かせ，外国語による聞くこと，読むこと，話すこと，書くことの(　②　)を通して，簡単な情報や考えなどを理解したり表現したり伝え合ったりするコミュニケーションを図る資質・能力を次のとおり育成することを目指す。
>
> (1) 外国語の音声や語彙，表現，文法，言語の働きなどを理解するとともに，これらの(　③　)を，聞くこと，読むこと，話すこと，書くことによる実際のコミュニケーションにおいて活用できる技能を身に付けるようにする。
>
> (2) コミュニケーションを行う目的や場面，(　④　)などに応じて，日常的な話題や社会的な話題について，外国語で簡単な情報や考えなどを理解したり，これらを活用して表現したり伝え合ったりすることができる力を養う。
>
> (3) 外国語の背景にある文化に対する理解を深め，聞き手，読み手，話し手，書き手に配慮しながら，(　⑤　)に外国語を用いてコミュニケーションを図ろうとする態度を養う。

(2) 次の文は「第2　各言語の目標及び内容等」「英語」「1　目標」「(5)　書くこと」である。(　①　)～(　③　)にあてはまる語句を書きなさい。

ア　関心のある事柄について，簡単な語句や文を用いて(　①　)に書くことができるようにする。 イ　日常的な話題について，事実や自分の考え，気持ちなどを整理し，簡単な語句や文を用いて(　②　)のある文章を書くことができるようにする。 ウ　社会的な話題に関して聞いたり読んだりしたことについて，考えたことや感じたこと，その(　③　)などを，簡単な語句や文を用いて書くことができるようにする。

(3)　次の文は「第2　各言語の目標及び内容等」「英語」「3　指導計画の作成と内容の取扱い」の(1)の一部である。(　①　)～(　④　)にあてはまる語句を書きなさい。

(1)　指導計画の作成に当たっては，小学校や(　①　)における指導との(　②　)に留意しながら，次の事項に配慮するものとする。 ア　(　③　)など内容や時間のまとまりを見通して，その中で育む資質・能力の育成に向けて，生徒の主体的・対話的で(　④　)の実現を図るようにすること。

(☆☆☆◎◎◎◎)

【高等学校】

【1】高等学校学習指導要領「第2章　各学科に共通する各教科」「第8節　外国語」について，次の(1)～(3)の問いに答えなさい。

(1)　次は「第1款　目標」である。(　①　)～(　⑧　)にあてはまる語句を書きなさい。同じ番号には同じ語句が入るものとする。

外国語によるコミュニケーションにおける見方・(　①　)を働かせ，外国語による聞くこと，読むこと，話すこと，書くことの言語活動及びこれらを結び付けた(　②　)な言語活動を通して，情報や考えなどを的確に理解したり適切に表現した

り伝え合ったりするコミュニケーションを図る資質・能力を次のとおり育成することを目指す。

(1) 外国語の音声や語彙，表現，文法，言語の働きなどの理解を深めるとともに，これらの知識を，聞くこと，読むこと，話すこと，書くことによる(　③　)のコミュニケーションにおいて，(　④　)や(　⑤　)，(　⑥　)などに応じて適切に活用できる技能を身に付けるようにする。

(2) コミュニケーションを行う(　④　)や(　⑤　)，(　⑥　)などに応じて，日常的な話題や社会的な話題について，外国語で情報や考えなどの概要や要点，(　⑦　)，話し手や書き手の意図などを的確に理解したり，これらを活用して適切に表現したり伝え合ったりすることができる力を養う。

(3) 外国語の背景にある文化に対する理解を深め，聞き手，読み手，話し手，書き手に配慮しながら，主体的，(　⑧　)に外国語を用いてコミュニケーションを図ろうとする態度を養う。

(2) 次は「第2款　各科目　第1　英語コミュニケーションⅠ」「1　目標」「(1)　聞くこと」の「ア」である。(　　)にあてはまる語句を書きなさい。

日常的な話題について，話される速さや，使用される語句や文，情報量などにおいて，(　　)を活用すれば，必要な情報を聞き取り，話し手の意図を把握することができるようにする。

(3) 次は「第2款　各科目　第1　英語コミュニケーションⅠ」「2　内容」「(3)　言語活動及び言語の働きに関する事項」「①　言語活動に関する事項」「エ　話すこと[やり取り]」の「(ア)」である。(　①　)~(　③　)にあてはまる語句を書きなさい。

身近な出来事や家庭生活などの日常的な話題について，使用する語句や文，やり取りの(　①　)な進め方が十分に示される状況で，情報や考え，気持ちなどを(　②　)話して伝え合う活動。また，やり取りした内容を(　③　)して発表したり，文章を書いたりする活動。

(☆☆☆◎◎◎◎)

解答・解説

【中高共通】

【1】(1)　エ　　(2)　ア　　(3)　イ　　(4)　エ

〈解説〉170～180語程度のパッセージと質問文を聞き，問題用紙に印刷された選択肢から解答を選ぶ4択問題である。パッセージはAとBの2本あり，それぞれ2つずつ質問がある。放送はパッセージ，質問とも1回のみである。　(1)　スクリプトの第1パラグラフの2文目にあるthere is a longstanding assumptionに着目する。その内容が続くthat節で示されており，後続する文で具体的に説明されている。この箇所が選択肢エのcertain complex of physical conditionsに該当する。　(2)　スクリプトの第3パラグラフの1文目にあるUsing a riverbed made of foam rather than real rockに着目する。アのsoft materialとは，本文のreal rockと対比的に用いられているfoamを言い換えたもの。　(3)　スクリプトの第1パラグラフに着目する。空港の位置は変わっていないにも関わらず，1960年代に比べて飛行機のフライト時間が長くなっていることが説明されている。　(4)　スクリプトの第3パラグラフの最後の文にあるthere's no pressure on airlines to become more efficientに着目する。よって，エ「航空会社が改善の努力をしなくなる」が適切。

【2】Because a lot of people accused the café of reverse sexism.

〈解説〉150語程度のパッセージを聞き，問題用紙に印刷された質問文を読み，英文1文で答える記述式問題である。放送は1回のみなので，集中して聞き取らなければならない。質問は「なぜカフェのオーナーはバッシングの標的になったのか」。punching bagは「叩かれ役，袋だたきの対象」。スクリプトの第1パラグラフ1文目にあるaccused of reverse sexismに着目する。同パラグラフ2文目にあるように，メルボルンにあるヴィーガン(完全菜食主義)・カフェのオーナーは，女性に対する優先席の提供と，男性に対する18％の追加課税を行い，それが逆性差別と批判されたのである。

【3】(1)　エ　(2)　ア　(3)　ア　(4)　ウ　(5)　イ

〈解説〉(1)　英文は「この発見はネバダ州南西の探鉱にはずみをつけ，その地域は隔てられた鉱山地域ではなく，巨大な鉱化帯の中心であったことがすぐにわかった」の意である。give impetus to～「～にはずみをつける(～を活性化させる)」。　(2)　英文は「私たちの町長は，陳腐なセリフを繰り返す俳優のように，やる気なさげに話す」の意である。languidly「物憂げに，やる気のない」。　(3)　英文は「早起きができないなら，どうして朝の勤務を引き受けたのか」の意である。feasible「実現可能な，～に適している」。　(4)　英文は「異なる民族の人々に加え，様々な料理がその町の多様性を具体的に示している」の意である。exemplify「～を実証する，～を例示する」。　(5)　英文は「両国は意見の相違を解決するためにその会議で会談した」の意である。iron out「(問題などを)解決する」。

【4】(1)　イ　(2)　エ　(3)　ウ　(4)　ア　(5)　ウ

〈解説〉(1)　英文は「文化や芸術は，プラハの春と言われる，検閲とソビエト支配が緩やかであった短期間に一時的に繁栄した」の意である。in short period「短期間に」。　(2)　英文は「暴力がテレビや映画に浸透しているが，私の祖父はそれが全く好きではない」の意である。

violenceは不可算名詞であり，代名詞はitで受ける。　(3)　英文は「芸術家はしばしば，教育か作品の制作に時間を費やすかの選択をしなければならない」の意である。「AかBの選択」を意味するchoice between A and Bが正しい形である。　(4)　英文は「他の彼の料理本で行っているのと同様に，新しい本の中でも，シェフのLouisは彼が料理の基本と考えることについて長々と説明をしている」の意である。offers lengthy explanationsをするのはhis other cookbooksではなくChef Louisであるため，Like in his other cookbooks の形に変える必要がある。

(5)　英文は「激しい感情の存在は，その原因が完全にはわからないが，いつも人を不安にさせる」の意である。makingはhuman beingsを目的語，そしてuneasyを補語としているため，weは不要である。

【5】(1)　①　エ　　②　キ　　③　オ　　(2)　She is so skillful that one or two days visit is enough in most cases.

〈解説〉(1)　まず，①ではBの直前の発話に着目する。「フードフェアに行きたいけれども，行けない」とあるため，その理由であるエ「Maria(ペットの猫の名前)を獣医に連れて行かないといけない」が適切。次に，②では次のBの発話に着目する。「よくわからないけど，まったく右前足を床につけようとしない」とあるので，Mariaの症状を尋ねる内容であるキが適切。③では次のAの発話に着目する。「私もSamuel先生は好きです。Samuel先生は，説明が上手ですね」とあるため，「Samuel先生の病院は評判がいい」という内容のオが適切。

(2)　(1)の空欄③の後にあるように，Aも飼い犬をSamuel先生の病院へ連れて行っていることがわかる。ここでのAの発話に続くBの発話はExactly.であり，Aの発話に同意していることがわかる。よって，Samuel先生の診療が優れていることを示す内容を書けばよいだろう。

【6】日本社会では，当事者同士の感情や情緒が大事であり，人間関係を形成するのに必ずしも言葉を必要としない。他者との関係性の中で自己が形成されるため，他者の状況や感情を理解すれば人間関係が形成

される。言葉を通じての相互理解が大前提である欧米社会に比べ，日本では論理的に言葉で説明しなくても，互いを理解することは十分可能である。(159字)

〈解説〉英文の日本語要約を160字で書く問題である。英文の重要な情報に着目して，重複する情報を整理しながら書けばよいだろう。最初に着目すべき点としては，第1パラグラフの1文目と4文目，そして第2パラグラフの2文目と3文目である。その上で，第2パラグラフの4文目以降で日本社会と欧米社会が対比的に書かれている箇所に着目し，必要な情報を加えてまとめればよいだろう。

【7】(1)　D　(2)　C　(3)　E　(4)　A　(5)　C　(6)　B

〈解説〉(1)　英文は「大英博物館は文化財を保護するために大変な努力をしている」の意であり，Dの1～2文目と対応する。　(2)　英文は「文化財を鑑賞するには快適な公共交通機関が重要である」の意であり，Cの1文目と対応する。　(3)　英文は「文化財が見つかった場所で見ることができれば，生徒たちはもっと勉強になるだろう」の意であり，Eの1文目と対応する。　(4)　英文は「人々が自分たちの文化財を鑑賞するために権利を得なければならないのはおかしい」の意であり，Aの1～2文目と対応する。　(5)　英文は「主な目的が大英博物館ではないとしても，多くの旅行者がロンドンを訪れている」の意であり，Cの2文目と対応する。　(6)　英文は「(考古学上の人工)遺物はそれが作られた国では重要ではないかもしれない」の意であり，Bの4文目と対応する。

【8】ふだんはのんきで，人と争ったりしない人が，ちょっと他の運転手や歩行者に挑発されただけで，突然自分のことだけしか考えられない人になり，A地点からB地点に行くまでに「不必要な」邪魔は入れさせないと決心してしまうことがある。そして，一切割り込ませはしないのである。

〈解説〉英文の基本的な形はA normally easy-going, non-argumentative

person may suddenly become a person,であり，at the slightest...and pedestrians,が動詞句を，また，unable to consider...interruptionsがa personを修飾している。そして，ダッシュに続く部分は，これまでの内容を言い換えて説明している。

【9】(1)　A　オ　　B　エ　　C　イ　　(2)　(a)　You have to learn how to use information efficiently rather than just memorizing it. At the same time, you have to be careful not to trust computers too much.〈29〉　　(b)　I would like to learn Geography in 2050. One reason is that our environment is continuing to change. We may lose some of the lands because of the rise in sea level, while the earth can create a new land after a volcanic eruption. I can learn something new in every class. Another reason is that by learning about geographic features of the world, we might be able to predict disasters like earthquakes and be prepared for them.〈78〉

〈解説〉(1)　まず，Aの前に「機械化による大量失業の不安は19世紀に遡るが，それは現在までに現実になってはいない。また，産業革命以降，機械によって失われた仕事に対して新しい仕事も作られ，平均的な生活水準は劇的に向上している」とある。そこで，オ「しかし今回は違って，現代においては機械学習が世界を変えると考えられる」を選ぶ。次に，Bの前に「しかしながら，AIは人の感情の理解を含め，ますますこれらのスキルでも人間を凌駕し始めている」とある。そこで，「身体的にも認知機能的にも人類が機械に対して優位に立てる点が見当たらない」ことを示すエを選ぶ。最後に，Cの前に「彼ら(＝よい運転手，銀行家そして弁護士)は，都会のジャングルではなくアフリカのサバンナに適応するような，経験則，手っ取り早い方法，そして時代遅れの回路に依存している」とある。そこで，「よい運転手，銀行家そして弁護士が誤りをおかしてもおかしくない」とあるイを選ぶ。(2)　(a)および(b)のどちらについても，与えられた英文を参考にして書くことが無難であろう。英文で書かれているほどではなくても，2050年は現代よりも機械化が進んでいることを念頭において答えればよい。まず，(a)について，少なくとも現代において機械が完璧に行えていないような，情報や機械を活用する能力を身につけることの重要性を論じればよいだろう。次に，(b)について，どの教科を選択してもよいが，機械化がいっそう進行する社会において，学ぶ理由をしっかり説明できる教科を選びたい。

【中学校】

【1】(1) ① 見方　② 言語活動　③ 知識　④ 状況　⑤ 主体的　(2) ① 正確　② まとまり　③ 理由　(3) ① 高等学校　② 接続　③ 単元　④ 深い学び

〈解説〉新学習指導要領に関する問題であり，空欄に適語を補充する形式である。多くは学習指導要領の基本的な内容が問われており，学習指導案を作成する際にも意識すべき点である。新学習指導要領の全体像を把握するため，同解説外国語編の「第1章　総説　2　外国語科改訂の趣旨と要点」にも目を通しておくとよいだろう。

【高等学校】

【1】(1) ① 考え方　② 統合的　③ 実際　④ 目的　⑤ 場面　⑥ 状況　⑦ 詳細　⑧ 自律的　(2) 多くの支援　(3) ① 具体的　② 即興で　③ 整理

〈解説〉新学習指導要領に関する設問である。新学習指導要領の全体像を把握するため，同解説外国語編・英語編の「第1部　外国語編　第1章　総説　第2節　外国語科改訂の趣旨及び要点」にも目を通しておくとよいだろう。

2019年度　実施問題

【中高共通】

【1】[リスニングテスト]

ただいまから，リスニングテストを始めます。これから読む英文の内容に関して，5つの質問をします。それぞれの質問の後に読まれる(a)，(b)，(c)，(d)の4つの選択肢の中から，答えとして最も適切なものを1つ選び，記号で答えなさい。英文と質問，選択肢は，全体をとおして2回読みます。聞きながらメモを取ってもかまいません。それでは始めます。

The global music industry soared a record 8.1 percent in 2017 as digital sales for the first time made up the majority of revenue thanks to the streaming boom, the industry said Tuesday.

Recorded music grossed $17.3 billion in 2017 with digital music — until the previous year roughly equal to physical sales worldwide — amounting to 54 percent of the revenue, the IFPI global body said in its annual report.

The 8.1 percent growth marks the third consecutive year of expansion and the fastest pace since the IFPI, the International Federation of the Phonographic Industry, began compiling data, the group's CEO, Frances Moore, told reporters on a conference call.

But the industry still is only about two-thirds of the value it was in the 1990s before the rise of the Internet and the scourge of pirated music sent the music business into a 15-year slump, Moore said.

The resurgence is almost entirely due to the rapid growth of streaming services including Spotify, Deezer and Apple Music, which have given the industry a badly needed new source of revenue.

The report said that 176 million people around the world paid for streaming subscriptions by the end of 2017, with 64 million joining throughout the year

— and there is plenty of room to grow on a global level.

Physical sales tumbled again but one bright side was vinyl, which remains a sliver of the market but grew 22.3 percent as records find a renewed market among audiophiles.

Stu Bergen, the CEO for international and global commercial services at the Warner Music Group, warned that the music industry should not become "complacent" and pledged that record labels would invest their revenue to develop new talent.

"We've fought too hard to get here and, after 15 years of decline, there's still plenty of room to grow," Bergen said on the conference call.

He voiced guarded optimism about China, where revenue jumped 35.3 percent as international labels increasingly penetrate the billion-plus market.

The growth, however, comes from a small base, with China only the 10th largest music market.

In one point of concern, Japan — the world's second largest music market — saw revenue decline by three percent.

The slump was paradoxically due to the continued strength of CD sales in Japan, where physical music makes up 72 percent of the market, with digital revenue not providing the same injection of growth as elsewhere.

"It's just a question of time. It's a traditional society and the move towards digital is slower than in some countries," Moore said. (428)

Questions

(1) According to the passage, what happened in 2017?

(a) Digital sales grew by 8.1 percent.

(b) The third biggest expansion of the growth was recorded.

(c) 17.3 billion people enjoyed streaming services.

(d) Digital music accounted for more than half of the sales.

(2) According to the passage, which is NOT true about the global music industry?

(a) It finally recovered to the level of the 1990s.

(b) Previously the Internet caused hard times.

(c) It didn't grow as expected for more than a decade.

(d) It has found a new way to improve earnings.

(3) According to the passage, which is true about the global music industry?

(a) It will reduce streaming subscription prices.

(b) It can develop more markets globally.

(c) Physical sales will be terminated soon.

(d) It will set up new investment companies.

(4) According to the passage, what is true about the trend in Chinese music industry?

(a) 35.3 percent of its sales is from domestic music.

(b) It didn't accept internationalization as it should have.

(c) It grew ten times larger over 15 years.

(d) Its revenue soared by about one third.

(5) According to the passage, what is true about the Japanese music market?

(a) CD sales declined by three percent over a year in 2017.

(b) Streaming services worked well enough to stimulate this slow-reacting market.

(c) Digital sales account for less than 30 percent of its revenue.

(d) The specialist in this passage is skeptical about its positive change.

【REPEAT】

これでリスニングテストを終わります。

(☆☆☆☆◎◎◎◎◎)

【2】次の各文の(　　)にあてはまる最も適切なものを，ア～エから1つ選び，記号で答えなさい。

(1) The political climate today is extremely (　　): no one can predict what the electorate will do next.

ア malevolent イ pertinent ウ volatile
エ claustrophobic

(2) Although the new evidence seems to ( ) the defendant of the breaking and entering charges, there is still the matter of the assault.

ア vindicate イ fabricate ウ exacerbate エ pervade

(3) Refusing to give in to the ( ), Jason stood his ground and ignored the hate mail and threats.

ア intimidation イ appellation ウ panacea エ sinecure

(4) These statistics tell the tale of an industry that is ( ) misusing antibiotics in an attempt to cover up filthy, unsanitary living conditions among animals.

ア prudently イ gallantly ウ cogently エ rampantly

(5) Some foreign governments appear to be happy to ( ) continued human rights abuses.

ア cook up イ gloss over ウ pick on エ tip off

(☆☆☆☆☆◎◎◎)

【3】次の各文の下線部ア～エの中で，誤っている箇所を1つ選び，記号で答えなさい。

(1) When the ball struck him ア<u>in the face</u>, the player イ<u>was collapsed</u> ウ<u>but</u> his teammates エ<u>carried on playing</u>.

(2) ア<u>It is acceptable</u> for workers イ<u>to eat</u> lunch at their desks on the ウ<u>condition that</u> they eat only エ<u>while the designated</u> lunch hour.

(3) ア<u>Recently</u> the company has supplied イ<u>all employee</u> with a mobile phone, ウ<u>whereas</u> a few years ago エ<u>only managers</u> had them.

(4) Behind the house ア<u>there is</u> one broken-down shed and イ<u>one pile of rubble</u> ウ<u>that</u> need エ<u>to be carted</u> to the town dump.

(5) To ア<u>see the Statue of Liberty</u> and イ<u>taking pictures</u> ウ<u>from the top</u> of the Empire State Building are two reasons エ<u>for visiting</u> New York City.

(☆☆☆◎◎◎◎)

【4】次の対話文の(　1　)～(　5　)にあてはまる最も適切な英文を，ア～クから選び，記号で答えなさい。ただし，同じ選択肢を2度使わないこと。

A : Hello, Jo. Come in and take a seat. I wanted to talk to you about your essay on weather control.

B : Right. What did you think?

A : Well, let's start by looking at your introduction. (　1　)

B : That's right, isn't it?

A : Well, you need to be careful here. (　2　) You need to specify that many experts believe this is the case, rather than saying, "This is how it is."

B : OK.

A : Then you look at the issues surrounding extreme weather, and how it has a negative effect in some countries.

B : (　3　)

A : No, not at all. It's very good, but I was slightly surprised when, in the same paragraph, you mentioned an advantage of extreme weather.

B : Not the right place for it?

A : Not really, no. In fact, I would question the need to put it there at all. (　4　)

B : Ah, I see what you mean. (　5　)

A : OK, then there's the section on weather-control programs.

ア　Yes, there is a lot of evidence that this is the case, but the issue is still controversial.

イ　I think I was going to elaborate on that, add more information, but I guess I forgot to do so.

ウ　I was worried that that section was a bit disorganized.

エ　Well, you summarize your main points and give a few points, which is great, but you then start talking about environmental systems.

オ　You say that global warming is causing extreme weather conditions around the world.

カ　I always have problems with the conclusion.

キ　At one point you're talking about droughts, hurricanes, floods, etc., and then suddenly you're talking about people being able to sunbathe on the beach in January.

ク　What I'd like to do is talk you through the process of cloud seeding.

(☆☆☆◎◎◎)

【5】次の英文を読んで，その趣旨を160字以内の日本語で書きなさい。ただし，句読点も字数に入れること。また，数字を書く場合は，1字につき1マス使用すること。

The processes of change in early twentieth-century life are most commonly presented in terms of technological inventions such as those in motorized transport, aviation, and radio, or sometimes by reference to new theoretical models such as Relativity and Psychoanalysis. But there were innovations in the sphere of language as well. Although now scarcely, remembered as an event of any cultural significance, the arrival of the crossword puzzle in 1924 may be seen as marking a new kind of relationship between the educated public and the vocabulary of the English language. It started as a newspaper trend, promoted by the offer of cash prizes, but it soon established itself as a national tradition, confirmed by the introduction of the first daily crossword in *The Times*, a British newspaper, in 1930. By this time, crossword fans were beginning to appear in fiction, too. Whether there is a connection between enthusiasm for the crossword and the 1930s boom in detective fiction, with its obvious puzzle-solving appeal, can only be guessed at. More certainly, the crossword encouraged a widespread interest in words. From their newspapers, readers were thus sent hurrying to dictionaries, which libraries complained they had repeatedly to replace because they were being roughly handled or even stolen by crossword lovers. The crossword, after all, relies strongly upon prior language regulation, including standard spellings, and the availability of widely respected dictionaries.

(☆☆☆◎◎◎)

【６】次の英文を読んで，(1)～(5)の問いに答えなさい。

"Heart disease is not a one- or two- gene problem," says Steven Ellis, a Cleveland Clinic (　A　). Ellis oversees a genetic study that collects DNA samples from patients who enter hospitals with atherosclerosis. Ellis suspects that dozens of genes contribute to a predisposition to heart disease. Of the several dozen genes, each may contribute just one percent to a person's total risk—an amount that may be compounded or offset by outside factors like diet. [　a　]

The point of tracking down all these small mutations, Ellis explains, is to create a comprehensive blood test—one that could calculate a person's genetic susceptibility by adding up the number of risky (and, eventually, beneficial) variables. Combined with other important factors, such as smoking, weight, blood pressure, and cholesterol levels, doctors could decide which (　B　), such as high-dose statins, and which ones are likely to benefit from exercise or other lifestyle changes. Some genes can already [　　], and whose won't. Assessing risk is crucial, Ellis says, because heart disease is often invisible. Fifty percent of men and 64 percent of women who die of heart disease die suddenly, without experiencing any previous symptoms. [　b　]

Although standard tests can detect atherosclerosis, they aren't foolproof. ①<u>They may reveal plaques, but give no indication whether or not they are life-threatening.</u> Tests like angiography, for example, in which doctors inject a dye into the bloodstream and track it with X-rays, can show how much blood is flowing through an artery, but cannot (　C　)—often the principal cause in a heart attack. [　c　]

Until there are tests, genetic or otherwise, that give a clearer measure of risk, everyone would be advised to exercise, watch their diet, and take statins for elevated cholesterol—the same advice doctors gave when the clogged-pipes model of heart disease was unchallenged. [　d　]

But statins, like any drug, carry the risk of (　D　): Muscle aches are a well-known effect, and periodic blood tests to check liver function are recommended. The fact is, many of us just like to eat cheeseburgers, lie back and watch TV, and get around in cars. And it's hard, says Leslie Cho, a director at the Cleveland Clinic, for a person to worry about a disease that hits ten years down the road—particularly since heart patients, unlike cancer patients, can't easily observe the progress of their disease. "②You've done damage over years, and it will take years to undo that damage. That's a very hard thing to sell," she says. "We do what we can, but then people go home."

③The good news is that genetic research continues to thrive. Should we want to, we will soon be able to know the state of our hearts—and our genes—in ever-growing detail. That knowledge, and what we do with it, could make the difference between dying at 65 and living until 80. The choice, increasingly, will be ours. [e]

(注) atherosclerosis アテローム性動脈硬化症 high-doze statins 高用量スタチン系薬剤 angiography 血管造影

(1) (A)～(D)に入る最も適した表現を，それぞれ次のア～エから1つ選び，記号で答えなさい。

A ア epidemiologist イ cardiologist ウ psychiatrist エ neuropathologist

B ア patients develop different characteristics
イ diseases are affected by drugs
ウ diseases require some routine procedures
エ patients need aggressive treatment

C ア expect the heart attack before detecting the symptoms
イ help plaques spot issues in the bloodstream
ウ discern the plaques embedded inside the artery wall
エ remove arterial cholesterol deposits in angiography

D ア side effects イ antibiotics ウ genetic triggers エ mutation

(2) 次の一文は，本文中から抜き出したものである。この一文が入る最も適切な位置を，[a]～[e]から選びなさい。

As one doctor commented, any person's heart attack risk is "50 percent genetic and 50 percent cheeseburger."

(3) 下線部①～③を日本語にしなさい。

(4) [　　]を補うように次の語句を並べ替えなさい。

[strongly to / level / predict / will / cholesterol / whose / respond / changes / dietary]

(5) この英文では，波線部は単に「帰宅する」という意味以上のことを表している。それはどのようなことか，本文の内容に合うように，"but the people" に続けて英語で書きなさい。

(☆☆☆☆◎◎)

【7】Explain your idea concerning the bar chart below in around 80 words and write your total number of words used inside ＜　＞ on the answer sheet.

The carbon footprint of Olympic electricity consumption

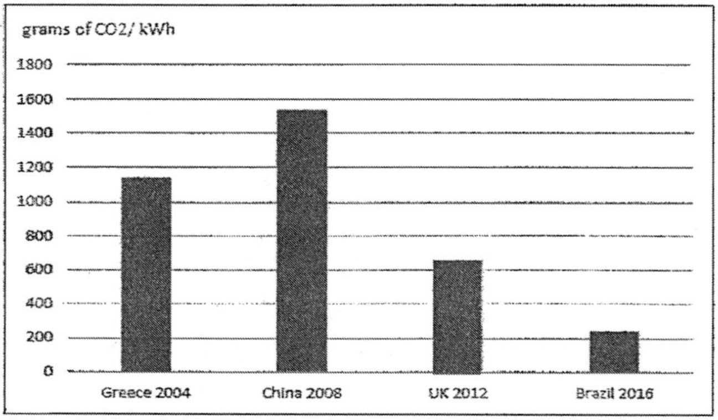

Data: Rio 2016 Carbon Footprint Management Report

(☆☆☆◎◎◎◎)

【中学校】

【1】中学校学習指導要領「第2章　各教科」「第9節　外国語」について，次の(1)～(3)の問いに答えなさい。

(1)　次の文は「第1　目標」の一部である。(　①　)～(　⑧　)にあてはまる語句を書きなさい。

> (1)　外国語の音声や語彙，表現，(　①　)，言語の働きなどを理解するとともに，これらの知識を，聞くこと，読むこと，話すこと，書くことによる実際のコミュニケーションにおいて活用できる(　②　)を身に付けるようにする。
> (2)　コミュニケーションを行う(　③　)や場面，状況などに応じて，日常的な話題や社会的な話題について，外国語で簡単な(　④　)や考えなどを理解したり，これらを活用して(　⑤　)したり伝え合ったりすることができる力を養う。
> (3)　外国語の背景にある(　⑥　)に対する理解を深め，聞き手，読み手，話し手，書き手に(　⑦　)しながら，主体的に外国語を用いてコミュニケーションを図ろうとする(　⑧　)を養う。

(2)　次の文は「第2　各言語の目標及び内容等」「英語」「1　目標」「(3)　話すこと[やり取り]」である。(　①　)～(　④　)にあてはまる語句を書きなさい。

> ア　(　①　)のある事柄について，簡単な語句や文を用いて(　②　)で伝え合うことができるようにする。
> イ　日常的な話題について，事実や自分の考え，気持ちなどを(　③　)し，簡単な語句や文を用いて伝えたり，相手からの質問に答えたりすることができるようにする。
> ウ　社会的な話題に関して聞いたり読んだりしたことについて，考えたことや感じたこと，その理由などを，簡単な語句や文を用いて(　④　)ことができるようにする。

(3)　次の文は「第2　各言語の目標及び内容等」「英語」「3　指導計画の作成と内容の取扱い」の一部である。(　①　)～(　④　)にあてはまる語句を書きなさい。

(3)　教材については，次の事項に留意するものとする。
ア　教材は，聞くこと，読むこと，話すこと[やり取り]，話すこと[(　①　)]，書くことなどのコミュニケーションを図る(　②　)・能力を(　③　)に育成するため，1に示す5つの領域別の目標と2に示す内容との関係について，単元など内容や時間のまとまりごとに各教材の中で明確に示すとともに，実際の言語の使用場面や言語の働きに十分配慮した(　④　)を取り上げること。

(☆☆☆◎◎◎◎◎)

【高等学校】

【1】高等学校学習指導要領「外国語」について，次の(1)～(3)の問いに答えなさい。

(1)　次は「第2款　各科目　第3　コミュニケーション英語Ⅱ」の「2　内容(2)」で示されている事項である。(　①　)～(　④　)にあてはまる語句を書きなさい。

ア　英語の音声的な特徴や内容の(　①　)などに注意しながら聞いたり話したりすること。
イ　論点や根拠などを明確にするとともに，文章の(　②　)や図表との関連などを考えながら読んだり書いたりすること。
ウ　未知の語の意味を推測したり背景となる知識を(　③　)したりしながら聞いたり読んだりすること。
エ　説明や描写の表現を工夫して相手に(　④　)に伝わるように話したり書いたりすること。

(2)　次は「第2款　各科目　第5　英語表現Ⅰ」の「1　目標」の英訳である。(　①　)～(　④　)に入る適切な語を英語で書きなさい。

To develop students' abilities to (①) facts, opinions, etc. from multiple (②) and communicate through (③) and a range of expression, while (④) a positive attitude toward communication through the English language.

(3) 次は「第3款　英語に関する各科目に共通する内容等」の「2」である。(①)~(④)にあてはまる語句を書きなさい。

英語に関する各科目の2の(1)に示す言語活動を行うに当たっては，中学校学習指導要領第2章第9節第2の2の(3)及び次に示す(①)の中から，それぞれの科目の目標を達成するのにふさわしいものを適宜用いて行わせる。その際，「コミュニケーション英語Ⅰ」においては，言語活動と効果的に関連付けながら，ウに掲げるすべての事項を適切に取り扱うものとする。

ア　語，連語及び慣用表現

(ア) 語

a 「コミュニケーション英語Ⅰ」にあっては，中学校で学習した語に400語程度の新語を加えた語

b 「コミュニケーション英語Ⅱ」にあっては，aに示す語に700語程度の新語を加えた語

c 「コミュニケーション英語Ⅲ」にあっては，bに示す語に700語程度の新語を加えた語

d 「コミュニケーション英語基礎」,「英語表現Ⅰ」,「英語表現Ⅱ」及び「英語会話」にあっては，生徒の(②)を踏まえた適切な語

(イ) 連語及び慣用表現のうち，(③)の高いもの

イ　文構造のうち，(③)の高いもの

ウ　文法事項

(ア) 不定詞の用法

(イ) 関係代名詞の用法

(ウ) (④)の用法

(エ)　助動詞の用法
(オ)　代名詞のうち，itが名詞用法の句及び節を指すもの
(カ)　動詞の時制など
(キ)　仮定法
(ク)　分詞構文

(☆☆☆◎◎◎◎◎)

解答・解説

【中高共通】

【1】(1)　(d)　　(2)　(a)　　(3)　(b)　　(4)　(d)　　(5)　(c)

〈解説〉(1)　放送される英文の長さは中程度である。今年度のトピックはデジタル時代における音楽業界の売り上げの変化についてであった。英文とその内容に関する質問および4つの解答肢を聞き，適切な解答を選択する問題である。英文・質問・選択肢ともに2回ずつ放送されるが，問題用紙には何も印刷されておらず，内容を事前に把握することはできない。メモを取ってもよいので，1度目は概要をつかみ2度目で細部まで聞き取れるよう集中して臨もう。数字が頻出するので，聞き逃さないように注意する必要がある。　(a)　8.1%売り上げが上昇したのは音楽業界全体なので誤り。　(b)　このような記述はない。(c)　17.3 billionという数字はスクリプト2文目にある音楽の総収益の額なので誤り。　(d)　スクリプト1文目のmade up the majority of revenueと一致する。　(2)　(a)　スクリプト4文目では「業界の売り上げは，まだ1990年代の3分の2である」と述べているので，「1990年代の売り上げと同等レベルにまで回復した」は誤り。　(3)　(b)　スクリプト第6文の内容と一致する。　(4)　(d)　スクリプトの最後から5文目にChina, where revenue jumped 35.3 percentと一致する。　(5)　(c)　スク

リプトの最後から2文目にin Japan, where physical music makes up 72 percent of the marketとあり，デジタル音楽は残りの28%とわかるのでこれが正解。

【2】(1) ウ　(2) ア　(3) ア　(4) エ　(5) イ

〈解説〉(1) ア　malevolent「悪意のある」，イ　pertinent「関連のある」，ウ　volatile「移り気な，不安定な」，エ　claustrophobic「閉所恐怖症の」。空欄の後の文は「有権者が次に何をするか誰も予測できない」とあるのでウが適切である。　(2) ア　vindicate「(無実を)証明する」，イ　fabricate「でっち上げる」，ウ　exacerbate「悪化させる」，エ　pervade「広がる」。there is still the matter of the assault「暴行事件がまだ残っている」とは逆の内容が空欄のあるAlthoughの節である。よってアを入れて「新しい証拠は不法侵入の容疑から被告の無実を証明すると思われるが」とすればうまくつながる。　(3) ア　intimidation「脅迫」，イ　appellation「呼称」，ウ　panacea「万能薬」，エ　sinecure「閑職」。カンマの後ろは「ジェイソンは一歩も引かずに嫌がらせの手紙や脅しを無視した」という意味で，前半の「(　　　)に屈することを拒み」とうまくつながるのはアとなる。　(4) ア　prudently「用心して」，イ　gallantly「勇敢に」，ウ　cogently「説得できるほどに」，エ　rampantly「猛烈に，はびこって」。文章に最も合うのはエとなる。(5) ア　cook up「でっちあげる」，イ　gloss over「隠す，軽く扱う」，ウ　pick on「いじめる」，エ　tip off「こっそり知らせる」。continued human rights abuses「続いている人権侵害」という悪事に結びつくのはイが適切である。

【3】(1) イ　(2) エ　(3) イ　(4) ア　(5) イ

〈解説〉(1) collapseは自動詞なのでイはcollapsedが正しい。　(2) the designated lunch hourは名詞句なのでエはwhileではなく前置詞duringを用いる。　(3) allは可算名詞の複数形を伴うのでイはall employeesとなる。　(4) one broken-down shed and one pile of rubbleが後ろに続くの

でアはthere areとなる。　(5)　andはto不定詞同士を結び付けているのでイは(to) take picturesとなる。

【4】(1)　オ　　(2)　ア　　(3)　ウ　　(4)　キ　　(5)　イ

〈解説〉教師と生徒の会話文の空欄補充問題である。　(1)　教師が生徒Joのエッセイの導入部分から話を始めようとしているので，エッセイの冒頭の文にふさわしいのは，オ「あなたは，地球温暖化が地球規模での異常気象の原因となっていると述べているのね」。　(2)　Bの発言のisn't it?に対応する答えは，アのYesから始まる文になる。　(3)　生徒が空欄で述べたことに対して次に教師がNo, not at all. It's very goodと返していることからウとカに絞られるが，ここではまだカの結論について述べているとは考えにくいのでウが適切である。　(4)　(3)から続いている，生徒のエッセイにまとまりがないことについて教師が述べている部分である。前後の脈絡がない内容を例示しているのは，キ「干ばつやハリケーンについて述べているのに，突然ビーチで日光浴できると書かれている」。　(5)　空欄の後で教師がOKと返していることからよい内容の発言が入ると考えられる，残った選択肢で肯定的な意味なのはイのみなのでこれが正解となる。

【5】20世紀初期の生活における変化の過程は，技術的発明という観点から示されるのが一般的だが，言語の領域でも数々の革新があった。クロスワードパズルは，教養のある人々と英語の語彙の間に新しい関係を築き，言葉に対する広い関心を促した。それは，以前から存在する言語の規則や，広く認められている辞書が使えることに強く依存している。(158字)

〈解説〉大きく3つの内容に分けて趣旨を書くとよい。1つ目の内容は本文第1文・2文の「20世紀初期の生活の変化の過程は技術的発明の観点だけでなく言語の領域でも革新があった」という内容である。2つ目の内容は第3文～6文のクロスワードパズルの普及についてである。3つ目の内容は第7文～9文のクロスワードパズルの普及の原因である。この3つを160字以内でまとめればよい。要約の問題では，詳細情報(具体例など)や過剰な情報を削除し，一連の動作を上位語に置き換えたり，トピックセンテンスを抜き出したりすることが重要である。具体的には，英字新聞の社説を200字以内で要約するといった練習をこなすことが挙げられる。

【6】(1) A イ　B エ　C ウ　D ア　(2) a

(3) ① 標準的な検査は血管に蓄積された老廃物を明らかにするかもしれないが，それらが命に関わるものかどうかを示すものではない。
② あなたの健康は何年もかけて損なわれてきており，回復するには何年もかかるだろう。それを納得させるのは大変難しいことだ。
③ 良いニュースは，遺伝子研究が順調に進んでいることだ。もし私たちが希望するなら，近いうちに，ますます詳細に心臓の状態を，さらには遺伝子の状態にいたるまで，知ることができるだろう。

(4) predict whose cholesterol level will respond strongly to dietary changes

(5) (but then people) go back to the previous lifestyle

〈解説〉(1) A 心臓病についてのコメントのためイの「心臓専門医」が入る。　B such as high-dose statins「高用量スタチン系薬剤といった」という語句が空欄直後にあり，エの，patients need aggressive treatmentの具体例とわかる。　C 空欄の後に「心臓病の主な原因」とあるので，悪い結果の意味を持つ，ウの「動脈内膜に堆積したプラークを識別する」が適切。　D 空欄の後に「筋肉痛がよく知られた作用である」とあり，アのside effects「副作用」を入れると前後がうまくつながる。　(2) 空欄aの前で，遺伝子が危険につながるのはどの人間もわずか1パーセントで，食事などの外的要因で増加したり相殺されたりするという内容が書かれており，それをわかりやすく言い換えたのが抜き出された一文である。　(3) ① Theyは前文のstandard tests「標準的な検査」を，plaques「プラーク」はatherosclerosis「アテローム性動脈硬化」を指す。give no indication whether～は「～かどうかを示すものではない」。　② do damageは「傷める，被害を及ぼす」という意味。undoは「回復する」，sellはここでは「(人に)納得させる」という特殊な意味で用いられている。　③　Should we want toはIf we should want toの倒置形である。want toの後にはbe able to know以下が省略されている。　(4)　空欄直後にwhose won'tがあることから関係詞whoseを空欄内で主語として使うことが予想できる。空欄内の動詞を見ると目的語を取れる他動詞はpredictのみである。changesは3人称単数現在のsがあるので動詞としては使えない。predictの後にwhose cholesterol levelを持ってきてこれがpredict内の節の主語となる。その他の語句を見るとrespond strongly toが結びつくことがわかり，willを伴って動詞となる。toの目的語はdietary changes「食事の変化」とすれば文が完成する。　(5)　homeは慣れ親しんだ自宅という意味であることから，慣れ親しんだ元の生活スタイルという意味で比喩的に用いられていると考えられる。「医者は出来るだけのことをしますが，人々は元の生活スタイルに戻ってしまいます」と述べているのである。

【7】According to this data, the CO_2 levels of the Olympic Games are gradually being reduced. For the host country, sustainability is increasingly important for the event. After China, the UK reduced the carbon footprint and Brazil managed to reduce it even further. Next Japan has to go further by using better carbon offset projects such as LED lighting, sustainable food and drink schemes. All of Japan should work together so that we can achieve this goal. I hope other countries will try as shown in this model. (87words)

〈解説〉ライティングは，テーマに関して時間内に正確に書くことが大切である。そのためには，まずゆっくりでもよいので規定の文字数の英作文を何度もこなし，文法や語彙の正確さ，流暢さを徐々に上げていく訓練が必要である。また，本問のテーマとして挙げられている「オリンピックでの電力消費における二酸化炭素排出量」については，2020年に日本がオリンピックの舞台になることもあり，日頃から新聞やニュースに目を通し自分の考えを持っておくことが大切である。

【中学校】

【1】(1) ① 文法 ② 技能 ③ 目的 ④ 情報 ⑤ 表現 ⑥ 文化 ⑦ 配慮 ⑧ 態度 (2) ① 関心 ② 即興 ③ 整理 ④ 述べ合う (3) ① 発表 ② 資質 ③ 総合的 ④ 題材

〈解説〉平成29年3月告示の「中学校学習指導要領」からの出題である。学習指導要領において，教科目標及び学年ごとの目標，内容，指導計画の作成と内容の取扱いは頻出である。必ず中学校学習指導要領及び同解説外国語編を並行して精読し，内容をしっかり理解した上で暗記しておくことが重要である。

【高等学校】

【1】(1) ① 展開 ② 構成 ③ 活用 ④ 効果的 (2) ① evaluate ② perspectives ③ reasoning ④ fostering (3) ① 言語材料 ② 学習負担 ③ 運用度 ④ 関係副詞

〈解説〉平成21年3月告示の「高等学校学習指導要領」からの出題である。学習指導要領において，教科目標及び学年ごとの目標，内容，指導計画の作成と内容の取扱いは頻出である。必ず現行の高等学校学習指導要領及び同解説外国語編・英語編を並行して精読し，内容をしっかり理解した上で暗記しておくことが重要である。なお，高等学校学習指導要領については，すでに平成30年3月告示の改訂版が出されている。今後は改訂版からの出題も考えられるので，同解説外国語編・英語編(平成30年7月)と併せて熟読されたい。

2018年度　実施問題

【中高共通】

【1】[リスニングテスト]

問題文及び5つの質問を聞き，各質問の後に読まれるa～dの4つの選択肢の中から，その質問に対する答えとして最も適切なものを1つ選び，記号で答えなさい。

ただいまから，リスニングテストを始めます。これから読む英文の内容に関して，5つの質問をします。それぞれの質問の後に読まれるa，b，c，dの4つの選択肢の中から，答えとして最も適切なものを1つ選び，記号で答えなさい。英文と質問，選択肢は，全体をとおして2回読みます。聞きながらメモを取ってもかまいません。それでは始めます。

Several centuries hence, climbers heading for Mount Fuji's summit will likely tread a forest trail for the first few hundred meters from the traditional departure point, now covered by sparse vegetation.

The upper limit of forest cover on the nation's highest peak is around 2,400 meters, roughly where the mountain's Fifth Station is situated and the highest point that vehicles can go.

But that elevation is expected to rise 500 years or so from now to around 2,800 meters on the southern flank of the 3,776-meter peak, according to a recent study.

Researchers believe that repeated eruptions had caused Mount Fuji's forest line, or the elevation above which no forest can grow, to recede, but that it will eventually revert to its original level of 2,800 meters.

Takashi Nakano and Taisuke Yasuda, researchers of the Mount Fuji Research Institute of the Yamanashi prefectural government, worked with

Yasuo Yamamura, a professor of plant ecology with Ibaraki University, to analyze aerial photos of Mount Fuji's flanks on the northern and southern slopes.

They compared photos taken in 1975 and 2002 to study how far forests had taken root.

The analysis showed that forest cover had risen 78 centimeters per year on the southern flank in a vertical direction and 41 cm on the northern flank.

If the current rates of rise remain the same, the forest line should reach an elevation of 2,800 meters in 500 years or so from now on the southern flank and in about 1,000 years on the northern flank, the researchers said.

It is the first estimate for the rates of rise, although it was understood that the forest cover has been gradually regaining lost ground.

The southern flank, where the forests are recovering faster, is more prone to fog, is more moist and gets more sunshine.

"The difference between the southern and northern flanks was probably caused by composite workings of various conditions," Nakano said. (329)

Questions

(1) According to the passage, which is true about an altitude of around 2,400 meters on Mt. Fuji?

(a) Several centuries ago, local people grew vegetables there.

(b) If you go there by car, you cannot go further.

(c) It's the upper limit of animals living in the forest.

(d) Five out of ten stations in total are situated there.

(2) Why did Mt. Fuji's forest line change?

(a) Because it erupted more than once.

(b) Because the number of climbers is increasing.

(c) Because trees were cut down for fuel.

(d) Because it has been affected by global warming.

(3) Which was true about the photos the three people used for the analysis?

(a) They climbed Mt. Fuji many times to take the photos.

(b) About 2,000 photos were taken for the purpose of the analysis.

(c) The photos taken in 1975 showed more kinds of trees.

(d) The photos of Mt. Fuji's flanks were taken from the sky.

(4) According to the passage, what would happen to the forest line on the northern flank of Mt. Fuji?

(a) It would fall, and researchers assumed it would reach an elevation of 2,800 meters.

(b) It would rise, and would rise at a rate of 78 centimeters per year.

(c) It would fall, but it wouldn't fall as low as 2,400 meters.

(d) It would rise, but it would take twice as long as on the southern flank.

(5) According to the passage, which is true about Mt. Fuji?

(a) The amount of sunshine determines whether its forest line will rise or fall.

(b) Many researchers have estimated the rates of change to Mt. Fuji's temperature.

(c) Its forest line has been reaching the point before the repeated eruptions.

(d) It's difficult to tell the difference between the southern and northern flanks.

【REPEAT】

これでリスニングテストを終わります。

(☆☆☆☆◎◎◎◎◎)

【2】次の各文の(　　)にあてはまる最も適切なものを，ア～エから1つ選び，記号で答えなさい。

(1) The state governor has (　　) a new policy which aims to reduce the amount of wasteful expenditure.

ア blended　イ instituted　ウ stimulated　エ deposed

(2) Excited and unafraid, the (　　) child examined the stranger with bright-eyed curiosity.

ア inquisitive　イ timorous　ウ apathetic　エ drowsy

(3) The stock market crash and the Great Depression that followed wreaked (　　) on the nation's banking system.

ア digression　イ zenith　ウ impunity　エ havoc

(4) The drones interrupted their rhythmic flights over the fields and began to fly about (　　).

ア erratically　イ plausibly　ウ contentiously

エ holistically

(5) They try not to worry excessively about the uncertainties in the future or to (　　) the traumatic events of the past.

ア put out　イ soak up　ウ dwell on　エ merge with

(☆☆☆◎◎◎◎)

【3】次の各文の下線部ア～エの中で，誤っている箇所を1つ選び，記号で答えなさい。

(1) The manager アrarely suggested that his employees take イbreak but he decided to do so ウwhen some of them complained of エtiredness.

(2) About a million and a half dollars アhave been spent イon repairing the road, but ウonly recently has the shoddy construction methods エbecome evident.

(3) The new library アis undoubtedly well イstocked and functional, ウbut no one can say that its atmosphere is anything like エthose of the old one.

(4) Energy from the solar panels アis economical and イenvironmental friendly, ウwhich will make it an important part of エthe electrical power industry in the future.

(5) アBeing lost in the mountains for two days イas a boy, Dave is ウalways careful to take a detailed map with him エwhen he sets out for a backpacking adventure in the wilderness.

(☆☆☆◎◎◎◎)

【4】次の対話文の(　1　)～(　5　)にあてはまる最も適切な英文を，ア～クから選び，記号で答えなさい。ただし，同じ選択肢を2度使わないこと。

A : Hi, Ben. (　1　) Is Mary excited?

B : (　2　) The school looks good, including this new gym. But I'm worried about some things.

A : I'm concerned, too. (　3　)

B : I know! There are just too many kids in the classes.

A : Yes. And there aren't enough computers for all of them.

B : (　4　) And often they have too much homework!

A : And I don't always have enough time to help. I really wish I had time.

B : I'm with you. We need more teachers.

A : Right! (　5　) Weren't you a teacher? How about volunteering at Minton?

ア　All summer she talked about starting sixth grade at Minton Middle School!

イ　Some schools and many districts have written policies regarding the degree of involvement parents should have in their children's homework.

ウ　Can you believe it's September and the first day of school already?

エ　Peter is in seventh, and his classes are huge.

オ　I know teachers often don't make enough money, but they have great schedules.

カ　Kids do not do so well in an impersonal environment on the first day of school.

キ　Did you come with up-to-date technology at your school?

ク　It seems like the kids just don't get enough attention in school.

(☆☆☆◎◎◎◎)

【5】次の英文を読んで，(1)～(5)の問いに答えなさい。

My 5-year-old son is beyond his years in many ways—with one big

(A). He still doesn't know how to turn on an iPad. In an effort to stave off a lifetime of device dependence, my husband and I have nurtured a screen-free environment in our home. ①It's kooky, but if you ask me, it's made all the difference in my children's development.

[a] Having both been raised in homes without televisions, our decision to limit screens came somewhat naturally to us. ②We wanted to delay technologically induced social isolation and encourage our children to develop skills that would serve them well in the real world. ③In our minds, childhood should be about fostering social interactions, encouraging creativity and responding to real-world stimuli.

[b] To cultivate a screen-free environment—if only for a few years—we've taken an old-fashioned approach. We bought a 1987 Golden Book Encyclopedia set on eBay. We've also (B) How does the sun move? That's a good question for Uncle Ariel, who studied chemistry in college. How do you build a door? Ask Uncle David, the contractor. Who created the world? As the self-appointed Bible scholar, that's my (C).

We aren't (D). The only way the children can survive the eight-hour drive to my Canadian parents' home in one piece is by watching "Sesame Street" on the TV screen in the back seat of our car. And when it's been weeks since they've seen their grandparents, we know that they have more to gain than lose by a video-chat session.

We're OK with making exceptions, so long as they remain only that.

[ ]. My children's concentration skills are strong. They can spend hours listening to tales of the gnarling and wizened trees of Narnia. They have learned how to share in household tasks, quickly becoming adept at polishing candlesticks, setting a table and folding napkins into stemware.

[c] Most important, the no-screen rule is bringing our children closer to our extended family. The practice of asking questions to humans rather than the Google search bar has generated interest in the talents of family members and friends.

[d] While my children don't have kiddie apps to master Mandarin or the fineries of classical music—at least not yet—they do a lot of questioning, imagining and creating.

I recognize that our hold on technology may only last for a few more years. ④<u>At some point, my children will ________________________</u>. Undoubtedly, device dependence lies ahead. But for now I am glad that they can learn to depend on their own minds and hearts—and on the special humans in their lives.

(1)　(A)～(D)に入る最も適した表現を，それぞれア～エから1つ選び，記号で答えなさい。

(A)　ア　ratification　　イ　bounty　　ウ　anomaly
　　　　エ　facet

(B)　ア　aggravated our relationship with "regional celebrities."
　　　　イ　developed a habit of contacting "local experts."
　　　　ウ　impeded the development of the faculties for "regional professionals."
　　　　エ　tarnished "local intellectuals" by asking questions.

(C)　ア　rabies　　イ　turf　　ウ　gadget
　　　　エ　valet

(D)　ア　humanitarians　　イ　socialists　　ウ　cosmopolitans
　　　　エ　absolutists

(2)　次の一文は，本文中から抜き出したものである。この一文が入る最も適切な位置を，[a]～[d]から選びなさい。

Albert Einstein said, "Imagination is more important than knowledge."

(3)　下線部①～③を日本語にしなさい。

(4)　次の語句を並べ替え，[　　　　　]に入る文を完成させなさい。

[in / and / have / invaluable / character / the gains / their development / been]

(5)　次の語句をすべて用いて，本文の内容に合うように下線部④の英文を完成させなさい。ただし，他に必要な語は自由に補うこと。
(skills / the digital world / need / succeed)

(☆☆☆☆◎◎◎◎◎)

【6】生徒一人一人がインターネットに接続できる電子機器を用いる授業を効果的に行うために，あなたが最も配慮しなければならないと考えることは何か，1つ取り上げ80語程度の英語で書きなさい。ただし，符号は語数に含めない。また，使用語数を書き入れること。

(☆☆☆☆◎◎)

【7】次の英文を読んで，その趣旨を160字以内の日本語で書きなさい。ただし，句読点も字数に入れること。

From now until the 2020 Tokyo Olympics, the Japanese government, along with a consortium of Non-Government Organizations, will be running the Sport for Tomorrow initiative. The goal of the initiative is to promote the benefits of playing sports and intercultural exchange. The initiative also entails the offering of courses in sports management to foreign students in Japan and anti-doping agency funding.

The Japanese government is not only promoting sport internationally, but domestically as well. Facing a rapidly aging population, promoting sport and exercise will be integral in maintaining the health of Japanese citizens as they get older. For a long time, it has not been uncommon to see coordinated stretch and exercise routines being done by employees in suits first thing in the morning, before starting a long shift. The exercise is important because the amount of hours many Japanese employees work and their resulting stress have been found to have incredibly negative effects on the employee's mental and physical health. The Japanese government has recognized this issue and is working to promote less work hours and more holidays, plus getting workers to be active and engage in sports to increase health and reduce stress.

Thanks to coordinated promotional efforts by the Japanese government, it is now becoming common to see groups of elders, out exercising together in public first thing in the morning. It is believed that the promotion of exercise in the workplace and in retirement has helped to contribute to the life longevity that many Japanese attain.

The Sport for Tomorrow initiative will only run until the 2020 Olympics, but due to the initiative, we may see more nations taking stronger stances to promote sport and exercise. If promoted properly, more people globally may live longer, healthier lives.

(注)　the Sport for Tomorrow initiative：SFTプログラム。2013年9月，国際オリンピック委員会(IOC)総会でのプレゼンテーションにおいて示した，スポーツ分野における我が国政府の国際貢献策(外務省HPより)。

(☆☆☆☆◎◎◎)

【中学校】

【１】中学校学習指導要領「第2章　各教科」「第9節　外国語」「第2　各言語の目標及び内容等」「英語」について，次の(1)～(3)の問いに答えなさい。

(1)　次の文は「2　内容」「(1)　言語活動　エ　書くこと」の一部である。(　①　)～(　④　)にあてはまる語句を書きなさい。

> (ア)　文字や符号を識別し，語と語の(　①　)などに注意して正しく書くこと。
> (イ)　語と語の(　②　)などに注意して正しく文を書くこと。
> (ウ)　聞いたり読んだりしたことについてメモをとったり，感想，(　③　)やその理由を書いたりなどすること。
> (エ)　(　④　)な場面における出来事や体験したことなどについて，自分の考えや気持ちなどを書くこと。
> (オ)　自分の考えや気持ちなどが読み手に正しく伝わるように，文と文のつながりなどに注意して文章を書くこと。

(2) 次の文は「2　内容」「(2)　言語活動の取扱い」「イ(イ)　第2学年における言語活動」である。(　①　)～(　④　)にあてはまる語句を書きなさい。

第1学年の学習を基礎として，言語の(　①　)や言語の(　②　)を更に広げた言語活動を行わせること。その際，第1学年における学習内容を繰り返して指導し定着を図るとともに，(　③　)を伝えたり，物事について(　④　)したりした内容などの中からコミュニケーションを図れるような話題を取り上げること。

(3) 次の文は「3　指導計画の作成と内容の取扱い」の(2)の一部である。(　①　)～(　⑧　)にあてはまる語句を書きなさい。

ア　(　①　)なものの見方や考え方を理解し，(　②　)な判断力を養い豊かな(　③　)を育てるのに役立つこと。 イ　外国や(　④　)の生活や文化についての理解を深めるとともに，言語や文化に対する関心を高め，これらを(　⑤　)する態度を育てるのに役立つこと。 ウ　広い(　⑥　)から国際理解を深め，国際社会に生きる日本人としての(　⑦　)を高めるとともに，(　⑧　)の精神を養うのに役立つこと。

(☆☆☆◎◎◎◎◎)

【高等学校】

【1】高等学校学習指導要領「外国語」について，次の(1)～(3)の問いに答えなさい。

(1) 次は「第2款　各科目　第2　コミュニケーション英語Ⅰ」の「3　内容の取扱い」で示されている事項である。(　①　)～(　④　)にあてはまる語句を書きなさい。

> (1)　中学校におけるコミュニケーション能力の基礎を養うための(　①　)な指導を踏まえ，聞いたことや読んだことを踏まえた上で話したり書いたりする言語活動を適切に取り入れながら，(　②　)の言語活動を有機的に関連付けつつ(　①　)に指導するものとする。
> (2)　(　③　)に応じて，多様な場面における言語活動を経験させながら，中学校や高等学校における学習内容を繰り返して指導し(　④　)を図るよう配慮するものとする。

(2)　次は「第2款　各科目　第6　英語表現Ⅱ」の「2　内容(2)」の一部の英訳である。(　①　)～(　④　)に入る適切な語を英語で書きなさい。

> A.　Speaking with due attention to the characteristics of English sounds, plot (　①　), etc.
> B.　Writing with due attention to passage structure, relation to charts and tables, expressions, etc., while (　②　) the points of the argument, evidence, etc., and reviewing and revising one's own writing.
> C.　Learning presentation (　③　), rules of debate and discussion, expressions used in these activities, etc., and applying them to real-life situations.
> D.　Making use of each other's ideas to solve problems, while respecting others' opinions and ideas and comparing each other's statements so as to (　④　) one's own mind.

(3)　次は「第4款　各科目にわたる指導計画の作成と内容の取扱い」の「2(1)」で示されている教材を取り上げる際に留意する必要がある4つの観点である。(　①　)～(　④　)にあてはまる語句を書きなさい。

ア　多様なものの見方や考え方を理解し，公正な(　①　)を養い豊かな(　②　)を育てるのに役立つこと。
イ　外国や我が国の生活や文化についての理解を深めるとともに，言語や文化に対する関心を高め，これらを尊重する態度を育てるのに役立つこと。
ウ　広い視野から国際理解を深め，国際社会に生きる日本人としての自覚を高めるとともに，(　③　)の精神を養うのに役立つこと。
エ　人間，社会，(　④　)などについての考えを深めるのに役立つこと。

(☆☆☆◎◎◎◎◎)

解答・解説

【中高共通】

【1】(1)　(b)　　(2)　(a)　　(3)　(d)　　(4)　(d)　　(5)　(c)

〈解説〉(1)　中程度の長さの英文と内容についての質問を聞き，適切な解答を選択する四択問題である。問題用紙には質問も選択肢も印刷されていないので，内容を事前に予測することはできない。放送は2度ずつありメモを取ってもよい。1度目は概要をつかみ2度目で細部まで聞き取れるよう集中して臨もう。なお，数字が頻出するので聞き逃さないように注意を要する。　(a)　スクリプト1文目の末尾にvegetation(草木，植生)という単語が出てくるが，vegetablesに関する描写はないので誤り。　(b)　スクリプト2文目のThe upper limit of forest以下の内容に即しているので正しい。　(c)　スクリプト中にはanimalsに関する描写はない。　(d)　スクリプト2文目に「2,400m付近はだいたい山の5合目が位置している場所」とは述べられているが，そこに10の合目のうち5つの合目があるとは言っていない。　(2)　(a)　スクリプト4文目の“repeated eruptions had caused Mount Fuji's forest line”と合っているため正解。他の選択肢は，それぞれ“number of climbers”“trees were cut down”“global warming”というスクリプト中に出てこない記述がある。(3)　スクリプト5文目の“to analyze aerial photos”から，航空写真を撮っていたことがわかる。これは，(d)の内容と合っている。他の選択肢は，それぞれ“many times”“about 2,000 photos”“more kinds of trees”というスクリプト中に出てこない記述がある。　(4)　スクリプト8文目の内容を問うている問題。もし現在の上昇率が変わらなければ，南の斜面では500年以内に，北の斜面では1,000年以内に森林のラインが2,800mの高さに達するだろうと述べられている。したがって(d)の内容が最も適切である。　(5)　(a)　スクリプト最後の文で「南の斜面と北の斜面の違いはさまざまな条件の複合的な働きによるものだ」と述べているので誤り。　(b)　富士山の気温についてはスクリプト中に出てこない。(c)は，スクリプト4文目で「やがて元の2,800mの水準まで戻るだろう」と述べられており，内容に即している。　(d)　スクリプト7文目で「1年間に上昇する距離が南の斜面と北の斜面で異なる」と述べられているため，誤りである。

【2】(1)　イ　(2)　ア　(3)　エ　(4)　ア　(5)　ウ

〈解説〉(1)　ア　blend「混ぜ合わせる」，イ　institute「定める，任命する」，ウ　stimulate「刺激する」，エ　depose「退ける」。この問いでは空欄の後に“a new policy”と続くためイが適切である。

(2)　ア　inquisitive「詮索好きな，知りたがりな」，イ　timorous「臆病な」，ウ　apathetic「無関心な」，エ　drowsy「眠そうな」。この問いでは，“with bright-eyed curiosity (好奇心で目を輝かせて)”とあるため，アが適切である。　(3)　ア　digression「脱線，余談」，イ　zenith「頂点，絶頂」，ウ　impunity「罰を受けないこと」，エ　havoc「大荒れ，大混乱」。wreak havoc on～は「～に大損害を与える」という意味の表現。ここでは“The stock market crash and the Great Depression that

followed (株式市場の急落とそれに続く大恐慌)" が主語である。
(4)　ア　erratically「不規則に」，イ　plausibly「もっともらしく」，ウ　contentiously「けんか腰で」，エ　holistically「総体的に」。"The drones interrupted their rhythmic flights (その無人機は規則的な飛行を中断した)" とあるため，アが適切である。　(5)　ア　put out「失わせる」，イ　soak up「吸収する」，ウ　dwell on「(過去を)振り返る」，エ　merge with「合併する」。空欄の後に "the traumatic events of the past (過去のトラウマとなっている出来事)" が続くため，ウが適切である。

【3】(1)　イ　　(2)　ウ　　(3)　エ　　(4)　イ　　(5)　ア
〈解説〉(1)　イはtake a breakが正しい表現。　(2)　ウは主語が複数形のthe shoddy construction methodsなので正しくはhave。　(3)　エは単数形のatmosphereを繰り返す語なのでthatが正しい。　(4)　イはfriendlyという形容詞を形容するため副詞でなければならない。正しくは，environmentally。　(5)　アは過去のことを表すため，havingを用いた分詞構文にしなければならない。正しくは，Having been lost。

【4】(1)　ウ　　(2)　ア　　(3)　エ　　(4)　ク　　(5)　オ
〈解説〉会話文の空所補充問題である。最初にAがBenにMaryの様子を聞いている。続くBenの発言には学校という言葉があるので，MaryはBenの娘だとわかる。以下，空欄以外の箇所をざっと読んでみると，新学期を迎えた子を持つ親同士が，学校についての不満を話しているとわかる。クラスに子どもが多すぎて，パソコンの台数が足りず，宿題が多すぎ，教師の数も足りないと言っている。この類の問題は，前後の会話の受けこたえから正答を推測していく必要がある。たとえば (3) の場合，その後に続くThere are just too many kids in the classes.「そのクラスには子どもがたくさんいすぎる」という文から，クラスの規模に言及している選択肢エを選ぶことが可能である。

【5】(1)　A　ウ　B　イ　C　イ　D　エ　(2)　d
(3)　①　それは風変わりなことだが，私に言わせれば，自分たちの子供の発達において大きな違いを生んだ。　②　科学技術が生み出す社会的な孤立化を抑え，現実の世界において子供たちに役立つ技能を育ませてやりたかった。　③　私たちが思うに，子供時代というものは，社交的関わりを深めたり，創意工夫が促進されたり，現実世界からの刺激に対応したりする時代でなければならない。　(4)　The gains in their development and character have been invaluable　(5)　(At some point, my children will) need to enter the digital world and learn the skills necessary to succeed there too(.)

〈解説〉(1)　A　ア　ratification「批准」，イ　bounty「博愛，奨励金」，ウ　anomaly「変則，例外」，エ　facet「側面」。筆者の5歳の息子は多くの点で年齢以上のことができるが，1つだけ大きな例外があって，iPadの電源を入れることができない。　B　のちに続く文で，さまざまな質問に対して周囲の人々が答えてくれている。このことを考えるとイの「『地域の専門家』と接触するクセがついた」が最も適切である。develop a habit doingは「～するクセがつく」という意味の表現。
C　ア　rabies「狂犬病」，イ　turf「なわばり，専門分野」，ウ　gadget「小物，小さな装置」，エ　valet「従者，(ホテルなどで世話をする)ボーイ」。第3段落で，何かわからないことがあったら，各分野に詳しい地元の人に聞くと述べている。　D　ア　humanitarian「人道主義者」，イ　socialist「社会主義者」，ウ　cosmopolitan「世界主義者」，エ　absolutist「絶対主義者」。パソコンやテレビを見ないscreen-freeの環境で子どもを育ててはいるが，長時間車で移動するときは子どもにテレビ番組を見せておとなしくさせるという記述である。つまり絶対的にscreen-freeを固守しているわけではないということ。　(2)　a～dのうち，dは後ろに「私の子どもたちは中国語をマスターするための子ども向けアプリやクラシック音楽の華美な装いを持っていないが，たくさんのことを質問したり想像したり造ったりする」とあり，アインシュタインの言葉と対応している箇所であることがわかる。

(3)　一つひとつの単語は難しくないため，文法関係(過去分詞を修飾する副詞や関係代名詞) をしっかり反映させた訳を書くことを心がけるとよい。　(4)　語句の中にhaveとbeenがあることから，主語が複数形の現在完了を用いた文であることが推察される。そこから，the gainsが主語であることを推測し，「何の」増加であるかをinで説明する文を作成すれば文が作成できる。gainsと複数形になっていることから，複数の物の増加を表していることが推察できる。　(5)　下線部④の前の文で「私たちがテクノロジーを抑制していることは，あと2～3年しか続かないことを認識している」とある。そのあと “At some point (いつか)” から文が始まっているため，キーワードをもとに，当該の部分には「子どもたちがテクノロジーの世界へ足を踏み入れる必要があること」や「その世界で成功するための技術を身につけること」といった内容が入ることが推察できる。キーワードを用いつつ，上述の内容をまとめられるよう適宜単語を補う必要があることに注意するべきである。

【6】Internet-capable devices have the potential to broaden the range of information available to students in class. However, it's important to make students aware of the possible risks inherent in using the Internet. For example, students should be trained to identify situation where it is not appropriate to share personally identifiable information. With clear rules in place to protect students, it is just as important for teachers to explain the purpose of the rules so that students are motivated to follow them. (81words)

〈解説〉ライティングは，テーマに関して時間内に正確に書くことが大切である。そのためには，まずゆっくりでもよいので規定の文字数の英作文を何度もこなし，文法や語彙の正確さ，流暢さを徐々に上げていく訓練が必要である。また，本問のテーマとして挙げられている「インターネットに接続できる電子機器 “Internet-capable devices”」といった教育関係の用語は，日ごろから教室英語の本や英語教育に関する雑誌などを読むことで身につけていくことが大切である。

【7】政府は，東京オリンピックに向けスポーツ振興を行っている。急速に高齢化が進む日本では，運動奨励による健康維持が不可欠である。また，スポーツは労働者の健康増進と長時間労働のストレス軽減にも役立つ。職場や退職後の運動促進が，日本人の長寿につながると考えられる。SFTプログラムを通じて，より長く健康的に暮らす人が増えるだろう。(160字)

〈解説〉要約の問題は，テキストに明示的に書かれている情報からそれを包括する情報へ統合することが重要である(例「朝から洗濯や掃除，仕事をし，夜遅くに帰宅した」→「忙しい1日だった」に統合)。そのためには，詳細情報(具体例など) や過剰な情報を削除し，一連の動作を上位語に置き換えたり，トピックセンテンスを抜き出したりすることが重要である。具体的には，英字新聞の社説を200字以内で要約するといった練習をこなすことが挙げられる。

【中学校】

【1】(1) ①　区切り　②　つながり　③　賛否　④　身近
(2) ①　使用場面　②　働き　③　事実関係　④　判断
(3) ①　多様　②　公正　③　心情　④　我が国　⑤　尊重　⑥　視野　⑦　自覚　⑧　国際協調

〈解説〉中学校学習指導要領において，教科目標及び学年ごとの目標，内容，指導計画の作成と内容の取扱いは頻出である。必ず現行の中学校学習指導要領及び同解説外国語編を並行して精読し，内容をしっかり理解した上で暗記しておくことが重要である。

【高等学校】

【1】(1) ①　総合的　②　四つの領域　③　生徒の実態　④　定着　(2) ①　development　②　clarifying　③　methods　④　broaden　(3) ①　判断力　②　心情　③　国際協調　④　自然

〈解説〉高等学校学習指導要領において，教科目標及び学年ごとの目標，内容，指導計画の作成と内容の取扱いは頻出である。必ず現行の高等学校学習指導要領及び同解説外国語編を並行して精読し，内容をしっかり理解した上で暗記しておくことが重要である。

2017年度　実施問題

【中高共通】

【1】[リスニングテスト]

問題文及び5つの質問を聞き，各質問の後に読まれるa～dの4つの選択肢の中から，その質問に対する答えとして最も適切なものを1つ選び，記号で答えなさい。

ただいまから，問題1のリスニングテストを始めます。これから読む英文の内容に関して，5つの質問をします。それぞれの質問の後に読まれるa，b，c，dの4つの選択肢の中から，答えとして最も適切なものを1つ選び，記号で答えなさい。英文と質問，選択肢は，全体をとおして2回読みます。聞きながらメモを取ってもかまいません。それでは始めます。

The number of foreign technical intern trainees who fled from workplaces in 2015 reached the highest level ever at 5,803, greatly surpassing the previous year's figure, according to a Justice Ministry survey.

The government believes that poor working conditions have resulted in these incidents in many cases. To counter this situation, the government plans to take legislative action to strengthen supervision in corporations and organizations that take on foreign trainees, aiming to stop an increase in the number of runaways.

The purpose of the foreign technical intern trainee system is for young foreign nationals to acquire the latest work skills in Japan and then use these skills in their home countries to aid economic development.

At the end of June last year, about 180,000 trainees were participating in the scheme.

The number of foreign trainees who fled in 2012 was 2,005. The number rose to 3,566 in 2013, and to 4,847 in 2014. In recent years, the number has risen annually by about a thousand.

By nationality, the largest number of trainees who ran away in 2015 were Chinese at 3,116, followed by 1,705 Vietnamese and 336 Myanmar nationals.

Sources close to the issue have pointed out that there are brokers who abuse the trainee system: these brokers introduce other jobs to foreign technical intern trainees and encourage them to leave their original workplaces. In some cases, foreign trainees have applied for refugee status after fleeing their workplaces with the aim of finding other jobs in Japan.

One of the reasons behind the problem is the awful treatment of foreign trainees by some of the companies and organizations that take part in the scheme.

The number of companies and organizations found to have engaged in misconduct, such as not paying a living wage, has been rising over the last five years. Last year, the number increased by 32 from the previous year to 273.

The sources said that there were some cases in which an employer paid a salary more than ¥1 million less than had been agreed, and foreign trainees were even physically hit, apparently for making low-quality products.

Last year, the Justice Ministry submitted a bill to the Diet to create a law for proper implementation of the foreign technical intern trainee system and protecting trainees under the system, which will contain penalty clauses for human rights violations against the trainees. The ministry wants the bill to pass as soon as possible. (404 words)

Questions

(1) In the passage, which is NOT included as a purpose of the technical intern trainee system for young foreigners?

(a) To help them to acquire the latest work skills.

(b) To economically support their countries, such as China, Vietnam and

Myanmar.

(c) To compensate for the labor shortage in their countries.

(d) To help them to be able to use better skills in their countries.

(2) How much was the increase of foreign trainees who ran away from their workplaces from 2014 to 2015?

(a) About five hundred.

(b) About one thousand.

(c) About two thousand.

(d) About five thousand.

(3) Why do some foreign trainees apply for refugee status?

(a) To cancel their debt.

(b) To get some money from their brokers.

(c) To leave Japan.

(d) To get a new job.

(4) Among the companies and organizations who took part in the scheme, how many were engaged in misconduct last year?

(a) 32

(b) 241

(c) 273

(d) 305

(5) According to the passage, what is the bill submitted by the Justice Ministry like?

(a) It contains a penalty for failing to protect trainees.

(b) It relaxes working visa requirements for people from Asia.

(c) It promotes a raise in salary for foreign trainees.

(d) It supports companies and organizations promoting human ights.

【 REPEAT 】

これでリスニングテストを終わります。

(☆☆☆☆☆◎◎◎)

【2】次の各文の(　　)にあてはまる最も適切なものを，ア～エから1つ選び，記号で答えなさい。

(1)　With the (　　) of the heat wave, sales of air-conditioners picked up.

ア　offshoot　　イ　onset　　ウ　outcome　　エ　fallout

(2)　Because one of our teammates failed to show up, we had to (　　) the judo team competition.

ア　terminate　　イ　abolish　　ウ　vacate　　エ　forfeit

(3)　The volcano has remained (　　) for over 200 years, but recently there have been signs that it is becoming active again.

ア　dormant　　イ　fluid　　ウ　vibrant　　エ　suspended

(4)　Fortunately, the debris flow by the heavy rain struck a (　　) populated area and no lives were lost.

ア　sparsely　　イ　massively　　ウ　severely　　エ　narrowly

(5)　Despite the writer's fame, the editor rejected his new story, saying that it did not (　　) to the magazine's high standards.

ア　look up　　イ　check off　　ウ　measure up　　エ　round off

(☆☆☆☆◎◎◎◎)

【3】次の各文の下線部ア～エの中で，誤っている箇所を1つ選び，記号で答えなさい。

(1)　A U.N. ア official who went to Vietnam to assess イ religious freedom said Thursday that security agents ウ closely monitored his visit, and people he wanted to meet were harassed and エ intimidating.

(2)　The branches of university, ア which イ long adhered to a "no-layoff" policy, began changing ウ its procedures エ under the pressure of financial losses.

(3)　The Obama administration on Monday launched ア a formal review of its electronic intelligence gathering イ in which has come under ウ widespread criticism since leaks エ by a former spy agency contractor.

(4)　Prenatal care and ア prevention of infection イ in mothers ウ at childbirth have $_{エ}$reduced down maternal mortality.

(5) My parents instilled thier moral values $_{ア}$for my sister and $_{イ}$me, $_{ウ}$enabling us, by the time we reached $_{エ}$our teen years, to know right from wrong.

(☆☆☆☆◎◎◎◎◎)

【4】次の対話文の(　1　)～(　5　)にあてはまる最も適切な英文を，ア～クから選び，記号で答えなさい。ただし，同じ選択肢を2度使わないこと。

A: I've found one of those personality tests on the Internet. (　1　)

B: Oh, those. They're a bit of a waste of time, aren't they? (　2　)

A: But they're quite good fun, aren't they?

B: Well, yes, especially if you do them with friends. (　3　)

A: That's true.

B: (　4　) I mean, I already know the answers, don't I? So, I'm not likely to get any surprises, like, oh, according to this test I'm happy —— I didn't expect that!

A: OK, I take your point. So what makes you happy?

B: (　5　)

A: Me too. But I need time on my own, as well.

ア　Anyway, why should I do a test that tells me how happy or healthy or successful I am?

イ　I did one on 'How healthy are you?' and the results were completely wrong.

ウ　It's impossible to find what you want, especially when it comes to psychology books.

エ　I would if I knew I could find something useful, but you know how disorganized it is there.

オ　You know, answer these questions to find out how happy you are.

カ　Oh, I don't know. Spending time with people I know and like, I guess. I need people around me.

キ　I think it's important that you shouldn't take them seriously, though.

ク　The advantage is that you're getting some exercise too, which is something I don't usually do.

(☆☆☆◎◎◎◎◎)

【5】次の英文を読んで，(1)～(5)の問いに答えなさい。

Meteorologists know that better than anyone. They make large numbers of forecasts and routinely check their accuracy —— which is why we know that one-and two-day forecasts are typically quite accurate while eight-day forecasts are not. With these analyses, meteorologists are able to sharpen their understanding of how weather works and tweak their models. [a] Then they try again. Forecast, measure, revise. Repeat. It's a never-ending process of incremental improvement that explains why weather forecasts are good and slowly getting better. There may be limits to such improvements, however, because weather is (A). ①The further out the forecaster tries to look, the more opportunity there is for chaos to flap its butterfly wings and blow away expectations. ②Big leaps in computing power and continued refinement of forecasting models may nudge the limits a little further into the future but those advances gradually get harder and the payoffs shrink toward zero. How good can it get? No one knows. But knowing the current limits is itself a success. [b]

In so many other high-stakes endeavors, forecasters are groping in the dark. They have no idea how good their forecasts are in the short, medium, or long term —— and no idea how good their forecasts could become. [c] That's because the forecast-measure-revise procedure operates only within the rarefied confines of high-tech forecasting, such as the work of macroeconomists at central banks or marketing and financial professionals in big companies. More often forecasts are made and then...nothing. ③Accuracy is seldom determined after the fact and is almost never done with sufficient regularity and rigor that conclusions can be drawn. The reason? Mostly it's a demand-side problem: The consumers of forecasting —— governments, business, and the public —— (B). So there is no measurement. Which means no revision. And without revision, there can be no improvement. Imagine a world in which people love to run, but they have no idea how fast the average person runs, or how fast the best could run, because runners have (C) —— stay on the track, begin the race when the gun is fired, end it after a specified distance —— and there are no independent race officials and timekeepers measuring results. How likely is it that running times are improving in this world? Not very. Are [ ]? Again, probably not.

"I have been struck by how important measurement is to improving the human condition," Bill Gates wrote. "④You can achieve incredible progress if you set a clear goal and find a measure that will drive progress toward that goal. This may seem basic, but it is amazing how often it is not done and how hard it is to get right." He is right about what it takes to drive progress, and it is surprising how rarely it's done in forecasting. [d] Even that simple first step —— setting a clear goal —— hasn't been taken.

(1) (A)～(C)に入る最も適した表現を，それぞれ次のア～エから1つずつ選びなさい。

(A) ア the lottery system of distributing subsidy
イ the hot bed of entrepreneurship
ウ the textbook illustration of nonlinearity
エ the obsolete telescope of fringe scientists

(B) ア don't demand evidence of accuracy
イ are hung up with the concept of precision
ウ don't appreciate the efficacy of forecasting
エ are content with mediocre results

(C) ア never received any compensation
イ fabricated performance data before
ウ been fully focused on their races

エ　never agreed to basic ground rules

(2)　次の一文は，本文中から抜き出したものである。この一文が入る適切な位置を，［ a ］～［ d ］から選びなさい。

[　At best, they have vague hunches.　]

(3)　下線部①～③を日本語にしなさい。

(4)　[　　]を補うように次の語句を並べ替えなさい。

[　physically capable / human beings / are / running / as / the best runners / as / fast　]

(5)　下線部④の条件として文中でビル・ゲイツが述べていること以外で，必要だとあなたが考えることを1つ取り上げ，それについて70語程度の英語で書きなさい。ただし，符号は語数に含めない。また，使用語数を書き入れること。

(☆☆☆☆◎◎◎◎)

【6】次の全文を英語に直しなさい。

大海原に出て陸が見えなくなる恐怖に耐えられなくては，新しい大陸に到達することはできない。そんなふうな言葉を何かで読んだ。

(☆☆☆☆◎◎◎◎)

【7】次の英文を読んで，その趣旨を120字以内の日本語で書きなさい。ただし，句読点も字数に入れること。

Music and language are universal, innate expressions of human cognition and communication. Their universality is evident in the fact that all cultures express themselves verbally and musically. Both are innate abilities that develop through personal interaction, as can be observed in the spontaneity with which children learn to act and interact musically and verbally from a very young age. But, specifically, how does the child acquire a language?

To learn a language, then, the child subconsciously abstracts the rules of the language structure and utilizes them to create his or her own novel sentences. Children do not just repeat the sentences they hear, but create new sentences by applying the rules they have abstracted from their language. A similar proposal can be made for the way in which children learn and create music. In order to learn and to create music, children abstract some of the rules of their musical culture and use them creatively. Just as they learn spontaneously the rules that allow them to originate an unlimited number of sentences, so they seem to learn the musical rules that allow them to create novel sequences in music.

Music and language are both modes of communication, yet they have different goals. Generally speaking, while the primary aim of language is to communicate thought, one of the main goals of music is to heighten emotions and express them aesthetically. Music is born out of the need to express ourselves and to communicate aesthetically through the abstractness and the characteristics of sound.

(☆☆☆☆◎◎◎)

【中学校】

【1】中学校学習指導要領「外国語」「第2　各言語の目標及び内容等」「英語」について，次の(1)～(3)の問いに答えなさい。

(1)　次の文は「2　内容」の「(1)　言語活動　ア　聞くこと」の一部である。(　①　)～(　④　)にあてはまる語句を書きなさい。

(ア)　強勢，イントネーション，区切りなど基本的な(　①　)の特徴をとらえ，正しく聞き取ること。

(イ)　(　②　)で話されたり読まれたりする英語を聞いて，情報を正確に聞き取ること。

(ウ)　質問や(　③　)などを聞いて適切に応じること。

(エ)　話し手に聞き返すなどして内容を確認しながら理解すること。

(オ)　まとまりのある英語を聞いて，(　④　)や要点を適切に聞き取ること。

(2)　次の文は「2　内容」の「(2)　言語活動の取扱い」「ア(ウ)　〔言語の働きの例〕」の一部である。(　①　)～(　④　)にあてはまる語句を書きなさい。

a　コミュニケーションを(　①　)にする

b　気持ちを伝える

c　(　②　)を伝える

d　考えや(　③　)を伝える

e　相手の(　④　)を促す

(3)　次の文は「3　指導計画の作成と内容の取扱い」の一部である。(　①　)~(　⑧　)にあてはまる語句を書きなさい。

ア　(　①　)なものの見方や考え方を理解し，(　②　)な判断力を養い豊かな(　③　)を育てるのに役立つこと。

イ　外国や(　④　)の生活や文化についての理解を深めるとともに，言語や文化に対する関心を高め，これらを(　⑤　)する態度を育てるのに役立つこと。

ウ　(　⑥　)から国際理解を深め，国際社会に生きる日本人としての(　⑦　)を高めるとともに，(　⑧　)の精神を養うのに役立つこと。

(☆☆☆☆☆◎◎◎◎)

【高等学校】

【1】高等学校学習指導要領「外国語」について，次の(1)~(3)の問いに答えなさい。

(1)　次は「第2款　各科目　第5　英語表現Ⅰ」の「2　内容(2)」で示されている事項である。(　①　)~(　⑥　)にあてはまる語句を書きなさい。

ア　(　①　)やイントネーションなどの英語の音声的な特徴，(　②　)，声の大きさなどに注意しながら話すこと。

イ　内容の要点を示す語句や文，(　③　)を示す語句などに注意しながら書くこと。また，書いた内容を(　④　)こと。

ウ　(　⑤　)の仕方や(　⑤　)のために必要な表現などを学習し，実際に活用すること。

エ　聞いたり読んだりした内容について，そこに示されている意見を他の意見と比較して共通点や相違点を整理したり，(　⑥　)をまとめたりすること。

(2)　次は「第2款　各科目　第3　コミュニケーション英語Ⅱ」の「2　内容(1)」の一部の英訳である。(　①　)～(　④　)に入る適切な語を英語で書きなさい。

A.　Understanding information, ideas, etc., and grasping the (　①　) and the main points by listening to introductions to specified topics, reports, dialogues, discussions, etc.
B.　Reading explanations, commentaries, stories, essays, etc. in accordance with the purpose such as rapid reading, intensive reading, etc. Reading aloud and (　②　) passages so that the meaning of the content is expressed.
C.　Drawing (　③　) through discussion, etc., on information, ideas, etc. based on what one has heard, read, learned and experienced.
D.　Writing (　④　) and cohesive passages on information, ideas, etc. based on what one has heard, read, learned and experienced.

(3)　次は「第4款　各科目にわたる指導計画の作成と内容の取扱い」の「2(1)」で示されている事項である。(　①　)～(　④　)にあてはまる語句を書きなさい。

教材については，外国語を通じてコミュニケーション能力を総合的に育成するため，各科目の目標に応じ，実際の言語の(　①　)や言語の(　②　)に十分配慮したものを取り上げるものとすること。その際，その外国語を日常使用している人々を中心とする世界の人々及び日本人の日常生活，風俗習慣，物語，地理，歴史，伝統文化や自然科学などに関するものの中から，生徒の(　③　)及び(　④　)に即して適切な題材を変化をもたせて取り上げるものとし，次の観点に留意する必要があること。(以下は省略)

(☆☆☆☆☆◎◎◎◎◎)

解答・解説

【中高共通】

【1】(1)　(c)　　(2)　(b)　　(3)　(d)　　(4)　(c)　　(5)　(a)

〈解説〉リスニングテスト：外国人技能実習制度についての出題である。制度の説明と課題について述べられているが，数字が頻出するので集中して聞く必要がある。2回読まれるので，1回目は概要をつかみ，2回目で聞き取れなかった箇所や細部をチェックするとよい。　(1)　スクリプト第3段落1文目のto acquire以下で(c)以外の内容が述べられている。　(2)　第5段落最後の文で「最近では1年間で約1000人増えている」とある。また，述べられている。したがって，約1000人が正解である。(3)　第7段落の最後で，「他の仕事を探す目的で」と述べられている。(4)　第9段落最後の文で「前年から32人増えて273人になった」と述べられている。32人と間違えないこと。　(5)　第11段落1文目後半のwhich以下がポイントである。「実習生への人権侵害に対する罰則条項が含まれている」と述べられている。

【2】(1)　イ　　(2)　エ　　(3)　ア　　(4)　ア　　(5)　ウ

〈解説〉(1)　カッコを含む部分は，「熱波の襲来とともに」の意味である。(2)　カッコを含む部分は，「柔道の団体戦をあきらめねばならなかった」の意味である。　(3)　カッコを含む部分は，「その火山は過去200年間活動休止状態だ」の意味である。　(4)　カッコを含む部分は，

「幸運にも，大雨による土石流は人があまり住んでいない地域を直撃した」の意味である。　(5)　カッコを含む部分は，「新作はその雑誌の高い基準に達していなかった」の意味で，measure upは「水準に達する」である。

【3】(1)　エ　(2)　ウ　(3)　イ　(4)　エ　(5)　ア

〈解説〉(1)　過去分詞のintimidatedが正解である。「苦しんで脅されていた」の意味となる。　(2)　主語がThe branchesと複数なので，所有格も複数形で受ける必要がある。ここは，itsとなっているので誤りである。theirが正しい。　(3)　前置詞のinは不要。「多方面の批判にさらされることになった電子情報の収集に関する公式見解」の意味で，whichの先行詞はgatheringである。　(4)「母体の死亡率を引き下げた」の意味であり，downは不要である。　(5)　アは，forではなく，instill A in〔into〕B「AをBに徐々に教え込む」という形で，inまたはintoを使用する。なお，instill B with Aとすることもできる。

【4】1　オ　2　イ　3　キ　4　ア　5　カ

〈解説〉1　直後のBでOh, those.「ああ，あれね。」と発言しているので，テストの内容について説明していることがわかる。　2　Bが「時間の無駄じゃないのか？」と発言しているので，自身の経験を話していることが類推できる。　3　直後でAがThat's true.と言っているので，AとBの一致点であることが類推できる。　4　BはI already know the answersと言っているので，「答えがわかっているから不要だ」と考えていることが類推できる。　5　直後にBが「私もそうだ。同様に自分自身の時間も必要だ。」と言っているので，これと関係するセリフはカが適切である。

【5】(1)　A　ウ　B　ア　C　エ　(2)　c　(3)　①　予想しようとする人がより先まで見通そうとすればするほど，無秩序がその蝶の羽をはためかせて予測を吹き飛ばしてしまう可能性が大きくなる。

② コンピュータの力の大躍進や，予想モデルの継続的な改良で，限界は少しだけ未来の方に推し進められるかもしれないが，そのような前進は段々と難しくなり，結果として得られるものはゼロに近づいていく。 ③ 事後に正確度が判定されることはめったにないし，結論を導き出すに足る規則性や厳密さをもって判定されることもほとんどない。 (4) the best runners running as fast as human beings are physically capable (5) I think that believing in your own potential is indispensable to achieving incredible progress in your life. However distant your goal may be, it is crucial not to set unreasonable limits on yourself. If you do, you may find that you've given up before you've even begun. You must believe that you can one day achieve whatever you set your sights on after taking on challenges and learning as much as you can along the way. (76語)

〈解説〉(1) A 第1段落5文目ForestからRepeatまでで，直線的な内容を述べている。ここでは，それと反対の状況を述べているのでウが適当。 B この部分の直後の2文Soからimprovementまでが結果を表している。「評価方法がなければ見直しはない。見直しがなければ改善はない。」と言っているので，アが適切である。 C 第2段落中ほどのImagineから同文のbecauseの前までで，「平均的な人がどれくらいの速さで走るか，最高の人がどれくらいの速さで走るべきかなんて誰も考えていない」という概要である。したがって，エが適切である。 (2) 指示された英文は，「せいぜいが，彼らはあいまいな予測をするだけである。」の意味である。この部分の前に来るのは，第2段落2文目andから同文文末のbecomeまでの「どうやれば予報が良いものになるかという対策はない」が適切である。 (3) ① ここでは，「the＋比較級，the＋比較級」がポイントである。「～すればするほど，ますます～」と訳さねばならない。いわゆる「バタフライ効果」に関係する言及である。 ② nudge「やんわりと押す」，payoff「報酬」。若干の明るい見通しはあるが，それも徐々にゼロになるという主旨である。
③ thatの先行詞はregularity「規則性」とrigor「厳密さ」である。
(4) 並べ替えた英文の意味は，「最高の走者は，人が肉体的に走れる

限界と同じぐらいに走っているのか？」という意味である。
(5)　正答では，まず，自分の可能性を信じることだと述べている。続いて，目標がどのように遠くに思えても，根拠のない理由で限界を設けてはだめだと続けて，そのような限界を設定した時点であきらめたことになる。いつかは実現すると信じることが必要だという主旨でまとめている。

【６】I once came across a maxim to the effect that one should not hope to reach a new continent unless one can overcome the terror of venturing into the infinite expanse of the ocean where no land is visible.
〈解説〉come across「遭遇する」，maxim「格言」，unless「もし…でなければ」。「そんなふうな言葉を何かで読んだ」の部分は，Iからthatまでで述べている。「(that以下)という趣旨の格言に遭遇した」と考えればよい。「耐えられなくては」の部分は，if one can'tと記述してもよい。

【７】音楽も言語も人間の認知とコミュニケーションの表現であり，人は相互作用の中でその能力を発達させる。潜在意識的に言語構造や音楽的文化の規則を抽出し，その規則を新しい文章や音楽の創造に用いる。言語は考えの伝達，音楽は情緒の美的表現を目的とする。(119字)
〈解説〉3つの段落をそれぞれ要約してまとめればよい。正答の第1文は，英文の第1段落第1文と第3文前半の要約である。正答の第2文は，英文の第2段落第1文the childからnovel sentencesまでの部分と，第4文の中ほどのchildrenからcreativelyまでの部分の要約である。正答の第3文は，英文の第3段落第2文のthe primaryからaestheticallyまでの部分の要約である。

【中学校】

【１】(1)　①　英語の音声　②　自然な口調　③　依頼　④　概要　(2)　①　円滑　②　情報　③　意図　④　行動
(3)　①　多様　②　公正　③　心情　④　我が国　⑤　尊重

⑥　広い視野　⑦　自覚　⑧　国際協調

〈解説〉(1)　「中学校学習指導要領　外国語」からの出題である。「聞くこと」の5項目を通して，英語の音声とはどのようなものであるかを理解し，その特徴をとらえながら聞き取ることができるようになること，また，話し手の気持ち，状況や場面によって強勢やイントネーションなどに変化があることを理解し，様々な状況に慣れて内容を聞き取ることができるようになることが必要である。　(2)　言語の働きについては，小学校と高等学校における分類との対応関係を分かりやすくするために統一を図り，5つに整理して，それぞれ代表的な例を示している。　(3)　題材の選択に関する3つの観点についての出題である。これからの国際社会に生きる日本人として，コミュニケーション能力を総合的に育成することが重要であり，そのためには，題材の選択にあたり，生徒の興味・関心を引き出して育てることができる適切なものを選択する必要がある。その際には，正しい理解が図れるように配慮することが大切である。

【高等学校】

【1】(1)　①　リズム　②　話す速度　③　つながり　④　読み返す　⑤　発表　⑥　自分の考え　(2)　①　outline　②　reciting　③　conclusions　④　coherent　(3)　①　使用場面　②　働き　③　発達の段階　④　興味・関心

〈解説〉(1)　①「リズム」とは，発話において他よりも目立って知覚される音や音節が規則的に繰り返されて起こる音声的刺激のことである。　②「話す速度」とは，その場の状況，聞き手の反応，話題，伝えようとする内容や気持ちなどに応じて発話する速さのことである。　③「つながり」とは，関連性のことであり，文と文，段落と段落の意味的・文法的な関連性を示す語句やフレーズがある。　④「読み返す」とは，誤解を招くような表現や無関係なことが書かれていないか，また，語句や文法などの間違いはないかなどに注意をするように指導することが必要である。　⑤「発表」とは，表現行動の一形態であり，メモに基づいての発表や何も見ないでの発表など，様々な方法を指導することが必要である。　⑥　この項目の後半が，意見を他の意見と比較して「自分の考え」をまとめるという内容である。その際には，考えの流れを明確にするためにフローチャートを利用するなどの工夫をする指導も必要である。　(2)　①から④の空欄部分は，日本語では以下のように記述されている。　①「事物に関する紹介や報告，対話や討論などを聞いて，情報や考えなどを理解したり，概要や要点をとらえたりする。」　②「説明，評論，物語，随筆などについて，速読したり精読したりするなど目的に応じた読み方をする。また，聞き手に伝わるように音読や暗唱を行う。」　③「聞いたり読んだりしたこと，学んだことや経験したことに基づき，情報や考えなどについて，話し合うなどして結論をまとめる。」　④「聞いたり読んだりしたこと，学んだことや経験したことに基づき，情報や考えなどについて，まとまりのある文章を書く。」　(3)　①から④の各項目は，4技能を総合的に育成する効果的な学習活動が可能となるように，十分に配慮するとともに題材の内容自体についても，十分に配慮することが必要であることを明示したものである。

2016年度　実施問題

【中高共通】

【1】[　リスニングテスト　]

ただいまから，リスニングテストを始めます。これから読む英文の内容に関して，5つの質問をします。それぞれの質問の後に読まれるa，b，c，dの4つの選択肢の中から，答えとして最も適切なものを1つ選び，記号で答えなさい。英文と質問，選択肢は，全体をとおして2回読みます。聞きながらメモを取ってもかまいません。

Robots are expected to take over human jobs in the next decade at a faster pace, as the technology becomes cheaper and smarter, according to a new study.

Companies will dedicate three times more money to the technology in the next ten years to offset rising labor costs, according to the Boston Consulting Group study. The growing investment will reduce the cost of manufacturing labor for the world's top exporters by 16 percent by 2025 and will result in cheaper products, the study found.

"For many manufacturers, the biggest reasons for not replacing workers with robots have been pure economics and technical limitations," said Michael Zinser, a partner at the Boston Consulting Group in a news release. "But the price and performance of automation are improving rapidly. Within five to ten years, the business case for robots in most industries will be compelling, even for many small and mid-sized manufacturers," he said.

The cost of using a certain type of robot, for example, fell from $182,000 in 2005 to $133,000 last year and will fall even further by 2025, the group predicts. As robots become smarter, they are able to take into account unexpected situations and respond using more complex algorithms. They are expected to take over one-quarter of industrial manufacturing tasks, up from 10 percent today.

"As labor costs rise around the world, it is becoming increasingly critical that manufacturers rapidly take steps to improve their output per worker to stay competitive," said Harold L.Sirkin, a BCG senior partner. "Companies are finding that advances in robotics and other manufacturing technologies offer some of the best opportunities to sharply improve productivity."

The company studied 21 industries in 25 countries and conducted interviews with experts, clients and analyzed industry reports.

Question

(1) According to the Boston Consulting Group study, what will companies do in the next ten years?

(a) They will invest more budget in automation.

(b) They will stop technological unemployment.

(c) They will do worldwide market research.

(d) They will continue offshoring technical support.

(2) According to a consultant, what is important in introducing robots in place of humans?

(a) Change in physical properties.

(b) Cost and operation of robotics.

(c) Labor-management policies.

(d) Closer economic relations.

(3) What is said about a certain type of robot?

(a) The number of them in manufacturing unexpectedly decreased in the last ten years.

(b) The cost of using them was reduced to less than $13,000 last year.

(c) Their performance is still inferior to that of humans in complex situations.

(d) Their proportion in industrial manufacturing tasks is expected to be one-quarter in the future.

(4) According to the passage, what must manufacturers do to succeed?

(a) Find the right time to invest in technology.

(b) Reform working environment for engineers.

(c) Replace robots with skilled workers.

(d) Improve their profit margins per worker.

(5) What did the Boston Consulting Group NOT do to do this research?

(a) It picked out one company from each country surveyed.

(b) It talked with people involved in these industries.

(c) It did research on various industries in multiple countries.

(d) It obtained information through industry papers.

【REPEAT】

これでリスニングテストを終わります。

(☆☆☆☆◎◎◎◎)

【2】次の各文の(　　)にあてはまる最も適切な語を，ア～エから1つ選び，記号で答えなさい。

(1) I hurt my knee playing football in university, and now it tends to (　　) in cold weather.

ア wind down　イ change over　ウ play off　エ act up

(2) Excavation, in essence, an act of (　　): to clear a site down to the lowest level means that all the upper levels are completely eliminated.

ア exploration　イ destruction　ウ spontaneity
エ validation

(3) The climb up the mountain was a long, (　　) one that left everyone out of breath.

ア arduous　イ terse　ウ adept　エ meager

(4) The property (　　) between the two landowners was resolved when a legal document showing the original boundaries was discovered.

ア wreck　イ contempt　ウ dispute　エ calamity

(5)　Because his delivery was (　　), the effect of his speech on the voters was nonexistent.

ア　plausible　　イ　halting　　ウ　vigorous　　エ　pertinent

(☆☆☆☆◎◎◎◎◎)

【3】次の各文の下線部ア～エの中で，誤っている箇所を1つ選び，記号で答えなさい。

(1)　ア<u>Because of</u> the long drought イ<u>citizens</u> were told that it was imperative that in the future they ウ<u>will</u> save as エ<u>much</u> water as possible.

(2)　Major ア<u>advertising</u> companies have イ<u>traditionally</u> volunteered ウ<u>its</u> time エ<u>to public</u> service accounts.

(3)　The bridal gown was ア<u>mostly</u> unique: イ<u>the bridegroom</u> designed ウ<u>it</u> and エ<u>his</u> mother wove the fabric.

(4)　He ア<u>sat down</u> イ<u>besides</u> the child and ウ<u>reassured</u> him that the monster was エ<u>merely</u> imaginary.

(5)　Scientific advances over the last fifty years ア<u>have led</u> to イ<u>changes in</u> health, agriculture and communication, and generally ウ<u>enhancing</u> socio-economic development and the quality of our エ<u>lives</u>.

(☆☆☆☆◎◎◎)

【4】次の対話文の(　1　)～(　5　)にあてはまる最も適切な英文を，ア～クから選び，記号で答えなさい。ただし，同じ選択肢を2度使わないこと。

A: I'm a nervous traveler and I don't like traveling internationally.

B: You could get travel insurance. Doing that would make you feel more secure, wouldn't it?

A: (　1　)

B: You could get insurance to cover mishaps on the trip, such as cancelled flights or missed connections and having your luggage lost, stolen, or damaged. It'll even cover your losses if your trip is cancelled.

A: (2)

B: In that case, you can get medical insurance to cover the costs of medical emergencies, even if you have to be medically evacuated in the event of serious injuries or illness.

A: (3)

B: And if things go terribly wrong, there's even insurance for if you become disabled or if there's an accidental death. They'll pay for repatriation of your remains or overseas funeral services.

A: (4)

B: The whole point is to make you less worried about bad things happening while you travel.

A: (5)

ア Oh, you're right. I could get really sick or injured.

イ The other car collided with mine without giving warning of its intention.

ウ Right, and right now the only insurance that seems to be foolproof is staying put.

エ Disabilities and death? Is that supposed to put my mind at ease?

オ It is important to obtain the best international travel medical insurance for your situation.

カ Maybe. What types of coverage are available?

キ I guess that would help, but I'm more nervous about something happening to me while I'm in another country.

ク I started to slow down but the traffic was more stationary than I thought.

(☆☆☆☆◎◎◎◎◎)

【5】次の英文を読んで，(1)～(4)の問いに答えなさい。

The (A)<u>banality</u> of evil shares much with the banality of heroism. ①<u>Neither attribute is the direct consequence of unique dispositional</u>

tendencies; there are no special inner attributes of either pathology or goodness residing within the human psyche or the human genome. Both conditions emerge in particular situations at particular times when situational forces play a compelling role in moving particular individuals across a decisional line from inaction to action. There is a decisive decisional moment when a person is caught up in a vector of forces that emanate from a behavioral context. Those forces combine to increase the probability of one's acting to harm others or acting to help others. Their decision may or may not be consciously planned or mindfully taken. Rather, strong situational forces most often impulsively drive the person to action. Among the situational action vectors are: group pressures and group identity, the diffusion of responsibility for the action, a temporal focus on the immediate moment without concern for consequences stemming from the act in the future, presence of social models, and commitment to an ideology.

A common theme in the accounts of European Christians who helped the Jews during the Holocaust could be summed up as the 'banality of goodness.' What is striking over and over again is the number of these rescuers who did the right thing without considering themselves heroic, who acted merely out of a sense of common (B)decency. The ordinariness of their goodness is especially striking in the context of the incredible evil of the systematic (a) by Nazis on a scale the world had never before experienced.

The heroic action of Rosa Parks's refusal to sit in the 'colored' section in the back of an Alabama bus or of the first responders' rush to the World Trade Center disaster are acts of bravery that occur at particular times and places. In contrast, the heroism of Mohandas Gandhi or Mother Teresa consists of valorous acts repeated over a lifetime.

[　　] depending on how we are influenced by situational forces. The imperative becomes discovering how to limit, constrain, and prevent the situational and systemic forces that propel some of us toward social pathology. But equally important is the injunction for every society to foster a 'heroic imagination' in its citizenry. It is achieved by conveying the message that every person is a hero in waiting who will be counted upon to do the right thing when the moment of decision comes. The decisive question for each of us is whether to act in help of others, to prevent harm to others, or not to act at all. ②We should be preparing many laurel wreaths for all those who will discover their reservoir of hidden strengths and virtues enabling them to come forth to act against injustice and cruelty and to stand up for their principled values.

The large body of research on situational determinants of antisocial behavior reveals the extent to which normal, ordinary people can be led to engage in cruel acts against innocent others. However, in those studies and many others, while the majority obeyed, conformed, complied, were persuaded, and were seduced, there was always a (　b　) who resisted, dissented, and disobeyed. In one sense, heroism lies in the ability to resist powerful situational forces that so readily entrap most people.

(1) 下線部(A)・(B)の意味として適切なものを，それぞれア～エから1つずつ選びなさい。

(A) ア　an extreme unhealthy interest in something or worry about something

イ　to be ordinary and not interesting, because of a lack of new or different ideas

ウ　a planned series of actions for achieving something

エ　to make someone nervous and confused by making them hurry or interrupting them

(B) ア　polite, honest and moral behavior and attitudes that show respect for other people

イ　failure to take enough care over something that you are responsible for

ウ　a sudden short period when someone, especially a child,

behaves very angrily

エ　a state of great anxiety or excitement, in which you cannot control your behavior

(2)　(a)・(b)に入る最も適した語を，それぞれア～エから1つずつ選びなさい。

(a)　ア　genocide　イ　hospitality　ウ　spouse
エ　hostage

(b)　ア　priority　イ　mobility　ウ　minority
エ　credibility

(3)　下線部①・②を日本語にしなさい。

(4)　[　　]を補うように次の語群を並べ替えなさい。ただし文頭に来る語も小文字にしてある。

implies / any of us / heroes as / easily become / perpetrators of evil / as / could / that / this perception

(☆☆☆☆◎◎◎◎)

【6】次の(1)の全文及び(2)の下線部を英語に直しなさい。ただし，(1)の文中の「しどけない」は “shidokenai” とすること。

(1)　しどけない，という言葉を耳にすることは最近あまりない。服装や姿勢がだらしないさまをいう。逆に，無造作にくつろいだ様子が魅力的にみえるという使い方もある。

(2)　英語には文法がない，あるとしても，その文法には規則がないといわれることが多い。確かに英語には，名詞・動詞の語尾変化はないにひとしい。こうした語尾変化が文法上きわめて重要な役割を果たしている言語は多いけれども，英語はちがう。

(☆☆☆☆☆◎◎◎◎)

【7】次の英文を読んで，その趣旨を120字以内の日本語で書きなさい。ただし，句読点も字数に入れること。

Most learners will have certain beliefs about language learning and most of these beliefs are likely to be (at least partly) incorrect. Some may think that you can master a language in a few months, and others might believe that even years of suffering may not be sufficient. Some may think that you can only learn the L2 in the host environment, and others might believe that L2 learning in school contexts can be useful if a child starts early enough. Some may think that starting 'early' should mean about 8 or 9 years old, and others might believe that anything over 5 is already too late. Some may think that you need a special 'knack' for languages to be able to learn them, and others might believe that hard work and persistence should be enough. Some may think that grammatical errors are to be avoided at all cost, and others might believe that mistakes do not matter as long as one is fluent. The list is endless.

Of course, issues like the above are not unambiguous and even language experts have disagreements. Fortunately, applied linguistics has (more or less) reached a state of maturity where some of the most extreme views can be refuted with confidence. I believe that it is important that we do so because incorrect beliefs can become real barriers to the mastery of an L2. Unrealistic beliefs about how much progress to expect and how fast, can function like 'time bombs' at the beginning of a language course because of the inevitable disappointment that is to follow. Rigid convictions about what is important about a language and what's not, or what's the best way of learning, can clash with your teaching approach, thereby hindering progress. The best thing is to sort out some of the most far-fetched expectations and erroneous assumptions early on in the course.

(注)　L2: second language

(☆☆☆☆◎◎◎◎)

【中学校】

【1】中学校学習指導要領「外国語」「第2　各言語の目標及び内容等」「英語」について，次の(1)～(3)の問いに答えなさい。

(1) 次の文は「2　内容」の「(1)　言語活動　エ　書くこと」である。(①)～(④)にあてはまる語句を書きなさい。

(ア) 文字や(①)を識別し，語と語の区切りなどに注意して正しく書くこと。

(イ) 語と語のつながりなどに注意して正しく文を書くこと。

(ウ) 聞いたり読んだりしたことについてメモをとったり，感想，(②)やその理由を書いたりなどすること。

(エ) 身近な場面における(③)や(④)したことなどについて，自分の考えや気持ちなどを書くこと。

(オ) 自分の考えや気持ちなどが読み手に正しく伝わるように，文と文のつながりなどに注意して文章を書くこと。

(2) 「2　内容」の「(2)　言語活動の取扱い」「ア(ウ)〔言語の使用場面の例〕」について，「a　特有の表現がよく使われる場面」として示されている7つの場面から，4つを書きなさい。

(3) 次の文は「3　指導計画の作成と内容の取扱い」の(1)に示されている配慮事項の一部である。(①)～(⑧)にあてはまる語句を書きなさい。

ア　各学校においては，生徒や地域の実態に応じて，学年ごとの目標を適切に定め，3学年間を通して英語の目標の(①)を図るようにすること。

エ　文字指導に当たっては，生徒の(②)に配慮し(③)を指導することもできること。

オ　語，連語及び慣用表現については，(④)の高いものを用い，活用することを通して定着を図るようにすること。

カ　(⑤)の使い方に慣れ，活用できるようにすること。

キ　生徒の実態や(⑥)の内容などに応じて，コンピュータや情報通信ネットワーク，(⑦)などを有効活用したり，ネイティブ・スピーカーなどの協力を得たりなどすること。

また，ペアワーク，グループワークなどの(　⑧　)を適宜工夫すること。

(☆☆☆☆◎◎◎◎◎)

【高等学校】

【1】高等学校学習指導要領「外国語」について，次の(1)～(3)の問いに答えなさい。

(1) 次は「第2款　各科目　第6　英語表現Ⅱ」の「2　内容(1)」で示されている事項である。

(　①　)～(　⑥　)にあてはまる語句を書きなさい。

ア　与えられた(　①　)に合わせて，即興で話す。また，伝えたい内容を整理して(　②　)に話す。

イ　(　③　)を決め，様々な種類の文章を書く。

ウ　聞いたり読んだりしたこと，学んだことや経験したことに基づき，(　④　)や考えなどをまとめ，発表する。また，発表されたものを聞いて，質問したり意見を述べたりする。

エ　多様な考え方ができる話題について，(　⑤　)を決めて意見をまとめ，相手を(　⑥　)ために意見を述べ合う。

(2) 次は「第3款　英語に関する各科目に共通する内容等　2　ア」の一部の英訳である。

(　①　)～(　⑤　)に入る適切な数字または英語を書きなさい。ただし解答は1語とは限らない。

A. Vocabulary，(　①　) and common expressions

(a) Vocabulary

a. For English Communication I，about (　②　) new words should be added to those introduced in lower secondary schools.

b. For English Communication Ⅱ，about (　③　) new words should be added to those stipulated in a.

c. For English Communication Ⅲ，about (　④　) new words

should be added to those stipulated in b.

d. For Basic English Communication, English Expression I, English Expression Ⅱ and (⑤), appropriate words should be introduced with consideration to students' capacities so that they are not overburdened.

(3) 次は「第3款 英語に関する各科目に共通する内容等 3」で示されている事項である。

(①)〜(④)にあてはまる語句を書きなさい。

ア 現代の(①)な英語によること。ただし，様々な英語が(②)に広くコミュニケーションの手段として使われている実態にも配慮すること。

イ 文法については，(③)ものであることを踏まえ，言語活動と効果的に関連付けて指導すること。

ウ コミュニケーションを行うために必要となる語句や文構造，文法事項などの取扱いについては，用語や用法の区別などの指導が中心とならないよう配慮し，実際に(④)できるよう指導すること。

(☆☆☆☆◎◎◎◎)

解答・解説

【中高共通】

【1】(1) (a) (2) (b) (3) (d) (4) (d) (5) (a)

〈解説〉リスニングテストでは，名詞や数字の聞き取りには特に注意する。

(1) 第1段落と第2段落1文目のthe technologyからyearsまでがヒントである。 (2) 第3段落1文目のFor manyからlimitationsまでがヒントである。この部分は「人間をロボットに置き換えない理由」を示しているが，設問は「人間の立ち位置にロボットを導入するのに重要なこと」

となっており，視点が逆になっていることに注意。 (3) 正答の(d)は，第4段落最後の文と内容が一致する。(a)はdecreased以下，(b)はless than以下，(c)はinferior以下が本文と合致しない。 (4) 第5段落1文目のit isからcompetitiveまでがヒントである。 (5) 何をしなかったかを問う設問なので注意。第6段落のThe companyからcountriesまでがヒントである。この部分が(a)のone company from each country surveyedとは合致しない。

【2】(1) エ (2) イ (3) ア (4) ウ (5) イ

〈解説〉(1) 全文の意味は，「私は大学時代にフットボールで膝をけがした。その結果，今では寒くなるとそこがうずく」。 (2) 全文の意味は，「掘削とは，要するに破壊ということである。つまり，ある場所を最低部まで明らかにするということは，そこまでの部分を完全に除去するからだ」。 (3) 全文の意味は，「登山は，長くて苦労の多いものであり，誰もが息が苦しくなる」。 (4) 全文の意味は，「2人の地主間の所有権争いは，元々の境界を示す文書が発見されたときに解決した」。 (5) 全文の意味は，「彼の演説はもたついたので，投票者への効果はなかった」。

【3】(1) ウ (2) ウ (3) ア (4) イ (5) ウ

〈解説〉(1) この部分の時制は過去なので，wouldが正しい。 (2) 主語が複数形なので，theirが正しい。 (3) 「ユニークと言ってもいいほどだ」の意味なので，almostが正しい。mostlyは「主に。たいていは」の意の副詞である。 (4) 「その子のそばに」の意味なので，besideが正しい。besidesは「～の他にも」の意の前置詞である。 (5) 現在完了形の後半の叙述なので，過去分詞形のenhancedが正しい。

【4】(1) カ (2) キ (3) ア (4) エ (5) ウ

〈解説〉対話全体の流れは，Aの心配に対してBが次から次へと保険の説明をするというものである。選択肢のイとクは直接の関係がない。また，オは内容からBの発言だが，Bの発言中には空欄はない。したがって，これらを除いた選択肢から考えればよい。　(1)　Bが保険を勧めた直後のAの対応なので，カが自然である。　(2)　空欄直後のBの発言のmedical insurance以下がヒントである。　(3)　空欄直前のBの発言のin the event以下と，直後のifからwrongまでがヒントである。

(4)　空欄直前のBの発言1文目がヒントである。　(5)　空欄直前のBのmake以下がヒントである。stay put「動かないでいる」。

【5】(1)　A　イ　　B　ア　　(2)　a　ア　　b　ウ　　(3)　①　どちらの特性も，その人に特有な生来の傾向の直接的な結果ではない。というのも，人の心理や遺伝子の中には，病的な邪悪さや善良さという特別な内的傾向はどちらもないからである。　②　不正や残酷さに立ちむかい，信念に基づいた価値観を守るために，表立った行動をとることを可能にする，秘めた力や美徳の蓄えを自らに見出すすべての人に対して月桂樹の冠を用意しておくべきだ。　(4)　This perception implies that any of us could as easily become heroes as perpetrators of evil

〈解説〉(1)　A　第2段落1文目と，3文目のThe ordinarinessからgoodnessまでがヒントである。「全く平凡な。陳腐な」の意味である。

B「礼儀正しいこと。寛大さ」の意味である。　(2)　a　ナチスによる組織的な大虐殺のことである。アウシュビッツやダッハウなどの強制収容所が知られている。　b　第5段落2文目のwhileからseducedまでがヒントである。majorityに対応している。　(3)　①　文全体の構造は，「evilとheroismの両者ともに～でない」という否定があり，この内容に関してセミコロン以下で詳述されている，というものである。また，residing以下はeitherからgoodnessまでの部分を修飾している。

②　文全体の構造は，who以下がall thoseを修飾しているものであり，who以下では，strengths and virtuesをenabling以下が修飾する構造となっている。さらに，to actとto stand upが不定詞の副詞用法(目的)となっている。　(4)　第3段落の内容と第4段落1文目のhow以下がヒントである。状況によって，私たちは善にも悪にも成り得るという主旨である。

perpetratorは「(犯罪など)を犯す人。(悪事)を働く人」という意味。

【6】(1)　Nowadays we rarely hear the expression “shidokenai”. It means “sloppy” in dress or posture. However, it can also be used to describe the grace and charm of unaffected nonchalance.　(2)　It has often been said that English has no grammar, or that, if it has, there are no rules in it. English has indeed very few of the kind of inflections on the end of nouns and verbs.

〈解説〉(1)「しどけない」とは「着物の着方などが，人前に出られないほど，だらしない状態」である。以下に別解を示す。The expression “shidokenai” has not been heard recently. It means to be untidy in a person's dressing or posture. To the contrary, it has another meaning that a person looks attractive and nice while relaxed.　(2)　下線部の1文目について，以下に別解を示す。「文法」は解答例ではrulesで表現しているが，2文目にくる内容を踏まえ，このように書いてもよいだろう。It is usually pointed out that English grammar has various irregularity, and that in fact, its inflections of nouns and verbs depend on each word.

【7】多くの人は言語学習について何らかの考えを持っているが，それらのほとんどは間違っている。間違った考え方は第二言語の習得において大きな障壁となり得るので，無理な期待や間違った仮説は早いうちに取り除いておくことが最も大切なことである。(114字)

〈解説〉第二言語の習得についての論述である。第1段落では習得についての様々な言説が述べられ，第2段落の最初でそれらが誤りであると指摘している。そして，応用言語学の観点から対処方法を示している。これらをまとめて記述すればよい。knack「こつ」，refute「論駁する」。

【中学校】

【1】(1)　①　符号　②　賛否　③　出来事　④　体験
(2)　あいさつ，自己紹介，電話での応答，買物，道案内，旅行，食事，の中から4つ　(3)　①　実現　②　学習負担　③　筆記体

④　運用度　⑤　辞書　⑥　教材　⑦　教育機器　⑧　学習形態

〈解説〉中学校では，コミュニケーション能力の基礎を養うことを目標としている。そのため，英語を聞いたり，話したり，読んだり，書いたりする基礎的な言語活動をバランスよく計画的・系統的に行うことが大切である。　(1)　①　この指導事項は，「書くこと」の言語活動のうち最も基本的な技能の習熟を求めたものである。　②　この指導事項で，「その理由」が追加されたのは，今回の改訂において言語に関する能力の育成が重視されているためである。　③・④「身近な場面における出来事や体験したことなど」を例示したのは，そういった事柄については積極的に自分の考えや気持ちを書いて表現することが比較的容易であると考えられるからである。　(2)「言語の使用場面」について特に具体例を示しているのは，日常の授業において実際的な言語の使用場面の設定や，言語の働きを意識した指導において手がかりとなるように考慮したからである。　(3)　①　この配慮事項は，指導計画の作成に当たって，3学年間を通して英語科の目標の達成を図るため，各学校において学年ごとの目標を適切に定めることの必要性を示したものである。　②・③　文字指導については，アルファベットの活字体の大文字及び小文字の指導を基本とし，必要に応じて筆記体を指導してもよいとされている。　④　活用することを通して定着を図るためには，運用度の高いものについて，繰り返し言語活動を行うことが効果的と考えられている。　⑤　授業での自己表現活動を自発的に行ったり，家庭で教科書から離れた学習に取り組んだりするうえでは，この指導事項は必要不可欠である。　⑥・⑦　視聴覚機器を効果的に使うことによって教材が具体化され，生徒にとって身近なものとしてとらえられるようになるのである。　⑧　どのような工夫を行うにしても，目標を達成するのに効果的な授業が展開できる学習形態であることが求められる。

【高等学校】

【1】(1) ① 条件 ② 論理的 ③ 主題 ④ 情報 ⑤ 立場 ⑥ 説得する (2) ① collocations ② 400 ③ 700 ④ 700 ⑤ English Conversation (3) ① 標準的 ② 国際的 ③ コミュニケーションを支える ④ 活用

〈解説〉(1) ①「与えられた条件」とは，話題，話す時間や量などの他，言語の使用場面や言語の働きによる制約も意味する。 ②「論理的に話す」とは，論理に矛盾や飛躍がなく，適切な論拠をもって筋道の通る主張を展開することである。 ③ この指導事項は，読み手や目的に応じて，生徒の興味・関心に応じた様々な種類の文章を簡潔に書く活動を示している。実際に書く活動を始める前段階の活動も含めて指導することが想定されている。 ④ 話された内容を自分の知識や経験に基づいて分析したり，判断したり，評価したりするなど，多様な観点から物事を考察するよう指導することが必要である。

⑤・⑥ 教師は，生徒が議論を構築する際の材料となる適切な資料を提供したり，生徒自身がそれを探すことができるよう指導したりすることが必要である。 (2) ① この中項目の日本語版のタイトルは「語，連語及び慣用表現」である。「連語」とは，2つ以上の語が結びついて，あるまとまった意味を表すものを指す。 ② 中学校で学習した1,200語程度の語に400語程度の新語を加えて1,600語程度の語とするという意味である。 ③「コミュニケーション英語Ⅰ」までに学習した1,600語程度の語に700語程度の新語を加えて2,300語程度の語とするという意味である。 ④「コミュニケーション英語Ⅱ」までに学習した2,300語程度の語に700語程度の新語を加えて3,000語程度の語とするという意味である。 ⑤ with以下は「生徒に過度の学習負担を強いることのないように配慮した」の意味である。 (3) ①「標準的な英語」とは現在国際的に広く日常的なコミュニケーションの手段として通用している英語のことであり，方言などに偏らないよう留意する必要がある。 ② 語彙，綴り，発音，文法などに多様性があるということに気づかせる指導を行うという意味である。 ③ 文法は基盤

として必要であるが，文法をコミュニケーションとは別物と考えたり，これら2つを対立的に考えたりしないような指導をすることが大切である。　④　語句や文構造，文法事項などを，表現しようとしている意味や使い方として理解し，多様な活動に取り組む中で定着を図ることの重要性を示している。

2015年度　実施問題

【中高共通】

【1】[リスニングテスト]

問題文及び5つの質問を聞き，各質問の後に読まれる(a)～(d)の4つの選択肢の中から，その質問に対する答として最も適切なものを1つ選び，記号で答えなさい。

英語リスニングテスト台本

ただいまから，問題1のリスニングテストを始めます。これから読む英文の内容に関して，5つの質問をします。それぞれの質問の後に読まれる(a)，(b)，(c)，(d)の4つの選択肢の中から，答えとして最も適切なものを1つ選び，記号で答えなさい。英文と質問，選択肢は，全体をとおして2回読みます。聞きながらメモを取ってもかまいません。それでは始めます。

As the people born during the postwar baby boom have begun entering the later stages of their lives, one out of every four people in Japan is now aged 65 or older. Working out measures to address the challenges posed by the nation's rapid aging — a situation without parallel in the rest of the world — is an unmistakably urgent matter.

The Internal Affairs and Communications Ministry released population estimates as of October 1, 2013, in which people aged 65 and over comprised more than 25 percent of the population for the first time. Nearly 31.9 million had celebrated their 65th birthday. Japan's population has contracted for a third straight year, and the working-age population has fallen below 80 million for the first time in 32 years.

The aging of society brings with it ballooning social security costs, including expenditures for medical and nursing care. Japan's social security system, as it exists today, is hardly sustainable and threatens to undermine Japan's social and economic vigor. The situation is grave indeed. In 2025, as the baby-boom generation passes the age of 75, the number of people needing medical and nursing care will undoubtedly rise even higher.

But as the number of older people continues to swell, there are limits to the number of elderly that can be cared for at facilities for the aged and hospitals. Expenditures covered by the nursing care and health insurance systems are likely to increase, leading to a further rise in benefit payments.

The situation calls for arrangements for integrated nursing care and medical services to be provided in the home, allowing the elderly to live at home for as long as reasonably practical. The government must also back construction of new housing to accommodate older people, including those with lower incomes.

Older people who receive no help from family are likely to face great difficulty living on their own if and when they encounter even minor physical or mental issues. Symptoms of dementia and other disorders also tend to be overlooked. Building neighborhood frameworks of mutual support to take the place of absent families is indispensable in coping with this situation.

We hope to see older people who are in good health and spirits take on volunteer and other activities for the benefit of their communities. Such contributions will add meaning to their lives, and at the same time reduce the likelihood that they will need nursing care services, thereby helping rein in social welfare expenditures for the nation as a whole.

Question

(1) According to the statistics, what was the population of people aged 65 and over in 2013?

(a) About 25 million.

(b) About 32 million.

(c) About 39 million.

(d) About 42 million.

(2) What will become of Japan in about 10 years?

(a) A working generation will get more jobs in the field of social welfare services.

(b) Japan's social security system will be fully designed.

(c) Japan's economy will have drastically declined.

(d) More people will need medical and nursing care.

(3) Among the following four statements, which is true concerning Japan's population?

(a) Japan's population will increase in the next ten years.

(b) More than 25 percent of the population is now 65 years old or older.

(c) The number of the working-age population has become more than 80 million for the first time.

(d) Many developed nations are more rapidly aging than Japanese society.

(4) What is needed for the elderly who receive no help from family?

(a) Support from their community.

(b) Regular interviews by governmental officials.

(c) The service of their diet.

(d) The construction of more new hospitals.

(5) What should be done in order to reduce the cost of the social welfare?

(a) To build more and new housing for the elderly.

(b) To make educational programs for the elderly.

(c) To provide the elderly with the opportunity of volunteer activities.

(d) To cure dementia and other disorders of the elderly.

【REPEAT】

これでリスニングテストを終わります。

(☆☆☆◎◎◎)

【2】次の各文の(　　)にあてはまる最も適当なものを，ア～エから1つ選び，記号で答えなさい。

(1) Everyone says that the boy is the very (　　) of his father.

ア body　イ image　ウ figure　エ person

(2) The researchers' latest findings are significant and are expected to be a (　　) in the treatment of cancer.

ア dropout　イ bundle　ウ condolence　エ breakthrough

(3) According to the traffic report, more than thirty cars (　　) due to the thick fog on the freeway.

ア collided　イ diverged　ウ disputed　エ violated

(4) Trains in Tokyo are sometimes packed with commuters so (　　) that those waiting on a platform find it impossible to board their train.

ア weirdly　イ densely　ウ devoutly　エ sparsely

(5) The lecturer waited patiently for the noise in the auditorium to (　　) before starting his talk.

ア smooth out　イ count off　ウ carry over　エ die down

(☆☆☆◎◎◎)

【3】次の各文の下線部ア～エの中で，誤っている箇所を1つ選び，記号で答えなさい。

(1) ア Dislike the gorilla, the イ male adult chimpanzee weighs ウ under 100 エ kilograms.

(2) She vacuumed ア the floors and イ cleaned ウ the glasses of the windows エ all by herself.

(3) Her mother ア brought up on the old saying that early to bed and early to rise イ would give health, wealth, and wisdom, ウ insisting that her son エ go to bed earlier.

(4) ア The new equipment that イ was installed recently in the physics laboratory cost over ウ ten million yen エ each.

(5) No writer ア ever puts down anything on イ paper that he or she knows

ウ for certain エ it is good or bad.

(☆☆☆◎◎◎)

【4】次の対話文の(1)~(5)にあてはまる最も適切な英文を，ア~クから選び，記号で答えなさい。ただし，同じ選択肢を2度使わないこと。

A: Have you gotten used to life and school over here?

B: Yes, I enjoy my life so far. The students of my school are kind, smart and supportive.

A: (1)

B: (2)

A: (3)

B: I also face the difficulty of accent and pronunciation. Especially, I think I'm speaking English with a Japanese accent. What can I do to improve that?

A: (4)

B: (5)

A: The important thing is to be polite while delivering your message using clear words that get your point across.

ア You mean you have gotten used to your life in this country. Did you get some guidance on your language ability for improvement from your team members?

イ You are hitting your head against the language barrier. I know how that feels. English is my second language too. At my house we speak Portuguese all the time.

ウ I'm glad to hear that. But you scarcely said a word during the discussions.

エ I had a lot of things to say. It is not so difficult to speak English because it is the common business language. But it is difficult to think of what I should tell to others.

オ　It makes me happy to hear you say that. Your words make me even more determined to improve my English ability.

カ　Sorry, but that's true. Sometimes it's difficult for me to give my opinion in English. I can't find the right words to express what I want to say.

キ　Well, that's a big challenge, but don't worry about that. Honestly, I feel you're already talking more and more like a native.

ク　You should learn how to speak English at a natural speed. It is more important than the individual pronunciation of each word.

(☆☆☆◎◎◎)

【5】次の英文を読んで，(1)～(4)の問いに答えなさい。

I said that physics is the study of (　A　) things, and this may seem strange at first. Physics appears to be a (　B　) subject, because the ideas of physics are difficult for us to understand. Our brains were designed to understand hunting and gathering, mating and child-rearing: (　a　). We are ill-equipped to comprehend the very small and the very large; things whose duration is measured in picoseconds or gigayears; particles that don't have position; forces and fields that we cannot see or touch, which we know of only because they affect things that we can see or touch. We think that physics is (　B　) because it is hard for us to understand, and because physics books are full of difficult mathematics. But the objects that physicists study are still basically (　A　) objects. They are clouds of gas or tiny particles, or lumps of uniform matter like crystals, with almost endlessly repeated atomic patterns. They do not, at least by biological standards, have intricate working parts. Even large physical objects like stars consist of a rather limited array of parts, more or less haphazardly arranged. ①<u>The behaviour of physical, nonbiological objects is so simple that it is feasible to use existing mathematical language to describe it, which is why physics books are full of mathematics.</u>

Physics *books* may be (　B　), but physics books, like cars and computers, are the product of biological objects - human brains. The objects and phenomena that a physics book describes are simpler than a single cell in the body of its author. And the author consists of trillions of those cells, many of them different from each other, organized with intricate architecture and precision-engineering into a working machine capable of writing a book. ②Our brains are no better equipped to handle extremes of complexity than extremes of size and the other difficult extremes of physics. Nobody has yet invented the mathematics for describing the total structure and behaviour of such an object as a physicist, or even of one of his cells. What we can do is understand some of the general principles of how living things work, and why they exist at all.

This was where we came in. We wanted to know why we, and all other (B) things, exist. And we can now answer that question in general terms, even without being able to comprehend the details of the complexity itself. To take an analogy, most of us don't understand in detail (b). Probably its builders don't comprehend it fully either: engine specialists don't in detail understand wings, and wing specialists understand engines only vaguely. Wing specialists don't even understand wings with full mathematical precision: they can predict how a wing will behave in turbulent conditions, only by examining a model in a wind tunnel or a computer simulation - the sort of thing a biologist might do to understand an animal. But however incompletely we understand how an airliner works, we all understand by what general process it came into existence. It was designed by humans on drawing boards. The other humans made the bits from the drawings, then lots more humans (with the aid of other machines designed by humans) screwed, rivetted, welded or glued the bits together, each in its right place. [ ] to us, because humans built it. The systematic putting together of parts to a purposeful design is something we know and understand, for we have experienced it at first hand, even if only with our childhood Meccano or Erector set.

(注) Meccano, Erector　組み立ておもちゃのブランド名

(1)　(　A　)・(　B　)に入る1語を，それぞれ下のア～エから1つずつ選びなさい。

(　A　)　ア　minimal　イ　delicate　ウ　simple
エ　fragile

(　B　)　ア　complicated　イ　versatile　ウ　gradual
エ　vague

(2)　(　a　)・(　b　)に入る最も適した表現を，それぞれ下のア～エから1つずつ選びなさい。

(　a　)　ア　a world in which unpalatable truth frequently prevails over falsehood in the end
イ　a world whose velocity is too high to be explained by the ordinary rotation
ウ　a world with people pursuing the enhancement of the results relating to safety issues
エ　a world of medium-sized objects moving in three dimensions at moderate speeds

(　b　)　ア　where a physicist relates an airliner
イ　how an airliner works
ウ　how a biologist explains an airliner
エ　where an airliner develops

(3)　下線部①・②を日本語にしなさい。

(4)　[　　]を補うように下の語群を並べ替えなさい。ただし文頭に来る語も小文字にしてある。

[existence is / into / an airliner / the process / not fundamentally / which / came / mysterious / by]

(☆☆☆◎◎◎)

【6】次の文の下線部(1)・(2)を英語に直しなさい。

(1)人類が獲得した第一の叡智。それは，「今」だけではなく，「未来」を慮(おもんばか)る能力です。そして，「自分」だけではなく，「将来の世代」の利益までも想像し，そのために行動する力です。(2)人類が新たな地平を拓くきっかけとなった農耕社会の成立は，「目の前の今」ではなく「収穫の時」を待つ，という未来を見る視点を人類が獲得できたからこそ，もたらされたものなのです。

(☆☆☆◎◎◎)

【7】次の英文を読んで，その趣旨を140字以内の日本語で書きなさい。ただし，句読点も字数に入れること。

Like most psychologists, William James, the American philosopher and physician and one of the founders of modern psychology, was particularly interested in human psychology, which he thought consisted of certain basic elements: thoughts and feelings, a physical world which exists in time and space, and a way of knowing about these things. For each of us, this knowledge is primarily personal and private. It comes from our own thoughts, feelings, and experience of the world, and may or may not be influenced by scientific facts about these things. For this reason, it is easy for us to make judgements about psychological matters using our own experience as a touchstone. We behave as amateur psychologists when we offer opinions on complex psychological phenomena, such as whether brain-washing works, or when we espouse as facts our opinions about why other people behave in the ways that they do: think they are being insulted, feel unhappy, or suddenly give up their jobs. However, problems arise when two people understand these things differently. Formal psychology attempts to provide methods for deciding which explanations are most likely to be correct, or for determining the circumstances under which each applies. The work of psychologists helps us to distinguish between inside information which is subjective, and may be biased and unreliable, and the facts: between our preconceptions and what is 'true' in scientific terms.

Psychology, as defined by William James, is about the mind or brain, but although psychologists do study the brain, we do not understand nearly enough about its workings to be able to comprehend the part that it plays in the experience and expression of our hopes, fears, and wishes, or in our behaviour during experiences as varied as giving birth or watching a football match. Indeed, it is rarely possible to study the brain directly. So, psychologists have discovered more by studying our behaviour, and by using their observations to derive hypotheses about what is going on inside us.

(☆☆☆◎◎◎)

【中学校】

【1】中学校学習指導要領「外国語」「第2　各言語の目標及び内容等」「英語」「2　内容」について，次の(1)・(2)の問いに答えなさい。

(1)　次の文は「(1)　言語活動　イ　話すこと」である。(　①　)～(　④　)にあてはまる語句を書きなさい。

主として次の事項について指導する。

(ア)　(　①　)，イントネーション，区切りなど基本的な英語の音声の特徴をとらえ，正しく発音すること。

(イ)　自分の考えや気持ち，(　②　)などを聞き手に正しく伝えること。

(ウ)　聞いたり読んだりしたことなどについて，(　③　)したり意見を述べ合ったりなどすること。

(エ)　(　④　)を用いるなどのいろいろな工夫をして話を続けること。

(オ)　与えられたテーマについて簡単なスピーチをすること。

(2)　次の文は「(2)　言語活動の取扱い」の一部である。(　①　)～(　⑫　)にあてはまる語句を書きなさい。

ア　3学年間を通じ指導に当たっては，次のような点に配慮するものとする。

(ア)　実際に言語を使用して互いの考えや気持ちを伝え合うなどの活動を行うとともに，(3)に示す言語材料について理解したり(　①　)したりする活動を行うようにすること。

(イ)　実際に言語を使用して互いの考えや気持ちを伝え合うなどの活動においては，(　②　)な場面や(　③　)に合った(　④　)な表現を自ら考えて言語活動ができるようにすること。

イ　生徒の学習段階を考慮して各学年の指導に当たっては，次のような点に配慮するものとする。

(ア)　第1学年における言語活動

小学校における外国語活動を通じて(　⑤　)面を中心としたコミュニケーションに対する(　⑥　)な態度などの一定の(　⑦　)が育成されることを踏まえ，身近な言語の(　⑧　)や言語の(　⑨　)に配慮した言語活動を行わせること。その際，自分の気持ちや身の回りの(　⑩　)などの中から(　⑪　)な表現を用いてコミュニケーションを図れるような(　⑫　)を取り上げること。

(☆☆☆◎◎◎)

【高等学校】

【1】高等学校学習指導要領「外国語」について，次の(1)～(3)の問いに答えなさい。

(1)　次は「第2款　各科目　第7　英語会話」の「3　内容の取扱い」である。(　①　)～(　⑥　)にあてはまる語句を書きなさい。

(1)　中学校におけるコミュニケーション能力の(　①　)を養うための総合的な指導を踏まえ，実際の会話に即した(　②　)を多く取り入れながら，聞いたり話したりする能力の向上を図るよう指導するものとする。

(2)　読むこと及び書くこととも(　③　)に関連付けた活動を行うことにより，聞くこと及び話すことの指導の(　④　)を高めるよう工夫するものとする。

(3) 生徒の(　⑤　)に応じて，多様な場面における言語活動を経験させながら，中学校や高等学校における学習内容を(　⑥　)て指導し定着を図るよう配慮するものとする。

(2) 次の英文は「第2款　各科目　第5　英語表現Ⅰ」の「2　内容(2)」である。(　①　)~(　④　)に入る適切な語を英語で書きなさい。

A. Speaking with due attention to the characteristics of English sounds such as rhythm and intonation, speed, (　①　), etc.

B. Writing with due attention to phrases and sentences indicating the main points, connecting phrases, etc. and (　②　) one's own writing.

C. Learning presentation methods, (　③　) used in presentations, etc. and applying them to real-life situations.

D. Forming one's own opinion by comparing what one has heard or read with opinions from other sources, and identifying (　④　) and differences.

(3) 次は「第4款　各科目にわたる指導計画の作成と内容の取扱い2(4)」である。(　①　)~(　④　)にあてはまる語を書きなさい。

各科目の指導に当たっては，指導方法や(　①　)を工夫し，ペア・ワーク，(　②　)などを適宜取り入れたり，(　③　)やコンピュータ，情報通信ネットワークなどを適宜指導に生かしたりすること。また，ネイティブ・スピーカーなどの協力を得て行うティーム・ティーチングなどの授業を積極的に取り入れ，生徒のコミュニケーション能力を育成するとともに(　④　)を深めるようにすること。

(☆☆☆◎◎◎)

解答・解説

【中高共通】

【1】(1) (b)　(2) (d)　(3) (b)　(4) (a)　(5) (c)

〈解説〉設問および選択肢を含めた聞き取りが必要なため，聞き逃しがないよう日頃から放送によるテストの練習を重ね，落ち着いて本番に臨むようにしたい。英文は2回読まれるので，聞き取れない箇所があった時でも慌てずに，以降の放送内容が頭に入らなくなるという事態を避ける。英文中に出てくる数値や人名などの名詞は聞き取りのポイントとなることが多い。　(1)　英文中では第2段落2文目で31.9 millionと具体的に述べられているが，選択肢ではおおよその数しか述べられない。したがって，解答は最も近いものを選択しなければならない。
(2)　第2段落で2013年10月1日時点の65歳以上人口の割合を述べたことを受け，約10年後の2025年の予測について述べた第3段落最後の文に対応する設問である。　(3)　日本の人口について正しく述べたものを選択する問題。正答の(b)に対応する箇所は，第2段落1文目である。
(a)　第4段落で老齢人口が増え続けることは述べられているが，日本の人口全体が増えるとは述べられていない。　(c)　第2段落最後の文で，日本の人口が3年連続で減少し，生産年齢人口は32年で初めて8000万人を割り込んだと述べられている。　(d)　第1段落最後の文で，日本の高齢化は世界でも比類のないものだと述べられている。
(4)　elderly who receive no help from family「家族からの援助がない高齢者」については第6段落に述べられており，同段落の最後の文をもとに解答を導ける。設問の選択肢が直接的に述べられているわけではないのでやや難しいが，(a)以外の選択肢は比較的容易に削除できる。
(5)　social welfare「社会福祉」に言及している第7段落の最後の2文をもとに解答を導ける。

【2】(1)　イ　　(2)　エ　　(3)　ア　　(4)　イ　　(5)　エ

〈解説〉(1)　the very image of A「Aにそっくりな人」。　(2)　dropout「途中退学者」，bundle「束」，condolence「弔辞」，breakthrough「大発見」。　(3)　選択肢の語はそれぞれ原形では，collide「衝突する」，diverge「分岐する」，dispute「議論する」，violate「違反する」。　(4)　weirdly「異様に」，densely「密集して」，devoutly「熱心に」，sparsely「まばらに」。　(5)　smooth out「解決する」，count off「順に番号を言う，数えて出す」，carry over「残存する」，die down「静まる」。

【3】(1)　ア　　(2)　ウ　　(3)　ウ　　(4)　エ　　(5)　エ

〈解説〉(1)　設問のように前置詞や接続詞のlikeを否定する場合はdislikeではなくunlikeを用いる。　(2)　この場合，ガラスは不可算名詞なので複数形にしない。　(3)　主節の目的を表しているので，分詞構文ではなくto不定詞等を用いるのが適切。　(4)　主語が複数形ならeachは数量表現の直後で問題ないが，単数形の場合eachは通常主語の前につける。　(5)　下線部イの後のthatは従属節中のitの位置に入る関係代名詞なので，itは省略するのが正しい。

【4】1　ウ　　2　カ　　3　イ　　4　キ　　5　オ

〈解説〉情報が少ないので，確実に解答できる箇所から解答していきたい。まず，直前に疑問文のある4が容易に解答できるだろう。4の直前でのBの質問は，「いかにしてアクセントや発音を向上させられるか」。それに対する答えとしては，キが適切であろう。また，それに対するBの応答である　5は，オが適切となる。残る3つでは，3が解答しやすいだろう。3の直後のBのセリフ1文目のalsoから，(　3　)は直後の文と似た内容を述べているはずなので，イを選ぶことができる。そして，1は直前のBの発言が現状肯定的であることからウを選び，それをもとに2にカを選択することができる。

【5】(1) A ウ B ア (2) a エ b イ

(3) ① 物理的かつ非生物学的な物体の動きは非常に単純なので，それを記述するために従来の数学的言語を使用することは可能である。また，そういうわけで物理学の本には至る所に数学が用いられる。

② 我々の脳は，極端な大きさやその他の物理学上の極端に難しいことを扱うようにできていないのと同様に，極端な複雑さを扱うようにもできていない。物理学者のような物体の全体構造や動き，それどころかその物理学者のたった一つの細胞の全体構造や行動であったとしても，それを記述できるような数学を発明した人は誰もいない。

(4) The process by which an airliner came into existence is not fundamentally mysterious

〈解説〉長文読解問題では，本文を読む前に問題文や語注など，本文以外の情報を頭に入れておきたい。本文を読む前に問題文に目を通せば，解答に必要な読み方がおのずと理解できるだろう。

(1) A minimal「最小限の」，delicate「繊細な」，simple「単純な」，fragile「もろい」。 B complicated「複雑な」，versatile「万能な」，gradual「漸進的な」，vague「曖昧な」。 (2) a 空欄の直前にコロン(：)があるので，前の文の内容を説明しているものが入ると判断できる。 b 空欄の直後の1文から，空欄の直前のdetailがどういうことかを読み取ることができれば容易に解答できるだろう。 (3) ① so ～ thatの構文である。1文であるが長いので，whichの前でいったん区切って，「～，それで…」のように訳すとわかりやすい。 ② 1文目はno better ～ than …「…できないのと同様に～できない」の訳し方がポイント。2文目は文法的には簡単な文である。物理学者自体を物体と見なしている点に注意して訳せばよい。

(4) 語群中のexistence isのexistenceを主語と考えてしまうと文ができあがらない。The process ～ is not … mysterious (to us,)という大筋をみつけること。come into A「Aになる」。

【6】(1)　One of the first pearls of wisdom humans gained was power to give adequate thought to not only the "now," but also the "future."

(2)　Agricultural society, which prompted human beings to open a new vista, was made possible through the long-term perspective toward the future that human beings acquired when they waited for the harvest instead of thinking solely about immediate concerns.

〈解説〉英作文の問題では，知っている単語，構文を駆使して背伸びしすぎない無難な英文を書くことを心がけよう。非英語母語話者にとって，直感の働かない外国語を誤りなく正確に書くことは非常に困難であり，微妙なニュアンスの差異による違和感などを見過ごしてしまう場合が多い。英作文では，見たことのない英文は書かないことが鉄則である。その意味で，英文を多く見ることは英作文をするうえで最も重要なトレーニングである。重要な文法や語法が含まれる英文等の例文暗記がよいだろう。　(1)　和文英訳では，あまり意訳しすぎず，求められていると思われる文法事項を駆使することができれば理想的である。この問題では，「AだけでなくB」の形が大枠であり，これに修飾語等を付け加えていくことが基本的な作業であろう。模範解答のように1文にしてもよいが，2文で答えても問題はないだろう。　(2)　解答例はやや説明的に述べているが，(1)と同様にnot A but Bの形で英文をつくり，和文中で「　」で括られた語句は英文中でも"　"で括って示すのが無難だろう。

【7】心理学は思考や感情についての学問である。人は個人的な思考や感情，経験をもとに心理学的問題を考えることが多いが，心理学はそれが主観的なものか科学的なものか識別してくれる。ただ，直接，脳を見ることは無理なので，心理学者は行動研究や観察を通して研究を進めてきたのである。(132字)

〈解説〉英文の日本語要約なので，本文の言い回しを使いつつも，自然な日本語に構成し直す能力が問われている。また，文量も140字と非常に少なめであることからも，本文の要旨を短文に圧縮し，趣旨を伝える高度な日本語力が求められていることは明白だろう。ポイントとしては，解答文の大枠を考えてから本文を読むことである。まず，本文を概観すると，段落が2つに分けられていることから，それぞれの段落の主張を読み取るべきことが想像できるだろう。140字という文字制限を考えると，それぞれの段落の主題を1つずつ含めるのが理想であり，最低限目指すべきところであろう。

【中学校】

【1】(1) ① 強勢　② 事実　③ 問答　④ つなぎ言葉
(2) ① 練習　② 具体的　③ 状況　④ 適切　⑤ 音声　⑥ 積極的　⑦ 素地　⑧ 使用場面　⑨ 働き　⑩ 出来事　⑪ 簡単　⑫ 話題

〈解説〉中学校学習指導要領(平成20年3月告示)「外国語」からの出題である。この設問のように語群がない場合も多いので，語句の正確な暗記が求められる。この設問で問われている箇所は全て重要な箇所であるが，なかでも，小学校における外国語活動との関連について述べた箇所は，今回の中学校学習指導要領から登場した重要な箇所なので，その理念とともに語句を正確に暗記しておきたい。特に，小学校で目指されているのは「コミュニケーション能力の素地」であり，中学校の「コミュニケーション能力の基礎」と区別して正確に覚えておきたい。

【高等学校】

【1】(1) ① 基礎　② 言語活動　③ 有機的　④ 効果　⑤ 実態　⑥ 繰り返し　(2) ① volume　② reviewing　③ expressions　④ similarities　(3) ① 指導体制　② グループ・ワーク　③ 視聴覚教材　④ 国際理解

〈解説〉平成21年3月告示の高等学校学習指導要領の改訂では，科目編成が大きく改められており，それぞれの特徴が問われることは今後も十分考えられる。科目の種類は，大別すると，「コミュニケーション英語」，「英語表現」，「英語会話」である。それぞれ，どこに共通の理念があり，どこが異なるのか，しっかりと理解しておきたい。語群が示されない場合も多いので，語句の正確な暗記が求められる。また，たとえば本問(1)①の「中学校におけるコミュニケーション能力の基礎」という箇所に似た表記として，平成20年3月告示の小学校学習指導要領「外国語活動」の「第1　目標」に「コミュニケーション能力の素地」があるなど，校種ごとの目標，指導内容，指導計画の作成と内容の取扱いの表記の微妙な違いもおさえておきたい。

2014年度　実施問題

【中高共通】

【1】[リスニングテスト]

問題文及び5つの質問を聞き，各質問の後に読まれるa～dの4つの選択肢の中から，その質問に対する答えとして最も適切なものを1つ選び，記号で答えなさい。

英語リスニングテスト台本

ただいまから，問題1のリスニングテストを始めます。これから読む英文の内容に関して，5つの質問をします。それぞれの質問の後に読まれるa，b，c，dの4つの選択肢の中から，答えとして最も適切なものを1つ選び，記号で答えなさい。英文と質問，選択肢は，全体をとおして2回読みます。聞きながらメモを取ってもかまいません。それでは始めます。

The Ministry of the Environment on Feb. 1 put the Japanese eel on the list of endangered species after determining that it will face a high risk of extinction in the wild in the near future due to overfishing, aggravated rivers and other habitats.

But the designation did not come with legal restrictions and catches and trade will not be regulated. Japan is believed to be the world's largest eel consuming country and experts are calling for a tightening of measures to protect the species.

As part of a review of its Red List of threatened species, the Ministry classified the Japanese eel into the category of IB threatened species, and now it is on par with the Japanese huchen, a member of the salmon family, and the blue-spotted mud hopper.

The Japanese eel had been listed as one of the species whose data have been deficient, but an analysis of up-to-date catches and the discovery of locations and timing of spawning as well as other ecological details prompted the ministry to put the Japanese eel near the top of the Red List.

According to the Fisheries Agency, catches of adult Japanese eel peaked at 3,387 tons in 1961 before dwindling to 267 tons in 2009. Catches of elvers of the Japanese eel for aquaculture totaled 232 tons in 1963 before nose-diving to only 6 tons in 2010.

The Ministry attributes the sharp fall mainly to overfishing and construction of weirs and dams which have prevented the number of Japanese eels from growing. In addition, the El Nino phenomena featuring high levels of sea surface temperatures along the equator in the Pacific is said to move Japanese eels' spawning grounds from waters off the Mariana Islands to the south, making it difficult for them to move toward the north with the help of ocean currents.

The latest designation puzzled eel farmers and other parties familiar with the Japanese eel.

An official at the Lake Hamanako eel farm cooperative in Hamamatsu, Shizuoka Prefecture, said the cooperative did not receive any advance notice of the Red List designation. Although the eel fry catch continues to decline, the classification as an endangered species seems too strong, the official said, adding, however, that the cooperative welcomes the Red List posting if it leads to conservation.

The cooperative is concerned about a sharp rise in the prices of eel fry because it has promoted eels which have been cultured for more than 100 days and which have weighed more than 150 grams as "Lake Hamanako eels."

Question

(1) What changed concerning the Japanese eel after the ministry reviewed the Red List of threatened species?

(a) The yearly catches and trade in the Japanese eel were regulated.
(b) More tightening measures were taken in order to protect it.
(c) It was classified into the same category as the Japanese huchen.
(d) More Japanese people agreed on the legal restriction on catching the Japanese eel.

(2) What was NOT analyzed before the decision to put the Japanese eel near the top of the Red List?
(a) The numbers of the eel caught every year.
(b) The location of Japanese eel's spawning sites.
(c) The Japanese eel's spawning time.
(d) The Japanese eel's relations with other fishes.

(3) How has the situation concerning the Japanese eel changed in Japan?
(a) Japan is no longer the world's largest eel-consuming country.
(b) The blue-spotted mud hopper became a more endangered species in number than the Japanese eel.
(c) The number of adult Japanese eels in 2009 catches decreased to less than 300 tons.
(d) Annual catches of Japanese eel for eating were lessened to only 6 tons in 2010.

(4) What is incorrect as one of the causes which have prevented the Japanese eel population from growing?
(a) The rise of the temperature around the Sea of Japan.
(b) The change of their spawning grounds.
(c) Overfishing.
(d) Construction of weirs and dams.

(5) Why did the designation concern eel farmers?
(a) Because they need more days to grow eel fry.
(b) Because the prices of eel fry might go up sharply.
(c) Because the designation might lead to the ban of eating eel fry.
(d) Because more parties might catch the Japanese eel illegally.

【REPEAT】

これでリスニングテストを終わります。

(☆☆☆☆◎◎◎)

【2】次の各文の(　　)にあてはまる最も適切な語を，ア～エから1つ選び，記号で答えなさい。

(1) All animals accompanying passengers must go through (　　) before entering the country.

ア quarantine　イ suspension　ウ restriction

エ detention

(2) Even though he is famous in his own country, the singer is (　　) unknown on the international stage.

ア identically　イ keenly　ウ vacantly　エ virtually

(3) Relaxation in a natural setting can have a (　　) effect on one's physical as well as mental health.

ア fiscal　イ salutary　ウ malign　エ residual

(4) A neighbor called the police upon seeing a stranger (　　) through her backyard last night.

ア retrieve　イ swagger　ウ prowl　エ disguise

(5) In an effort to clean up its image, the government is set to establish an ethics committee to (　　) corrupt party officials.

ア weed out　イ tie up　ウ string out　エ rack up

(☆☆☆◎◎◎)

【3】次の各文の下線部ア～エの中で，誤っている箇所を1つ選び，記号で答えなさい。

(1) The book was ア<u>so long</u> that イ<u>I wondered that</u> I would ウ<u>be able to</u> エ<u>get through</u> all of it.

(2) The report I read said that 60 percent ア<u>of all French people</u> firmly felt that the United States イ<u>should not have used</u> bombs ウ<u>unless</u> the country

had no other means to defend エthemselves.

(3) If you devoted ア<u>half as much time</u> and energy to solving problems イ<u>as you do</u> ウ<u>to worry about</u> them, エ<u>you wouldn't have any problems</u>.

(4) ア<u>Dismissing</u> a century ago イ<u>as immoral</u>, the author's masterpiece ウ<u>has continued to touch</u> the minds and hearts of readers エ<u>around the world</u>.

(5) ア<u>I would</u> イ<u>appreciate very much</u> if ウ<u>you would show me</u> how to put エ<u>the machine back together</u>.

(☆☆☆◎◎◎)

【4】次の対話文の(1)～(5)にあてはまる最も適切な英文を，ア～クから選び，記号で答えなさい。ただし，同じ選択肢を2度使わないこと。

A: Thank you for your time today. I know you're very busy. You look a little tired.

B: (1)

A: (2)

B: Thank you for asking. I immensely enjoy doing my job because it's the work I love. The work I do is very, very interesting.

A: I'm happy to know that you enjoy doing what you do. But, working too hard without relief can be depressing.

B: (3)

A: (4)

B: (5)

A: Sounds interesting. I'd love a vacation like that.

ア Exactly. It's relaxing and gives me new vitality and energy. I'm a kind of an explorer.

イ I know. Achieving a work-life balance is very important in order to do a good job. I can have everything done by the end of this month. So, next month, I'm going to take a leave of absence.

ウ Yes, I can't afford to take time off from work. But I'm delighted to be working here. Is there anything that I can help you with?

エ　That's right. Managing the project I'm concerned with is creating a lot of work. I lead a busy life.

オ　Oh, I intend to take a few days off too. Why don't we learn yoga? I learned it before. It was very wonderful and I would be interested in taking more lessons.

カ　That's good. Do you have any plans? I hear you love to travel in areas where most people don't go.

キ　I learned it before. It was interesting, but I want to do a more vigorous exercise. It's good to shed excess weight.

ク　It's good to work hard, but you sometimes need to cut yourself some slack. What can I do to lend a hand?

(☆☆☆◎◎◎)

【５】次の英文を読んで，(1)～(5)の問いに答えなさい。

Vocabulary is learned incrementally and this obviously means that lexical acquisition requires multiple exposures to a word. ①This is certainly true for incidental learning, as the chances of learning and retaining a word from one exposure when reading are only about 5% - 14%. Other studies suggest that it requires five to sixteen or more repetitions for a word to be learned. If recycling is neglected, many partially known words will be forgotten, wasting all the effort already put into learning them. Fortunately, this recycling occurs naturally as more frequent words appear repeatedly in texts and conversations. This repetition does not happen to nearly as great an extent for less frequent words, so teachers should look for ways to bolster learner input to offset this. (　a　) seems to be one effective method.

For explicit learning, however, recycling has to be consciously built into any study program. Teachers must guard against presenting a word once and then forgetting about it, or else their students will do the same. This implies developing a more structured way of (　b　) that reintroduces words repeatedly in classroom activities. Learning activities themselves need to be designed to require multiple manipulations of a word, such as in vocabulary notebooks in which students have to go back and add (c) about the words. Understanding how memory behaves can help us design programs that give maximum benefit from revision time spent.

L2 learners benefit from (d) of explicit teaching and incidental learning. Explicit teaching can supply valuable first introductions to a word, but of course not all lexical aspects can be covered during these encounters. The varied contexts in which learners encounter the word during later incidental meetings can lead to broader understanding of its collocations, additional meaning senses, and other higher-level knowledge. In addition, repeated exposure will help to consolidate the lexical aspects first learned.

Additionally, explicit teaching is probably essential for the most frequent words of any L2, because ②they are prerequisites for language use. The learning of these basic words cannot be left to chance, but should be taught as quickly as possible, because they open to the door to further learning. Less frequent words, on the other hand, may be best learned by reading extensively, because there is just not enough time to learn them all through conscious study. Thus, explicit teaching and incidental learning complement each other well, with each being necessary for an effective vocabulary program.

It is probably worth considering adding a vocabulary learning strategies component to your vocabulary program. You will not be able to teach all the words students will need, and even the input generated by extensive reading has its limitations. Students will eventually need to effectively control their own vocabulary learning. A list would give some idea of the range possible, but research has shown that to be effective training must be tailored to your particular situation, taking into account the age, motivation, proficiency, and desires of your students. ③Also, it appears that learners naturally mature into using different strategies at different times of their life, so it seems reasonable to introduce them to a variety of strategies and let them decide which ones are right for them.

(注) L2 : second language

(1) 下線部①の論拠を2つ，本文に即して簡潔に日本語で説明しなさい。

(2) 本文の流れに合うように，(a)～(d)に入る語句を次のア～エからそれぞれ1つずつ選び，記号で答えなさい。ただし，同じ記号を2度使わないこと。(文頭に来る語も小文字にしてある。)

ア additional information　　イ extensive reading

ウ presenting vocabulary　　エ a complementary combination

(3) 下線部②が表していることを，下線部中のtheyの内容を明らかにした上で日本語で説明しなさい。

(4) 下線部③を日本語に直しなさい。

(5) 次の英文が本文の要約となるように，(ア)～(エ)に入る1語を英語で書きなさい。

Understanding key notions of how vocabulary is acquired can help us deliver more realistic and effective vocabulary teaching. Words can be learned from (ア) teaching, or they can be learned (イ) while students' attention is on the meaning of the discourse. In either case, words are learned (ウ). This means that they need to be met numerous times before they are acquired, and so repetition needs to be built into vocabulary learning. Expanding rehearsal is the most time-effective way to manage the review of (エ) known vocabulary that has been explicitly considered. Students need to take some responsibility for their own vocabulary learning, making it necessary to introduce them to vocabulary learning strategies so that they can do this more effectively.

(☆☆☆◎◎◎)

【6】次の日本文を英語に直しなさい。

世界情勢が急激に変化し，国内的にも世界的にも広範な問題が表面化しつつある中，地球温暖化のような未曾有な問題を克服し，持続可能な発展を達成する鍵として，様々な国々が科学技術や技術革新における政策を積極的に推し進めようとしている。

(☆☆☆◎◎◎)

【7】次の英文を読んで，その趣旨を120字以内の日本語で書きなさい。ただし，句読点も字数に入れること。

One feature of American English that was not anticipated is that, apart from vocabulary, foreign influence is not discernible. It sometimes occurred to British observers in the nineteenth century that American English would eventually diverge significantly from the British variety because so many Americans were of some linguistic stock other than English. But no such effect took place. Certainly, foreign speech habits had no effect on native English pronunciation. The "broken English" of immigrants was mimicked for purposes of humor, but would hardly be imitated seriously, even subconsciously. The numbers and prestige of the established, native English-speaking community protect its language from phonological "mixing." So, too, with syntactic structures. Foreign patterns translated into English are perceived as unidiomatic. Examples turn up in print for humor's sake, like the Pennsylvania Dutch "The butter is all," the Swedish "cook coffee," or the urban Yiddishisms: "You should live so long," or "So all right already," but such patterns are not incorporated into the native system.

A limited number of vocabulary items aside, the American whirlpool has swallowed many foreign languages without being affected by them. The process is still going on, inexorably working and inevitably to end in a society that is monolingual in English. Children born to foreign parents who share streets and playgrounds with English-speaking children learn perfect English from their peers. They instinctively know better than to imitate the imperfect

English of their parents. In large, mixed communities the third generation prefers to know nothing of the grandparents' Polish, Hungarian, or Italian. Foreign languages survive longer in communities that successfully maintain isolation from the American mainstream, like the prosperous Pennsylvania Dutch farming area, the Cajun French area in Louisiana, or the French communities in New England along the Canadian border.

(☆☆☆◎◎◎)

【中学校】

【1】中学校学習指導要領「外国語」「第2　各言語の目標及び内容等」「英語」「2　内容」について，次の(1)～(3)の問いに答えなさい。

(1) 次の文は「(1)　言語活動　ウ　読むこと」である。(　①　)～(　④　)にあてはまる語句を書きなさい。

(ア) 文字や(　①　)を識別し，正しく読むこと。

(イ) 書かれた内容を考えながら黙読したり，その内容が表現されるように音読すること。

(ウ) 物語のあらすじや説明文の(　②　)などを正確に読み取ること。

(エ) 伝言や手紙などの文章から書き手の意向を理解し，(　③　)に応じること。

(オ) 話の内容や書き手の意見などに対して感想を述べたり賛否やその理由を示したりなどすることができるよう，書かれた内容や(　④　)などをとらえること。

(2) 「(3)　言語材料　エ　文法事項」について，「(ア)文，(イ)文構造，(ウ)代名詞，(エ)動詞の時制など」に続いて(オ)～(ケ)として5つ示されている中から4つ，書きなさい。なお，「(オ)」，「(カ)」など各文法事項の前につけられているカタカナの部分は書かなくてよい。

(3) 次の文は「(4)　言語材料の取扱い」である。(　①　)～(　⑧　)にあてはまる語句を書きなさい。

ア　発音と(　①　)とを関連付けて指導すること。

イ　文法については，(　②　)を支えるものであることを踏まえ，(　③　)と効果的に関連付けて指導すること。

ウ　(3)のエの文法事項の取扱いについては，用語や用法の(　④　)などの指導が中心とならないよう配慮し，実際に(　⑤　)できるように指導すること。また，語順や(　⑥　)などにおける日本語との違いに留意して指導すること。

エ　英語の(　⑦　)を理解させるために，関連のある(　⑧　)はまとまりをもって整理するなど，効果的な指導ができるよう工夫すること。

(☆☆☆◎◎◎)

【高等学校】

【1】高等学校学習指導要領「外国語」について(1)～(3)の問いに答えなさい。

(1)　次は「第2款　各科目　第3　コミュニケーション英語Ⅱ」の「2　内容(2)」に示されている指導上の配慮事項を示している。(　①　)～(　⑧　)にあてはまる語句を書きなさい。

ア　英語の(　①　)な特徴や内容の(　②　)などに注意しながら聞いたり話したりすること。

イ　論点や(　③　)などを明確にするとともに，文章の構成や(　④　)との関連などを考えながら読んだり書いたりすること。

ウ　未知の語の意味を(　⑤　)したり背景となる知識を(　⑥　)したりしながら聞いたり読んだりすること。

エ　説明や(　⑦　)の表現を工夫して相手に(　⑧　)に伝わるように話したり書いたりすること。

(2)　次の英文は「第2款　各科目　第5　英語表現Ⅰ」の「2　内容(1)」を表している。(　①　)～(　④　)に入る適切な語を英語で書きなさい。

The following language activities, designed for specific (　①　) situations in order to encourage students to apply their abilities to understand and convey information, ideas, etc., should be conducted in English.

A. (　②　) speaking on a given topic. Speaking concisely in a style suitable for the audience and purpose.

B. Writing brief passages in a style suitable for the audience and (　③　).

C. Summarizing and presenting information, ideas, etc., based on what one has heard, read, learned and (　④　).

(3)　次は「第3款　英語に関する各科目に共通する内容等　2」の「ア　語，連語及び慣用表現」を示している。(　①　)，(　②　)にあてはまる語句を書きなさい。

(ア)　語

d　「コミュニケーション英語基礎」，「英語表現Ⅰ」，「英語表現Ⅱ」及び「英語会話」にあっては，生徒の(　①　)を踏まえた適切な語

(イ)　連語及び慣用表現のうち，(　②　)の高いもの

(☆☆☆◎◎◎)

解答・解説

【中高共通】

【1】(1)　c　(2)　d　(3)　c　(4)　a　(5)　b

〈解説〉(1)　本文中でthe Ministry classified the Japanese eel into the category of IB threatened species, and now it is on par with the Japanese huchen … と述べられていることから c が適切である。　(2)　本文中で an analysis of up-to-date catches and the discovery of locations and timing of spawning as well as other ecological details prompted the ministry to put the Japanese eel near the top of the Red List. と述べられていることから，dだけ本文中で分析対象として挙げられていない。　(3)　本文中ではcatches of adult Japanese eel peaked at 3,387 tons in 1961 before dwindling to 267 tons in 2009.と述べられていることから，cが正解である。 (4) 本文中でThe Ministry attributes the sharp fall mainly to overfishing and construction of weirs and dams which have prevented the number of Japanese eels from growing. と述べられており，選択肢の中でincorrectなのはaである。

(5) 本文中でThe latest designation puzzled eel farmers and other parties familiar with the Japanese eel. と述べた後から，The cooperative is concerned about a sharp rise in the prices of eel fry … と述べられている。このことから，理由は価格が急激に上がるかもしれないと思っているからであると分かる。

【2】(1) ア (2) エ (3) イ (4) ウ (5) ア

〈解説〉(1) quarantine「検疫(所)」，suspension「つるすこと，停止，停学」，restriction「制限」，detention「拘置，居残り」 「全ての動物が入国前に通らなければならない」のはアである。 (2) identically「完全に同じように」，keenly「熱心に，抜け目なく」，vacantly「ぼんやりと」，virtually「実質的には，事実上，～も同然」 virtually unknownで「知られていないも同然」である。 (3) fiscal「会計の」，salutary「有益な，健康に良い」，malign「有害な」，residual「残りの，未解決の」 relaxationが主語であり，effectを形容することからイが適切である。 (4) retrieve「取り戻す」，swagger「自慢する」，prowl「(餌・獲物などを求めて)うろつく」，disguise「変装する」 知覚動詞 see＋O＋原形不定詞で「O が～するのを見る」である。見知らぬ人が庭で何をしていたかを考えるとウが適切である。 (5) weed out「(雑草を)引き抜く，(好ましくないものを)取り除く」，tie up「固く縛る」，string out「つるす，(話などを)引き伸ばす」，rack up「(得点などを)得る，蓄積する」 不定詞の目的語が corrupt party officials「腐敗した政党役員」であり，文頭にも In an effort to clean up its image とあることから，アが適切である。

【3】(1)　イ　(2)　エ　(3)　ウ　(4)　ア　(5)　イ

〈解説〉(1)　wondered の後の接続詞は if もしくは whether であるべきである。　(2)　再帰代名詞は主語もしくは目的語を同一文中で指す時に用いられる。このことを踏まえると，主語である the country を指していると考えるのが自然であるので，themselves ではなく itself である。　(3)　ウの to は devote とともに用いられる前置詞であるから，to worry about ではなく，to worrying about でなければならない。　(4)　分詞構文であるから，従属節での主語は主節の主語と一致しているはずである。このことを鑑みると，the author's masterpieceがdismiss「退ける」のか退けられるのかを考えれば退けられるという受動態でなければならないことが分かる。よって，Dismissing ではなく Dismissed が適切である。　(5)　appreciate は他動詞であるから目的語を取らなければならない。通例，I would appreciate it if S V ～ という形で用いられる。

【4】1　エ　2　ク　3　イ　4　カ　5　ア

〈解説〉1　空欄1の直前にある You look a little tired. に対する返答が含まれているものが正答となる。エは，その発言に対する適切な応対と疲れている理由を述べていることから，1に相応しい。　2　空欄2の直後に Thank you for asking. とあることから，何かを尋ねたことが分かる。疑問文が含まれている選択肢はウとク(オは勧誘と見なし，カは Do you have any plans? に対して Thank you. とは答えないので除外する)であるが，ウは空欄1に続かない(Yes / No疑問文で終わっていない)ため，ここではクが適切である。　3　空欄3の直前に working too hard without relief can be depressing. とある意味，助言とも取れる発言がある。イは，その助言に対して I know. で受けており，relief の具体例として I'm going to take a leave of absence. と休みを取ることを述べていることから，この選択肢が最も適切である。　4　休暇を取ることを受けて，それに対する応対として That's good. と答えているカが最も適切である。その後に Do you have any plans? が続くのも自然である。　5　空欄4に入る選択肢カの I hear you love to travel in areas where most people don't go. に対する応答が含まれるものが正答となる。ここではアが最も適切である。

【5】(1) (解答例) 読む際に一度見ただけの語彙を習得できる確率は5%から14%だということ。/ ある語を習得するのには，5回から16回あるいはそれ以上繰り返すことが必要だと主張する研究があること。
(2) a イ b ウ c ア d エ (3) (解答例) どんな第2言語でも，最高頻度の語は，その言語を使う時にそれがなければ始まらないような語である。 (4) (解答例) また，学習者たちは，人生のその時その時に応じて違った方略を使うように自然に成長するようなので，様々な方略を経験させ，どれが自分に合っているのか決めさせるのも理にかなっているように思える。 (5) ア explicit
イ incidentally ウ incrementally エ partially

〈解説〉(1) 下線部①に続く，as the chances of learning and retaining a word from one exposure when reading are only about 5%－14%.という部分と，その次の文の Other studies suggest that it requires five to sixteen or more repetitions for a word to be learned. という部分が根拠となる。
(2) a 空欄に続く部分の one effective method というのが，何のための method なのかは直前を見ると teachers should look for ways to bolster learner input to offset this. とあり，この this はその前の repetition does not happen to nearly as great an extent for less frequent words を受けていると考えられることから，イの extensive reading がそこから脱却するための1つの方法と述べている文であることが分かる。 b 空欄 b の後ろに続く reintroduces words repeatedly in classroom activities がヒントになる。この修飾を受ける名詞であるからウが適切である。 c 空欄前の add と後の about the words がヒントである。このことからアの additional information が適切である。 d 空欄後に of と of の前置詞句の中に and で結ばれた構造があることがヒントである。このことから combination を含むエが適切である。 (3) they は直前の部分の the most frequent words を指している。they が複数名詞を受ける前方照応の代名詞であることを踏まえると，複数名詞は直前部分にこの語句しか見当たらない。prerequisite は「前提条件」という意味である。
(4)　初めの it は that 以下を指し示す形式主語であり，後の it も to 不定詞以下を指す形式主語である。reasonable「理にかなっている」，strategy「方略」，right for A「Aに合っている」　(5)　ア・イ　第4段落最終文に explicit teaching and incidental learning complement each other well, with each being necessary for an effective vocabulary program とある。ウ　空欄の含まれる文の構造から，空欄には副詞が入ることが予想される。また，続く文に This means that they need to be met numerous times before they are acquired と説明がある。　エ　第1段落第4文に If recycling is neglected, many partially known words will be forgotten とある。この文を逆に取れば，If recycling is not neglected, many partially known words will not be forgotten. となる。

【6】(解答例)　With the state of affairs in the world undergoing drastic changes and a range of problems coming to the fore both domestically and on a global scale, as the key to overcoming unparalleled problems, such as global warming and achieving sustainable development, various countries are actively developing policies in science technology and innovation.
〈解説〉このように1文が長い日本文を英語に直す際は，主語を見極めることが非常に重要である。そして，副詞節になる部分はどこか，英語における SVO などの核となる部分はどこかを見分ける。＜　＞が副詞節，[　] が核となるまとまりとして分けると以下のようになる。＜世界情勢が急激に変化し，国内的にも世界的にも広範な問題が表面化しつつある中,＞　＜地球温暖化のような未曾有の問題を克服し，持続可能な発展を達成する鍵として,＞ [様々な国が科学技術や技術革新における政策を積極的に推し進めようとしている]。　また,「未曾有」のように日本語特有の表現は,「今までに経験したことのないような」と言い換えることにより書きやすくなる。

【7】(解答例)　アメリカ英語に他言語の影響が見えないのは，英語の母国語話者たちのコミュニティの威信や数の多さが他言語との混合を防いできたからだ。アメリカ社会の中で他言語は淘汰され，アメリカの本流から孤立した社会においてのみ他言語は残存するのである。

〈解説〉120字以内という字数制限から，各段落の内容を60字程度でまとめなければならない。パラグラフの構造上，1つのパラグラフに1アイデアが原則であるので，各パラグラフにおけるキーセンテンスを見つけるとよい。第1段落のThe numbers and prestige of the established, native English-speaking community protect its language from phonological "mixing."の部分と第2段落のForeign languages survive longer in communities that successfully maintain isolation from the American mainstream … の部分がそれにあたると考えられる。for example などで示される例示は要約の際省かれることが多い。

【中学校】

【1】(1)　①　符号　　②　大切な部分　　③　適切　　④　考え方

(2)　形容詞及び副詞の比較変化 / to不定詞 / 動名詞 / 現在分詞および過去分詞の形容詞としての用法 / 受け身　の中から4つ　　(3)　①　綴り　　②　コミュニケーション　　③　言語活動　　④　区別　⑤　活用　　⑥　修飾関係　　⑦　特質　　⑧　文法事項

〈解説〉学習指導要領に掲載されている「第2　各言語の目標及び内容等」「英語」「2　内容」の「(1)言語活動」の聞くこと，話すこと，読むこと，書くことの部分，「(3)言語材料　エ　文法事項」および「(4)言語材料の取扱い」の部分は頻出である。それぞれの項目を正確に覚えておきたい。

【高等学校】

【1】(1)　①　音声的　　②　展開　　③　根拠　　④　図表
⑤　推測　　⑥　活用　　⑦　描写　　⑧　効果的
(2)　①　language-use　　②　Impromptu　　③　purpose
④　experienced　　(3)　①　学習負担　　②　運用度

〈解説〉英語表現Ⅰ・Ⅱやコミュニケーション英語Ⅰ・Ⅱの学習指導要領の目標や内容，指導上の留意点などはしっかり整理して覚えておきたい。特に高校では英文での理解が必要になってくることから，日本語と英語を対照して整理しておくとよいだろう。括弧抜きにされるところは例年の傾向と照らし合わせながら予想し，自ら問題を作って練習するのもよいだろう。

2013年度　実施問題

【中高共通】

【1】リスニングテスト

問題文及び5つの質問を聞き，各質問の後に読まれるa～dの4つの選択肢の中から，その質問に対する答えとして最も適切なものを1つ選び，記号で答えなさい。

英語リスニングテスト台本

ただいまから，問題1のリスニングテストを始めます。これから読む英文の内容に関して，5つの質問をします。それぞれの質問の後に読まれるa，b，c，dの4つの選択肢の中から，答えとして最も適切なものを1つ選び，記号で答えなさい。英文と質問，選択肢は，全体をとおして2回読みます。聞きながらメモを取ってもかまいません。それでは始めます。

People who ate chocolate a few times a week or more weighed less than those who rarely indulged, according to a U.S. study involving a thousand people.

Researchers said the findings, published in Archives of Internal Medicine, do not prove that adding a candy bar to your daily diet will help you shed pounds. Nor did the total amount of chocolate consumed have an impact.

But the researchers, led by Beatrice Golomb, from the University of California San Diego, said it was possible that antioxidants in chocolate could be behind health benefits, including lower blood pressure and cholesterol, as well as decreased body weight. She also said, “People assume that chocolate is bad because it comes with calories and it’s typically eaten as a sweet.”

She and her colleagues used data from a study on cholesterol-lowering drugs that surveyed 1,000 healthy adults on typical eating habits, including how often they ate chocolate. The participants, who ranged from 20 years old to 85 years old, ate chocolate an average of twice per week and had an average body mass index, or BMI, of 28, which is considered overweight but not obese.

The researchers found people who ate chocolate with greater frequency tended to eat more calories than those who ate less. But even so, chocolate lovers tended to have a lower body weight.

That was still the case after researchers accounted for age and gender, as well as how much they exercised.

The effect worked out to a 2.3 kilogram-to 3.2 kilogram-difference between people who ate five servings of chocolate a week compared to those who did not eat any, Golomb said. However, it was only how often they ate chocolate, rather than the total amount, that was linked to their weight.

Eric Ding, a nutritionist at the Harvard Medical School who was not involved in the study, said, "This new study is relatively small and could not prove cause-and-effect, so it is hard to take any lessons from the findings." But the key for chocolate lovers seems to be considering calories and knowing that not all chocolate is created equal.

Question

(1) According to Golomb's research, what can be a health benefit of eating chocolate?

(a) Relaxing.

(b) Reducing stress.

(c) Lowering blood pressure.

(d) Improving eating habits.

(2) In the study conducted by Golomb and her colleagues, what kind of people were the subjects?

(a) People who had the habit of walking.

(b) People who ate chocolate everyday.

(c) People who were suffering from obesity.

(d) People who were healthy adults.

(3) As the result of their experiment, what did the researchers find about chocolate lovers?

(a) They tended to have a lower body weight.

(b) They tended to eat more sweets.

(c) They tended to intake low-calorie food.

(d) They tended to suffer from serious diseases.

(4) What was the difference in weight in kilograms between people who ate chocolate five times a week and people who did not eat any?

(a) 1.2 to 2.3.

(b) 2.1 to 2.3.

(c) 2.3 to 3.2.

(d) 1.2 to 3.2.

(5) According to the passage, which statement is true?

(a) Adding a candy bar to their daily diet will help people reduce weight.

(b) Dr. Golomb thought that people tend to see chocolate as bad.

(c) The total amount of chocolate people ate was linked to their weight.

(d) Dr. Ding joined this experiment to support Dr. Golomb's research.

【REPEAT】

これでリスニングテストを終わります。

(☆☆☆☆◎◎◎)

【2】次の各文の(　　)に当てはまる最も適切な語を，ア～エから1つ選び，記号で答えなさい。

(1) A person skilled in the (　　) of animal tracks can tell not only the species and size of the creature, but also approximately when it passed by.

ア translation　　イ interpretation　　ウ realization
エ inscription

(2) The dishonest salesman used a variety of tricks to (　　) customers into buying his overpriced products.

ア wring　　イ bond　　ウ lure　　エ nurture

(3) The sports commentators agreed that the athlete's small size was (　　) since she was easily the strongest competitor in the judo tournament.

ア deceptive　　イ dubious　　ウ receptive　　エ intimidating

(4) Allen is retiring today, so we'd like to give him this small gift as a (　　) of our appreciation.

ア refund　　イ token　　ウ venue　　エ voucher

(5) An accomplice created a (　　) so that the shoplifter could slip the stolen jewelry into her pocket unnoticed.

ア reversion　　イ violation　　ウ suspension　　エ diversion

(☆☆☆☆◎◎◎)

【3】次の各文の下線部ア～エの中で，誤っている箇所を1つ選び，記号で答えなさい。

(1) The Prime Minister ア requested that the Finance Minister イ be more careful because whatever he ウ says to the press or even privately to his colleagues often エ have an impact on the stock market.

(2) In Japan, household. appliances, such as air conditioners and refrigerators, have ア gotten bigger and more effective イ while using less energy, ウ owing to a government program that constantly エ rises efficiency standards.

(3) Fast food and convenience stores now play key roles in daily life. Adults have built ア a material rich society, イ with the result that children are becoming over-nourished and ウ getting fat エ for lack of exercise.

(4) ア Originally イ cultivating in India, the banana was brought to the Americas by ウ the Portuguese who found エ it in Asia.

(5)　I am really ア<u>grateful to</u> all the people イ<u>who offered</u> information ウ<u>without which</u> the data for this book エ<u>had never</u> been gathered.

(☆☆☆◎◎◎)

【4】次の対話文の(　1　)～(　5　)にあてはまる最も適切な英文を，ア～キから選び，記号で答えなさい。ただし，同じ選択肢を2度使わないこと。

A : I hear you have a lot of hobbies.

B : (　　　1　　　)

A : (　　　2　　　)

B : It was interesting, but I am thinking of learning flamenco now. It looks exciting.

A : Oh, I love it, too. But unlike you, I am the kind of person who sticks to one hobby, and only one. It's been my passion for ten years.

B : (　　　3　　　)

A : (　　　4　　　)

B : (　　　5　　　)

A : That would be no problem, but I recommend you to go to my dancing school. I've been there for six years. Why don't you come with me? Then you can learn a lot.

ア I stayed in Spain for nine months when I was young. I saw it then and was fascinated by it.

イ You mean you don't have any hobbies at all? I know you were learning cooking.

ウ Didn't you say you were learning dancing flamenco? Did you quit it?

エ Only dancing flamenco is my hobby now. I'm going to quit learning cooking and start learning it.

オ Yes, in a sense, I do. But to tell the truth, I am the type who can't keep one hobby up for long.

カ Then I'm sure you can dance it very well. Would you train me in your free time?

キ Really? I never knew that. That's quite impressive. How did you get into that?

(☆☆◎◎◎)

【5】次の英文を読んで，(1)～(5)の問いに答えなさい。

Language is, essentially, a means of relating two different kinds of patterns or forms of representation — sound and meaning. The representation of language sounds, the phonological system, is an external representation; the representation of meanings, the semantic system, is an internal representation. The means of relating the two is a language's syntactic system.

We can think of the external and internal representations as involving different codes. The external, phonological code is the one in which language is transmitted from one person to another, from speaker to hearer. On the other hand, the internal, semantic code is the one in which speakers and hearers represent the meanings, or messages, of the sentences they produce and understand. A language's syntactic system is essentially a means of relating a representation in one of these codes to a representation in the other. That is, the syntactic system provides a translation from the phonological representation of a sentence into its semantic form and vice versa. ①There is rarely a direct relation between a representation in the phonological code and one in the semantic code, and those rare cases where there is involve units no larger than words. Meaning is conveyed from person to person linguistically only when the speaker translates the meaning he wishes to convey into an external form and the listener translates that form back into a representation of the meaning.

[　　　　　②　　　　　]

Now, let's look at the nature of language from another aspect. The external code, the highly structured phonological system, is unique to language and serves almost no function other than its linguistic one. Occasionally, the close relationship between the external code and the translation process has led people to speak as if the code itself were language. (　a　) This is a confusion between speech and language.

The internal code, on the other hand, is probably not unique to language. This code appears to serve functions in addition to its linguistic ones. (　b　) The semantic code involves concepts and propositions of the sorts involved in thought. Language is one way, though not necessarily the only way, of translating these representations into an external code. Language is one means of expressing what we think. Translation from the internal, semantic code to the external code is, of course, not necessary. (　c　) And in some cases a translation can be performed only with great difficulty. We sometimes have trouble finding the appropriate form for expressing what is represented in the internal code. ③<u>In cases where the translation does occur, we tend to think of the internal code as semantic and a part of language. When translation into the external code of language does not occur, we tend to think of the internal code as a general cognitive code. The semantic and cognitive codes are interrelated, perhaps identical.</u> (　d　) We might think of this code as being the interface between language and thought, the place where the two meet.

If the internal representations that underlie language are the same kind as those involved in thinking, then it seems likely that there will be close relationships between the kinds of phenomena we observe in language and those we observe in some other kinds of cognitive functioning. ④<u>This</u> suggests that we might learn a great deal about language and language processing from considering certain other aspects of cognitive functioning, For example, it might be helpful to view the processes involved in a child's acquiring language as reflections of those underlying general cognitive development.

(1)　下線部①を日本語にしなさい。

(2)　次は[　②　]に入る英文である。(　ア　)～(　ウ　)に入る1語を英語で書きなさい。

Thus, it is the (　ア　) and external codes as well as the means by which (　イ　) between them are accomplished that constitute language. A language can be thought of as both the two codes and the set of rules or procedures for turning a representation in one of them into a representation in the (　ウ　).

(3)　次の文が入る最も適切な場所を，(　a　)～(　d　)の中から選んで記号で答えなさい。

We often think without speaking.

(4)　下線部③を日本語にしなさい。

(5)　下線部④のThisの内容を日本語で説明しなさい。

(☆☆☆☆◎◎◎)

【6】次の日本語で，下線部(1)・(2)を英語に直しなさい。

(1)経済・社会環境の変化や人々の意識の変化などにより，家族，地域，職場のつながりは弱まっているといわれている。一方で，現代の経済生活や社会の姿に合った新しいつながりの形も生まれてきている。(2)家族が個室にこもらないように家づくりに工夫を施し，自然な形で家族が触れ合う機会を作るような例もある。

(☆☆☆☆◎◎◎)

【7】次の英文を読んで，その趣旨を100字以内の日本語で書きなさい。ただし，句読点も字数に入れること。

In many meetings, much time is spent on presentations — too much. Many reports could have been submitted to group members in writing or on a one-to-one basis. And of the essential presentations, a large number are poorly prepared and delivered.

Most oral presentations are given to inject new ideas and information into a group's problem-solving and decision-making. Poor presentations waste participants' time even after they are delivered because the relevant information is not in a form that can help the group in its deliberation, and so people spend a lot more time wheel-spinning, trying to reorganize and digest it before they can make a decision.

What's so difficult about making a presentation, anyway? All you have to do is to get up in front of a group and say what you want people to know, and they will get the message. Wrong! You may say X, but they may hear Y. And what's worse, they may think that Y really means Z. Communicating is a two-way street. You haven't communicated until you know that the other person has heard you correctly and comprehended what you really mean.

Communicating is also problem-solving. The situation you want to change is the difference between what you know and what you think someone else knows. Until you have changed the situation to a point where you believe the other person knows what you wanted him or her to know, you haven't solved your communication problem. And you can't do that without some feedback, some response from the other person. It's like trying to find out what's wrong with a child. Until the child responds in some way, by talking, nodding, pointing, or crying, you won't know what's wrong. Problem-solving is trial and error. But until you know the results of one trial, how can you decide what to do next?

To solve a presentation problem, you must consider the total interchange between you and your audience, not just what you do and say during your report. You must analyze the situation and design your presentation. You must ask yourself the questions: what, why, where, how, and how many.

(☆☆☆☆◎◎◎)

【中学校】

【1】中学校学習指導要領(平成20年3月告示)「外国語」「第2　各言語の目標及び内容等」「英語」について，次の(1)～(3)の問いに答えなさい。

(1)　「2　内容　(2)　言語活動の取扱い　ア(ウ)[言語の働きの例]」について，「b　気持ちを伝える」として4つ示されている中から，3つ書きなさい。

(2)　次の文は「2　内容　(3)　言語材料」の一部である。(　①　)～(　③　)にあてはまる語句を書きなさい。

ア　音声

(ア)　現代の(　①　)

(イ)　語と語の連結による音変化

(ウ)　語，句，文における基本的な(　②　)

(エ)　文における基本的なイントネーション

(オ)　文における基本的な(　③　)

(3)　次の文は「3　指導計画の作成と内容の取扱い(2)」の一部である。(　①　)～(　⑧　)にあてはまる語句を書きなさい。

ア　(　①　)なものの見方や考え方を理解し,公正な判断力を養い(　②　)な心情を育てるのに役立つこと。

イ　外国や我が国の(　③　)や文化についての理解を深めるとともに，言語や(　④　)に対する関心を高め，これらを(　⑤　)する態度を育てるのに役立つこと。

ウ　広い視野から(　⑥　)を深め，国際社会に生きる日本人としての(　⑦　)を高めるとともに，(　⑧　)の精神を養うのに役立つこと。

【高等学校】

【1】新高等学校学習指導要領(平成21年3月告示)「外国語」について(1)～(3)の問いに答えなさい。

(1)　次は「第2款　各科目　第2　コミュニケーション英語Ⅰ　2　内容(1)」で示されている事項である。(　①　)～(　④　)にあてはまる語句を書きなさい。

ア　事物に関する(　①　)や対話などを聞いて，情報や考えなどを理解したり，概要や要点をとらえたりする。

イ　説明や物語などを読んで，情報や考えなどを理解したり，概要や要点をとらえたりする。また，聞き手に伝わるように(　②　)

する。

ウ　聞いたり読んだりしたこと，学んだことや経験したことに基づき，情報や考えなどについて，話し合ったり(　③　)をしたりする。

エ　聞いたり読んだりしたこと，学んだことや経験したことに基づき，情報や考えなどについて，(　④　)。

(2)　「第3款　英語に関する各科目に共通する内容等　1」において，[言語の働きの例]としてa～eまで5つ示されている。このうちaは「コミュニケーションを円滑にする」である。残り4つのうち，2つを書きなさい。

(3)　次は「第4款　各科目にわたる指導計画の作成と内容の取扱い2(1)」の一部である。(　①　)～(　⑥　)に入る語句をあとから選び，記号で答えなさい。

教材については，外国語を通じてコミュニケーション能力を(　①　)育成するため，各科目の(　②　)に応じ，実際の言語の(　③　)や言語の働きに十分配慮したものを取り上げるものとすること。その際，その外国語を日常使用している人々を中心とする世界の人々及び日本人の日常生活，風俗習慣，物語，地理，歴史，伝統文化や(　④　)などに関するものの中から，生徒の発達の段階及び(　⑤　)に即して適切な題材を(　⑥　)をもたせて取り上げるものとし，次の観点に留意する必要があること。

ア　国際理解	イ　自然科学	ウ　変化	エ　特徴
オ　目標	カ　学習内容	キ　指導方法	ク　使用場面
ケ　工夫	コ　興味・関心	サ　総合的に	シ　有機的に

(☆☆☆☆◎◎◎◎)

解答・解説

【中高共通】

【1】(1)　c　　(2)　d　　(3)　a　　(4)　c　　(5)　b

〈解説〉(1)　チョコレートの効能については第3段落の1文目のthat以降に説明があり，「チョコレートに含まれる抗酸化物質が，体重の減少と同様に，血圧やコレステロール値を下げるといった健康上の利益の背景にある」と述べられている。　(2)　実験の概要は第4段落で説明されており，研究対象は1,000 healthy adults on typical eating habits「典型的な食習慣を持つ1000人の健康な成人」とある。　(3)　実験結果は第5段落で「より高い頻度でチョコレートを食べていた人はカロリーを多く摂る傾向にあったものの，体重は減り易かった」と説明されている。　(4)　第7段落目に「チョコレートの効果によって，1週間に5回以上チョコレートを食べた人と，一度も食べなかった人の違いは2.3キロから3.2キロほどになった」とある。　(5)　bは第3段落のPeople assume ～ の文の内容と一致する。

【2】(1)　イ　　(2)　ウ　　(3)　ア　　(4)　イ　　(5)　エ

〈解説〉(1)　interpretation「解釈，判別」訳「動物の足跡の判別に長けた人は，その生物の種と大きさだけでなく，いつ頃それが通ったかまでわかる」　　(2)　lure ～ into …「～を…に誘惑する」訳「不誠実なセールスマンはあの手この手を使って，法外な値段の商品を客に買わせようとする」　　(3)　deceptive「人を欺くような，見かけによらない」訳「スポーツコメンテーターは，その選手は柔道大会で簡単に優勝したので，小さい体格は見かけによらないと同意した」　　(4)　token「しるし，記念品」訳「Allenは今日をもって退職するので，私たちは感謝のしるしとしてこの小さな贈り物を彼にあげようと思う」

(5)　diversion「そらせること」(ここでは店員の目を万引きからそらせることを指す)　訳「万引き犯が盗んだ宝石を気づかれずにポケットに

入れられるよう，共犯者は店員の目をそらせた」

【3】(1) エ　(2) エ　(3) ア　(4) イ　(5) エ

〈解説〉(1) have→has　because節の中の主語はwhatever ～ colleaguesで単数扱い。訳「首相は財務大臣に注意するよう言った。それは財務大臣が言うことは，それが報道関係者に対してでも，同僚に個人的に言ったことでも何でも，株市場に影響を与えてしまうからだ」

(2) rises→raises　riseは「上がる」という意味の自動詞。ここは後ろに目的語を伴って「～を上げる」という意味の他動詞でないといけない。訳「日本では，効率規準を常に上げている政府のプログラムのおかげで，エアコンや冷蔵庫といった家電がより大きく，効率的になっている」　(3) material rich→material-rich　名詞と名詞が連なって形容詞の役割をする際には，名詞と名詞をハイフンでつなぐ。訳「大人は物質が豊かな社会を作った。その結果，子どもたちは栄養過多になり，運動不足によって肥満になってきている」

(4) cultivating→cultivated　Originally cultivated in Indiaは分詞構文で，言い換えるとThough it was originally cultivated in Indiaとなる(itはthe bananaを指す)。訳「もともとバナナはインドで栽培されていたが，アジアでそれを発見したポルトガル人によって南北アメリカに持ち込まれた」　(5) had never→would have never been(couldでもよい)。whichはinformationを主語とする関係代名詞で，without ～ gatheredの意味は「その情報がなければこの本をまとめることは決してできませんでした」とならなければいけない。これは過去における仮定の話を表すので，助動詞の過去形＋have＋過去分詞の仮定法過去完了の形を用いなければならない。

【4】(1) オ　(2) イ　(3) キ　(4) ア　(5) カ

〈解説〉(1) Aが「あなたは趣味がたくさんあるって聞いたけど」と言っていて，オは「そう，ある意味ではね」と言っているので自然な応答となる(I doはI do have a lot of hobbiesを意味する)。　(2) Bの「でも実は1つの趣味を長く続けられなくて」に対し，イは「全然趣味がないってこと？料理を習っているって聞いたけど」という意味で自然な応答となり，次の「(料理は)面白かったんだけどね」にもつながる。
(3)　Aが「10年間それ(フラメンコ)に夢中なの」に対し，「本当に？知らなかった。素敵ね。なんではまったの？」と述べているキが自然な流れとなる。　(4)　フラメンコに夢中になった経緯をBが尋ねているので，スペインでの出来事を述べたアが応答として適切。　(5)　カは「時間があったら(フラメンコを)教えてくれる？」と質問していて，Aの「大丈夫よ(That would be no problem)」はこれへの応答となる。

【5】(1)　(解答例)　音声符号の表現と意味符号の表現の間に直接的な関係はほとんどなく，まれに関係があるような場合でも，単語以上の単位となることはない。　(2)　ア　internal　　イ　translations
ウ　other　　(3)　c　　(4)　(解答例)　実際に内的符号の外的符号への翻訳が行われたとき，我々はその内的符号を言語学的に意味を持つもの，すなわち言語の一部と考える傾向がある。言語的な外的符号への翻訳が行われない場合は，その内的符号を一般的な認知符号であると考える傾向がある。つまり意味と認知の符号は相互に関係していて，おそらく同一のものである。　(5)　(解答例)　もし，言語の根底にある内的表現と思考に関する内的表現が同種のものであるならば，言語の中で見られる現象と他の認知機能で見られる現象には密接な関係がありそうだということ。
〈解説〉(1)　rarely「めったに～ない」relation between A and B「AとBの間の関係」oneはrepresentationを指す。those rare cases where there is「それ(音声符号の表現と意味符号の表現の間の関係)がある珍しい場合」(whereは関係副詞)。no larger than ～「～以上になることはない」
(2)　1文目はit is ～ that …の強調構文。アはexternalと並列でcodesを修飾していることからinternalだとわかる。イは，themがinternal and external codesを指し，the means ～ accomplishedまでが「それらの間の(イ)が達成される方法」となるので，イにはtranslationが入るとわかる。

ただし，述語がareなのでtranslationを複数形にするのを忘れないように。ウはoneと対比になるように入れればよい。ここでoneとthe otherはexternal codeとinternal code(またはその逆)を指す。　(3)　We often think without speakingは空欄cの前文(Translation ～ necessary.)を言い換えたもの。Translation from the internal, semantic code to the external codeとは，考えていることを言葉にして表す(話す)ことを指す。　(4)　In cases where ～「～の場合には」(whereは関係副詞)。think of A as B「AをBと考える」「外的な符号への翻訳が行われる」とは，考えていることを言葉にして表すことを指す。「認知符号(cognitive code)」とは頭のなかで考えていることを指し，ここでは言葉に表されない思考を指す。interrelated「相互に関係がある」identical「同一な」　(5)　Thisは前文を指す。that underlie language「言語の根底にある」(thatは関係代名詞)。thoseはrepresentationsを指す。it seems likely that ～「～のようだ」we observe in languageはphenomenaにかかる。thoseはthe kinds of phenomenaを指す。抽象的な内容だが，つまり，言葉を話すことと頭を使う他の作業(計算，運動，料理など)は，頭の中の同じところを使って行っているのはないか，ということ。

【6】(1)　(解答例)　It is said that changes in the economic and social environments, and in people's attitudes, have led to a weakening in the ties between families, communities and workplaces.　(2)　(解答例)　There are examples of homes being designed in ways that prevent family members from becoming isolated, and provide them with chances to spend more time with each other in a natural way.

〈解説〉(1)　「～により」は原因を表すので，解答例のように「原因 lead to 結果」の表現やdue to ～を用いて表すことができる。「つながり」はtieの他に，relationshipやbondでもよい。「弱まる」はweakenで，weakeningは動名詞で「弱まり」の意味。　(2)「～のような例もある」はThere are examples of ～(where ～)で表す。「家族が個室にこもらないように」ということと「家族が触れ合う機会を作る」というのは同じ内容。そのために「家づくりに工夫を施す」と言っているので，英文でもその構造を反映させたい。解答例ではin ways that以下に上記の工夫の2つの目的(prevent ～ とprovide ～)が並列で書いてある。

【7】(解答例)　プレゼンテーションでは問題解決や意志決定に資するような情報伝達がなされなければならない。そのためには，発表者は周到に準備をし，聞き手と相互にコミュニケーションをとりながら行うことが重要である。(96字)

〈解説〉第1～2段落では問題提起として，近年行われているプレゼンテーションが本来の目的(ある人々の問題解決や意志決定に役立つ情報を与える)を果たしていないことが述べられている。続く第3～4段落ではプレゼンテーションが難しい理由(人によって解釈が異なる可能性がある)と，プレゼンテーションの目標(自分が意図する内容を相手が理解している)を述べている。最後の第5段落では，プレゼンテーションを正しく行うための方法(事前の準備と実際のプレゼンでの状況の判断)が述べられている。要約ではこれらの情報を字数制限内で書けばよい。

【中学校】

【1】(1)　礼を言う，苦情を言う，褒める，謝る，の中から3つ

(2)　①　標準的な発音　②　強勢　③　区切り　(3)　①　多様　②　豊か　③　生活　④　文化　⑤　尊重　⑥　国際理解　⑦　自覚　⑧　国際協調

〈解説〉(1)　「言語の働きの例」はaからeまであり，それぞれについてさらに詳しい働きの例と具体的な表現の例が示されている。「b 気持ちを伝える」では，Thank you. Thanks a lot.(礼を言う)，Stop that noise. Can you be quiet?(苦情を言う)，Good job. What a nice dress!(褒める)，I'm sorry. Please forgive me.(謝る)などが具体例として挙げられている。

(2)　アの「標準的な発音」とは，北米や英国の発音を指すのではなく「多様性に富んだ現在の英語の発音」と解説に説明がある。ウは，日本語とは異なる英語のリズムの重要性を訴えることを目的とする。オ

の区切りの認識は，読む・聞く・書く・話すの全てで重要だと解説では述べられている。　(3) 「3 指導計画の作成と内容の取扱い (2)」は教材の選定の観点を示した項目である。ア～ウはその3つの観点である。広く公平な視野，言語や文化を尊重する態度，国際協調の精神を育てることが，それぞれの観点の趣旨。

【高等学校】

【1】(1) ①　紹介　②　音読　③　意見の交換　④　簡潔に書く
(2)　気持ちを伝える，情報を伝える，考えや意図を伝える，相手の行動を促す，の中から2つ。　(3) ①　サ　②　オ　③　ク
④　イ　⑤　コ　⑥　ウ

〈解説〉(1)　高校は様々な科目があるが「コミュニケーション英語I」のみ必修となっているため，出題頻度は全国的に非常に高い。目標と内容はぜひ覚えておきたい。「事物に関する紹介」とは説明的な文章を指す。「聞き手に伝わるように音読する」のは，機械的な練習に陥りがちな音読も，相手を念頭に置くことでコミュニケーションを意識した活動になるため。ウはインプットとアウトプット(話すこと)の統合を目指した指導内容。エは，書くことに特化している点でウと異なる。
(2)　この5つの「言語の働きの例」は中学校の学習指導要領と共通しているが，高校ではそれぞれの働きの内容が多様に，かつ高度になっている。　(3) 「第4款 各科目にわたる指導計画の作成と内容の取扱い(2)」は教材の選定の観点を示した項目で，中学校の学習指導要領とほぼ共通した内容となっている。ア～エの4つの教材選定の観点があり，広く公平な視野，言語や文化を尊重する態度，国際協調の精神，人間・自然・社会への認識を育てるのに役立つもの，とある。

2012年度　実施問題

【中高共通】

【1】[リスニングテスト]

問題文及び5つの質問を聞き，各質問の後に読まれるa～dの4つの選択肢の中から，その質問に対する答えとして最も適切なものを1つ選び，記号で答えなさい。

(☆☆☆◎◎◎)

【2】次の各文の(　　)にあてはまる最も適切な語を，ア～エから1つ選び，記号で答えなさい。

(1) A team of rescue workers was (　　) to the crash sight to search for survivors.

ア dispatched　イ transmitted　ウ degraded　エ reprobated

(2) The good-humored joke (　　) the tension in the room.

ア reserved　イ dispelled　ウ allocated　エ berated

(3) The impact of the situation failed to touch him; he remained (　　) as a stone.

ア impassive　イ immaculate　ウ oppressive　エ truculent

(4) A heavy fog (　　) the valley, so that even nearby trees appeared as shadowy ghosts.

ア encountered　イ engrossed　ウ endowed　エ enveloped

(5) It would be (　　) to ask for a raise now; the boss is in no mood to grant our request.

ア specious　イ timely　ウ impolitic

エ　fortuitous

(☆☆☆◎◎◎)

【3】次の各文の下線部の意味を最もよく表している語を，ア～エから1つ選び，記号で答えなさい。

(1)　The present situation of the country is <u>precarious</u>.

ア　serene　　イ　uncertain　　ウ　injurious　　エ　prosperous

(2)　Some historians consider George Washington's cutting down a cherry tree <u>dubious</u>.

ア　authentic　　イ　educational　　ウ　unreliable

エ　anachronistic

(3)　We were surprised to be surrounded by many boys who all looked <u>malnourished</u>.

ア　exhausted　　イ　restive　　ウ　adamant　　エ　underfed

(4)　The manager is <u>dexterous</u> in handling angry customers.

ア　skillful　　イ　intelligent　　ウ　feckless　　エ　rigorous

(5)　No one could foresee the political <u>implications</u> behind the President's action.

ア　factors　　イ　influences　　ウ　references　　エ　derivations

(☆☆☆◎◎◎)

【4】次の英文を読んで，その趣旨を120字以内の日本語で書きなさい。ただし，句読点も字数に入れること。

Songs and singing have a great potential in foreign language teaching. The acceptance among students is high, the technical conditions for supplying audio files are sufficient and there are indications that the acquisition of language, in particular vocabulary, is enhanced by their usage. Concerning learning strategies of good test takers, the questionnaire did not yield a clear picture; listening to the supplied audio files seems to support test takers in the perceptive part of the vocabulary tests. About the learnability of vocabulary items, a bias concerning the item difficulty index has been identified, which was independent from the length of items or the time of its introduction : Items introduced through songs had in general a higher item difficulty index — they were easier — than items introduced through other materials. However, it is still unclear, whether this advantage comes solely from the mode of introduction, from frequency of encounter or from other reasons.

(☆☆☆☆◎◎◎)

【5】次の英文を読んで，(1)～(3)の問いに答えなさい。

Small-group exercises can be extremely effective for both active and reflective learners. (ア) Group work must be used with care, however : simply telling students to work together on problems or projects can do more harm than good. Most references on cooperative learning point out that students often respond negatively to group work at first, and that (イ) the benefits of the approach are fully realized when the group work is structured to assure such features as positive interdependence, individual accountability and appropriate uses of teamwork and interpersonal skills. When language students have been taught cooperative skills, they showed positive results in both language skill and (ウ) altruism.

(1)　下線部(ア)を日本語に直しなさい。

(2)　下線部(イ)を日本語に直しなさい。

(3)　下線部(ウ)の反意語を書きなさい。

(☆☆☆◎◎◎)

【6】次の英文の(　1　)～(　5　)にあてはまるもっとも適切な語をア～コから選び，記号で答えなさい。ただし，同じ選択肢を2度使わないこと。

Recent studies have researched the benefits of restricting calories in our diet. A study of adult monkeys showed that they were one-third as (　1　) to die from age-related diseases if they consumed 30 percent (　2　) calories than they did in their regular menu. Previous, well-publicized research had shown that restricting calories can (3) the life span of creatures ranging from flies to dogs, for reasons still (4). But the latest trial, led by a leading research institution, is the first to show officially that caloric restriction can improve (5) in primates.

ア unclear　イ fewer　ウ depress　エ more
オ abstract　カ survival　キ likely　ク experimental
ケ be　コ increase

(☆☆☆◎◎◎)

【7】次の対話文の(1)～(4)にあてはまる最も適切な英文をア～キから選び，記号で答えなさい。ただし，同じ選択肢は2度使わないこと。

A : I hear you have been working as a nurse. What's it like?

B : Working as a nurse is fascinating. I feel strongly I'm helping sick people and their families.

A : (1)

B : (2)

A : I respect you. If I were you, I would feel down. I'm afraid I couldn't keep it up.

B : When I started working, I was almost crushed by the pressures of my job, but I have become accustomed to the work now.

A : I'm afraid it would take me more time than you to get used to it.

B : (3)

A : I've wondered what it would be like to work in medicine, but I'm not confident I could.

B : Don't worry. Work is work. Though there is hardship in any work, it will prove worthwhile.

A : (4)

B : When the patients get well and leave the hospital, they and their family expressed gratitude to me. It gives me a warm feeling to know I've helped people.

ア　I guess you're right. What keeps you going?

イ　I've already told you about it time and time again. You should keep it in mind.

ウ　Yes. As for the work, the responsibility is heavy and I have to work very late.

エ　It must be very awesome to help people, but isn't it intense?

オ　What should I do now to work in medicine, especially at a hospital?

カ　How long do you think will it take for me to get used to it?

キ　Oh, I remember you said you were interested in working at the hospital before.

(☆☆◎◎◎)

【8】次の日本文を英語に直しなさい。

成長期にある子どもにとって，健全な食生活は，健康な心身をはぐくむために欠かせない。学校においては，家庭と連携し，生徒が食品の品質や安全性について，正しい知識や情報に基づいて自ら適切な判断ができるように，食に関する教育が行われている。

(☆☆☆◎◎◎)

【中学校】

【1】新中学校学習指導要領(平成20年3月告示)「外国語」「第2　各言語の目標及び内容等」「英語」について，次の(1)・(2)の問いに答えなさい。

(1)　次の文は「2　内容　(1)　言語活動　ア　聞くこと」である。(①)~(⑤)に当てはまる語句を書きなさい。

(ア)　強勢，イントネーション，(①)など基本的な英語の音声の特徴をとらえ，正しく聞き取ること。

(イ)　自然な口調で話されたり読まれたりする英語を聞いて，

(②)を正確に聞き取ること。

(ウ) (③)や依頼などを聞いて適切に応じること。

(エ) 話し手に(④)などして内容を確認しながら理解すること。

(オ) まとまりのある英語を聞いて，(⑤)や要点を適切に聞き取ること。

(2) 「2 内容 (2) 言語活動の取扱い ア (ウ)[言語の働きの例]」について，(A)・(B)のいずれか1つを選び，その記号を記入し，問いに答えなさい。

(A) 「a コミュニケーションを円滑にする」として4つ示されている中から3つ選び，書きなさい。

(B) 「c 情報を伝える」として4つ示されている中から3つ選び，書きなさい。

(3) 次の文は「3 指導計画の作成と内容の取扱い(1)」の一部である。(①)〜(⑧)に当てはまる語句を書きなさい。

ウ 音声指導に当たっては，(①)との違いに留意しながら，(②)などを通して2の(3)のアに示された言語材料を(③)して指導すること。

また，音声指導の補助として，必要に応じて(④)を用いて指導することもできること。

エ 文字指導に当たっては，生徒の(⑤)に配慮し(⑥)を指導することもできること。

オ 語，連語及び慣用表現については，(⑦)の高いものを用い，(⑧)することを通して定着を図るようにすること。

(☆☆☆◎◎◎◎◎)

【高等学校】

【1】次の(ア)〜(ウ)の文は，現行高等学校学習指導要領「外国語」の「第5 リーディング」「2 内容 (2)言語活動の取扱い ア 指導上の配慮事項」の一部である。(1)〜(3)にあてはまる語句を書きなさい。

(ア)　(　1　)の意味を推測したり，背景となる知識を活用したりしながら読むこと。

(イ)　文章の中でポイントとなる語句や文，(　2　)の構成や展開などに注意して読むこと。

(ウ)　目的や状況に応じて，(　3　)など，適切な読み方をすること。

(☆☆☆◎◎◎◎◎)

【2】次の文は，新高等学校学習指導要領(平成21年3月告示)「外国語」の「第2　コミュニケーション英語Ⅰ」と「第5　英語表現Ⅰ」の目標である。(　1　)～(　6　)にあてはまる語句を書きなさい。

「コミュニケーション英語Ⅰ」

英語を通じて，積極的にコミュニケーションを図ろうとする態度を育成するとともに，(　1　)や考えなどを(　2　)に理解したり適切に伝えたりする(　3　)を養う。

「英語表現Ⅰ」

英語を通じて，積極的にコミュニケーションを図ろうとする態度を育成するとともに，事実や意見などを(　4　)から考察し，論理の展開や(　5　)を工夫しながら(　6　)を養う。

(☆☆☆◎◎◎◎◎)

【3】新高等学校学習指導要領(平成21年3月告示)「外国語」の「第3款　英語に関する各科目に共通する内容等　3」には，言語材料を用いるに当たっての配慮事項が3つ示されている。これについて，(1)～(3)の問いに答えなさい。

(1)　様々な英語が国際的に広くコミュニケーションの手段として使われている実態に配慮しながら，どのような英語を用いることとされているか。

(2)　文法については，コミュニケーションを支えるものであることを踏まえ，どのように指導することとされているか。

(3)　コミュニケーションを行うために必要となる語句や文構造，文法事項などの取扱いについては，実際に活用できるように指導するために，どのような配慮をすることとされているか。

(☆☆☆◎◎◎◎◎)

解答・解説

【中高共通】

【1】(1)　d　(2)　c　(3)　b　(4)　a　(5)　d

〈解説〉スクリプト無し。問題文，質問，解答の選択肢すべてが放送で流れ，文字による手がかりはないので，とにかく聞き取りに集中することが必要である。問題数は多くないので，日頃の耳慣らしとリスニング問題集などの練習で対応できるであろう。メモを取りながら答えを予測しつつ聞く練習もしておきたい。

【2】(1)　ア　(2)　イ　(3)　ア　(4)　エ　(5)　ウ

〈解説〉(1)　主語が「救助隊が」で，be動詞により受動態になっている。空欄以下は「墜落現場に生存者捜索のため」で，「派遣された」が最も適切である。他の選択肢は，イ「送信／伝達された」，ウ「評判や評価を落とされた」，エ「避難された」という意味。　(2)　目的語が「室内の緊張感を」なので，「一掃した」のdispelledがあてはまる。他選択肢はそれぞれ，ア「予約する／留保する」，ウ「割り当てる」，エ「非難する」の意。　(3)　文前半は「その状況の衝撃も彼を動かすことはできなかった」，そして「彼は石のように～のままだった。」と続くので，空欄には状態を示す語が入る。　(4)　文後半に「傍にある木々も謎めいた幽霊のように見えた」とあるので，「深い霧」が谷を「覆った」とするenvelopedがあてはまる。他選択肢はア「(偶然に)遭遇する」，イ「没頭させる」，ウ「基金などを提供する」の意味。

(5)　文意は「いま給料の引き上げを頼むのは～だろう。上司は私達の要求を受け入れる気分ではないから」で,「得策でない」とするimpoliticが適切。他選択肢は,ア「見掛け倒しの」,イ「時機のよい」,エ「思いがけない」の意である。

【3】(1)　イ　(2)　ウ　(3)　エ　(4)　ア　(5)　イ

〈解説〉(1)　precariousは,ラテン語のprecārius「祈りによって,あるいは単なる好意によって獲得される」から来ていると言われ,「不確かな」さらに「不安定な・危険な」を意味する。最も近いのはuncertain。他選択肢はそれぞれ,ア「静かな・穏やかな」,ウ「傷つけるような,有害な」,エ「繁栄している・豊かな」である。　(2)　dubiousは「疑わしい・怪しい」で関連語はdoubt。どちらもラテン語のdubium「疑う」を語源とすると言われる。最も近いのは「頼りにならない」のウ。他選択肢は,ア「正真正銘の」,イ「教育的な」,エ「時代錯誤の」の意。(3)　malnourishedは「栄養不良の」の意。mal-は「悪い」を意味する接頭辞で,norishは「～に栄養を与える」,norishedで「栄養が与えられた(状態)」を意味する。同じく「栄養不良の」を意味するunderfed(under：劣った＋fed：養われた)が適切。他選択肢はア「疲れ果てた」,イ「反抗的な・落ち着かない」,ウ「固い・頑固な」の意。(4)「器用な,巧妙な」の意。ラテン語のdexter「右腕・器用な」が語源と言われる。「腕の良い,技術的に巧みな」を意味するアが最も近い。他選択肢は,イ「知性のある」,ウ「無益な・無能な」,エ「厳格な・正確な」の意味である。　(5)　implicationはimply「ほのめかす・暗示する」の名詞形。political implicationで「政治的影響・政治的意味あい」。political influencesで同等の意味になる。他選択肢は,ア「要因」,ウ「言及・参照・関連性等」,エ「派生・起源」の意。

【4】(解答例)　歌と歌唱には外国語教育における大きな潜在力がある。学習者による受容の度合いは高く，技術面でも可能であり，語彙の獲得も強化される。受験生の学習戦略においても音楽ファイル聴取は語彙テストの知覚面で受験生の助けになるようだ。
〈解説〉英文の構造として，冒頭に結論，次いで結論を強化するための論拠，例示，最後に必要に応じて要旨についての考察，というパターンがあり，パラグラフ個々にもこの構造があてはまる場合が多い。従って趣旨を書く場合に最も重要なパートは問題文の冒頭から論拠説明の前までと考え，解答の語数制限など，与えられた条件に応じて論拠，例示などをも加えて書くようにする。

【5】(解答例)　(1)　しかしながら，グループワークは注意をもって適用されるべきである。単に生徒に対して，ある課題や企画について共同作業をせよ，と命じるだけでは，ためになるよりもむしろ苦痛をもたらすだろう。　(2)　このアプローチの利点は，建設的な相互依存，個々の責任，そしてチームワークと対人能力の適切な活用，といった特性を確保したうえでグループワークが構築された場合に，十分に実現される。　(3)　misanthropy，egoism等
〈解説〉(1)　howeverはコロン以前の文全体にかかる。コロン以下の文の主語は，tellingからcanの前までである。　(2)　such ～ as …「…するような～」という意味で，as以下はsuchの後の名詞を意味上の主語とした節になる。　(3)　altruismは「利他主義・利他的行為」という意味。反意語としては「利己主義」を意味するegoism，「人間嫌い」を意味するmisanthropyなどが考えられる。

【6】1　キ　　2　イ　　3　コ　　4　ア　　5　カ
〈解説〉1・2　パラグラフ冒頭に，食事でのカロリー摂取制限の恩恵について書かれており，空欄1・2を含む文はそれをサポートする内容と考えられので，“カロリー増→加齢に関連する病気による死亡の可能性増加”，または“カロリー減→可能性低下”という図式が予測できる。

「序数または割合を表す数値＋as likely to ～」で「～する傾向が…(率・割合)」を意味するので1にはlikelyが入り，「死亡の可能性が3分の1」となる。それに対応するのは「より低いカロリー摂取」なので2にはfewerがあてはまる。　3　逆接の接続詞等はなく，続く文も同主旨と考えられるので，「カロリー摂取制限(restricting calories)」は「寿命(life span)」を「伸ばす(増す)可能性がある」という展開が予測できる。よって，あてはまるのは(can) increaseとなる。　4　同じ第3文のカンマの後にはfor reasons「～の理由で」とあるが，1語では理由説明は不可能なので，for reasons still unclear「理由はいまだ不確かで」とするア。　5　Butは直前のreasons still unclearを受けており，「理由はいまだ不確かだが，最近の調査は～を示した。」という文脈になっている。improve survivalで「生存期間を延ばす」の意。primatesは「霊長類」である。

【7】1　エ　　2　ウ　　3　キ　　4　ア

〈解説〉1　看護師の仕事についてBが，“I feel strongly I'm helping sick people ～.”と答えているので，“It must be very awesome to help people ～.”と受け止めているエが適切。　2　I respect you.という答が返ってきているので，質問やアドバイスは除外する。この返答に対応する言葉として，「責任は重く，遅くまで働かなければなりません」とのウがあてはまる。また，1に入ると思われるエの最後部分「激しい仕事ではないのですか？」に対する答としても，「はい，仕事としては責任が重く～」と，適切に繋がる。　3　Aが「私なら，慣れるのにあなたより長くかかるでしょう」と自分の話を持ち出したのを受け止め，「ああ，以前病院の仕事に関心があると仰しゃっていたのを覚えています」と返している。　4　最後のBのせりふで，「病人がよくなって退院する時，その人達や家族が感謝を示してくれる。人を助けたという温かい感じを受ける」と言っているので，“What keeps you going?”「あなたが仕事を続けている理由となっているのは何ですか？」という質問だったと判断できる。また，Bの「価値があるとわかる」に対して，Aの「あなたは正しいと思う」という繋がりも適切。

【8】(正答例)　For children in the growing stage, healthy dietary life is essential to cultivate a healthy mind and body. The dietary education, in which students learn to evaluate the quality and safety of food by themselves on the basis of correct knowledge and information, is conducted at school with the cooperation of their families.

〈解説〉英作問題については，個々の表現力や語彙によりいろいろな解答が考えられるので，あまり難しく考える必要はない。注意すべきは，文法的な誤りで不完全な英語となり意味が伝わらないこと，次に，元の文に近い形にこだわり，英語として不自然になってしまうことである。また，単語単位，フレーズ単位で元の文と対応する表現を思いつかなくても，知っている語の組み合わせで内容が伝わるように応用を利かせることが必要であり，そのためには日頃から英語を書くことに慣れておくこと，豊かな表現を自分のものにするために英語を多読する事が大事である。

【中学校】

【1】(1)　①　区切り　②　情報　③　質問　④　聞き返す　⑤　概要　(2)　A　呼びかける／相づちをうつ／聞き直す／繰り返す　のうちから3つ　B　説明する／報告する／発表する／描写する　のうちから3つ　(3)　①　日本語　②　発音練習　③　継続　④　発音表記　⑤　学習負担　⑥　筆記体　⑦　運用度　⑧　活用

〈解説〉(1)(2)(3)　全て指導要領そのままの穴埋めであり，この形式の出題は非常に多い。何度も読み返し，覚えこんでおけば難なく解けるが，サッと読んで内容を理解しただけで臨むと，必ずしも常識の範囲で解ける問題ばかりではないので思わぬ失敗をする可能性もある。何を問われても答えられるよう，よく読みこんで記憶しておくことが必須である。

【高等学校】

【1】1　未知の語　　2　段落　　3　速読や精読

〈解説〉全て指導要領本文そのままの穴埋めである。何度も読み返し，覚えこんでおけば難なく解けるが，サッと読んで内容を理解しただけで臨むと，必ずしも常識の範囲で解ける問題ばかりではないため，そのままの語を思いつかない可能性もある。しっかりと読み込んでおきたい。

【2】1　情報　　2　的確　　3　基礎的な能力　　4　多様な観点　　5表現の方法　　6　伝える能力

〈解説〉大問9と同様に，学習指導要領本文の空欄補充問題である。

【3】(1)　現代の標準的な英語。　(2)　言語活動と効果的に関連付けて指導すること。　(3)　用語や用法の区別などの指導が中心とならないよう配慮すること。

〈解説〉各項目の一部を問題箇所として抜いた文を読み，元の文にあった要素を補充するかたちとなっているが，いずれにせよ暗記のレベルまで読み込んでおけば解ける問題と言えるだろう。

2011年度　実施問題

【中高共通】

【1】ただいまから，リスニングテストを始めます。受審者は問題用紙(その1)の問題1を見なさい。これから読む英文の内容に関して5つの質問をします。a，b，c，dの4つの答えの中から最も適切なものを1つ選び，記号で答えなさい。英文を2回読んだ後，それぞれの質問を2回，選択肢を1回読みます。聞きながらメモを取ってもかまいません。それでは始めます。

In 2008, Starbucks coffee chain received adverse publicity for leaving taps running in all of their 10,000 outlets. This was calculated to use more than 23 million liters of public water a day -- enough to supply the entire population of Namibia for the same time period. After complaints, Starbucks changed its policy.

But this incident highlights the stark contrast between water-rich and water-poor regions. Spain and Australia have been experiencing drought for several years, which may hint at longer-term climate change. Should drought conditions continue, these countries have the capital reserves to invest in major water transfer schemes and water purification plants to remove salt from water.

In the Horn of Africa, notably in Ethiopia, failure of the seasonal rainfall and rising food prices have caused increasingly severe problems, with over 6 million people now in need of emergency aid. Expensive technological fixes are not an option.

In the UK, a person uses, on average, 150 liters of water per day, although domestic use only accounts for about 20% of total water use. Just one tap running for three minutes uses as much water as one African person, living in a drought-stricken area, does in one day. Many people walk miles to collect water -- women in Africa and Asia commonly carry 20 kg of water on their heads, equal to some airlines' luggage allowance. It is a big difference from simply turning on a tap for access to safe, clean water.

Too much water is being taken out of the hydrological cycle. Global consumption of fresh water is doubling every 20 years, mainly to meet agricultural and industrial demands for water, with the global spread of technology and development. The human output could be added to the standard diagrams of the hydrological cycle as abstraction rates increase.

The study of water resources is now an essential part of school education. Those in charge of education have recognized that water supply and demand is a vital issue : one that is of great interest to geographers at all levels of study and one that will energize students of all ages. As global climates change, some regions will suffer increasing water scarcity and stress, and conflicts will occur between users, possibly leading to water wars. Developing students' understanding of this fundamental resource must be an essential element of the school curriculum.

Question

(1) Why did the coffee chain receive adverse publicity?

a. They were running 100,000 coffee outlets using water to make coffee.

b. They received complaints about the water, but they ignored them.

c. They wouldn't change the policy to leave taps running all day long.

d. They used a large amount of the public's water inefficiently.

(2) How can some countries with long droughts such as Australia and Spain deal with the problem?

a. By investing in technological fixes like water purification plants.

b. By using the hydrological cycle to purify used water.

c. By depending on other countries for emergency aid.

d. By decreasing the agricultural consumption of water.

(3) How much water does a person in the UK use, on average, per day?

a. 50 liters.

b. 100 liters.

c. 150 liters.

d. 200 liters.

(4) Why should water issues be an essential element of the school curriculum?

a. Because it allows people in the UK to access water by turning on the tap.

b. Because it may lead to very serious problems like conflicts and wars.

c. Because it makes all regions in the world suffer increasing water scarcity.

d. Because it is part of a controlled assessment for the course.

(5) According to the passage, which statement is true?

a. A possible solution for severe problems in Ethiopia is to build a major water transfer scheme.

b. Global consumption of fresh water is increasing mainly because of domestic use in each country.

c. Some Africans in drought-stricken areas use as little water as one tap running for 3 minutes per day.

d. The human output of water has already been in the standard diagram of the hydrological cycle.

これでリスニングテストを終わります。

(☆☆☆☆☆◎◎◎)

【2】次の各文の(　　)にあてはまる最も適切な語を，ア～エから1つ選び，記号で答えなさい。

(1) To justify his ruling, the judge (　　) a similar case in court.

ア prescribed　イ cited　ウ declared　エ referred

(2) His speech was too (　　); its meaning escaped me completely.

ア ambiguous　イ jocose　ウ succinct　エ concise

(3) Since his clothes were soaked, his story of falling into the creek seemed ( ).

ア incredible　イ absurd　ウ plausible　エ diminutive

(4) The restaurant itself was beautiful and the service excellent, but the food was ( ).

ア inedible　イ outstanding　ウ conclusive　エ filling

(5) Politicians are not coerced into taxing the public; they do it of their own ( ).

ア reputation　イ appraisal　ウ graft　エ volition

(6) Do not undertake a daily program of ( ) exercise such as jogging without first having a physical checkup.

ア light　イ futile　ウ strenuous　エ token

(7) Putting in a new kitchen is known to be a good way to ( ) the resale value of a house.

ア enroll　イ enliven　ウ enforce　エ enhance

(8) The dangers often ( ) in firefighting keep many people from pursuing that line of work.

ア confronted　イ trivialized　ウ equipped

エ initialized

(9) The school's plan to make wearing uniforms optional faced a ( ) of opposition from the PTA.

ア cavalcade　イ sprawl　ウ wall　エ acrimony

(10) Thank you very much for your recommendation. It was ( ) in my getting the job.

ア interruptive　イ influential　ウ futile　エ escapade

(☆☆☆◎◎◎)

【3】次の英文を読んで，その趣旨を120字以内の日本語で書きなさい。ただし，句読点も字数に入れること。

In the Japanese EFL context where students normally share the same first language and where varying levels of motivation can exist, it is very important that we both encourage the meaningful use of English between students, and importantly provide them with the conversational strategies and tools to be successful in doing so. Given the appropriate tools and task conditions, students will have greater opportunities to engage in more meaningful interactions.

EFL students need to develop a new view of oral classes that does not involve a solely academic approach to the study of English. Rather, one that engenders a spirit of experimental risk-taking in order to achieve the fluency and communication skills which most of our students expect from their investment in language learning.

(注) EFL : English as a Foreign Language

(☆☆☆◎◎◎)

【4】次の英文を読んで，(1)・(2)の問いに答えなさい。

(ア)Perhaps the most obvious thing to say about conversation is that it is a cooperative interaction；participants must agree on a topic, they must take turns developing it and their contributions must be intelligible, relevant and truthful. Our human disposition to participate in such interactions is no trivial thing to be taken for granted. (イ) Just as human evolution provided biological bases underlying and shaping linguistic structures and processes, so it also provided a biological basis for this kind of cooperative social behavior.

(1) 下線部(ア)を日本語に直しなさい。

(2) 下線部(イ)を日本語に直しなさい。

(☆☆☆◎◎◎)

【5】次の英文の(1)～(5)にあてはまる最も適切な語をア～クから選び，記号で答えなさい。ただし，同じ選択肢を2度使わないこと。

Morality in action is a constant work in progress, (1) we understand its meanings by the consequences of our actions. What makes moral action even more difficult is that (　2　) consequences of actions are not easy to predict — they are moving pieces within a larger mosaic of general human (　3　) and nature. Moral action means taking a transactional view of activity, understanding (　4　) we do on as many different levels as possible and understanding the consequences of our activity from as many different (　5　) as possible.

ア　when　　イ　which　　ウ　what
エ　where　　オ　experiences　　カ　possible
キ　experiments　　ク　perspectives

(☆☆☆◎◎◎)

【6】次の対話文の(　1　)～(　4　)にあてはまる最も適切な英文を，ア～キから選び，記号で答えなさい。ただし，同じ選択肢を2度使わないこと。

A : Have you finished writing a report about global warming? The deadline is today.

B : (　1　)

A : Did you check some meteorological agency sites?

B : I've checked out... or rather visited several sites for that. They were very useful.

A : (　2　)

B : I know it. The same goes for radio, television, and other information tools.

A : In any event, we should pay closer attention to the information especially on the Internet.

B : Any information tool may present many problems unless we use it wisely.

A : Books and encyclopedias help us a great deal. I always use them when we examine something.

B : (　3　)

A : (　4　)

B : I don't deny it. Anyway, the most important thing is to use the many kinds of information tools wisely.

ア　No, I didn't do that, because I know many websites have much uncertain information on them.

イ　I agree with your opinions. Using the Internet is difficult.

ウ　However, some can be misleading because there is wrong and correct information on the same sites.

エ　That's true, but reading books captivates our curiosity. It's different from other learning methods.

オ　I've already checked some meteorological agency sites. They are very convenient.

カ　Yes. I found a great deal of information about it on the web. It helped me a lot.

キ　I'm afraid you are old-fashioned. We can get much information very easily on the web.

(☆☆◎◎◎)

【7】次の日本文を英語に直しなさい。

これからの学校には，産業構造・就業構造の変化や社会の要請に適切に対応し，生徒が，将来の基盤を築き，自立して生きていくことができるように，発達段階をふまえたキャリア教育・職業教育を推進することが求められています。

(☆☆☆☆◎◎◎)

【中学校】

【1】新中学校学習指導要領(平成20年3月告示)「外国語」「第2　各言語の目標及び内容等」「英語」「2　内容」について，次の(1)・(2)の問いに答えなさい。

(1)　次の文は「(1)　言語活動　エ　書くこと」である。(　①　)～(　⑤　)に当てはまる語句を書きなさい。

(ア)　(　①　)を識別し，語と語の区切りなどに注意して正しく書くこと。

(イ)　(　②　)　などに注意して正しく文を書くこと。

(ウ)　聞いたり読んだりしたことについてメモをとったり，感想，賛否や(　③　)を書いたりなどすること。

(エ)　身近な場面における出来事や(　④　)などについて，自分の考えや気持ちなどを書くこと。

(オ)　自分の考えや気持ちなどが読み手に正しく伝わるように，(　⑤　)などに注意して文章を書くこと。

(2)　次の(a)・(b)の問いに答えなさい。

(a)「(2)言語活動の取扱い」について，(A)・(B)のいずれか1つを選び，その記号を記入し，問いに答えなさい。

(A)　「ア(ウ)[言語の使用場面の例]　a　特有の表現がよく使われる場面」として7つ示されている中から3つ選び，書きなさい。

(B)　「ア(ウ)[言語の働きの例]　d　考えや意図を伝える」として7つ示されている中から3つ選び，書きなさい。

(b)　次の文章は「(4)言語材料の取扱い」についての事項である。(　①　)～(　⑧　)に当てはまる語句を書きなさい。

ア　(　①　)と綴りとを関連付けて指導すること。

イ　文法については，(　②　)を支えるものであることを踏まえ，(　③　)と効果的に関連付けて指導すること。

ウ　(3)のエの文法事項の取り扱いについては，(　④　)や(　⑤　)の区別などの指導が中心とならないよう配慮し，実際に(　⑥　)できるように指導すること。また，(　⑦　)や(　⑧　)関係などにおける日本語との違いに留意して指導すること。

(☆☆☆☆◎◎◎◎)

【高等学校】

【1】次の英文は，現行高等学校学習指導要領「外国語」の「第1款　目標」を表している。(　1　)～(　5　)に入る適切な語を英語で書きなさい。

To develop students' (　1　) communication abilities such as understanding information and the speaker's or writer's (　2　), and expressing their own ideas, (　3　) the understanding of language and culture, and (　4　) a positive (　5　) toward communication through foreign languages.

(☆☆☆☆◎◎◎◎◎)

【2】現行高等学校学習指導要領「外国語」「第6　ライティング」の後には，[言語の使用場面の例]が4つ示されている。「創作的なコミュニケーションの場面」以外の3つの場面を答えなさい。

(☆☆☆☆☆◎◎◎◎)

【3】新高等学校学習指導要領(平成21年3月告示)「外国語」の「第3款　英語に関する各科目に共通する内容等　4」について(　1　)～(　4　)にあてはまる語句を書きなさい。

英語に関する各科目については，その特質にかんがみ，生徒が(　1　)を充実するとともに，授業を実際の(　2　)とするため，授業は(　3　)を基本とする。その際，生徒の(　4　)を用いるよう十分配慮するものとする。

(☆☆☆☆◎◎◎◎◎)

解答・解説

【中高共通】

【1】(1)　d　(2)　a　(3)　c　(4)　b　(5)　c

〈解説〉リスニングでは，質問文の冒頭にある5W1Hに気をつけておくことが重要である。(1)　第1段落1文目 "for leaving taps running in all of their 10,000 outlets"から「10,000ある彼らの支店の全てで蛇口を開けっぱなしにしていたために」とある。このことから判断したい。

(2)　第2段落"Should drought conditions continue,～"の1文にその内容が書いてある。ちなみにこの文の訳は「万一干ばつが続くようなら，これらの国々は，主要な水移転計画と水から塩分を取り除くための水浄化プラントに投資する(invest in)ための政府準備金(the capital reserves)を持っている」である。"Should drought conditions continue,"の箇所は倒置形になっており，"If drought conditions should continue～"と同義である。(3)　第4段落1文目に記述がある。　(4)　最終段落の"As global climates change"から始まる文に書いてある。　(5)　cと同内容の記述は第4段落の"Just one～"の1文にある。エチオピアにおける解決方法については本文で記述がないのでaは不適である。bは第5段落に水消費量の増加は農業と工業のせいだとあるので不適である。dは第5段落の最後の1文に「(水の)抽出率(＝abstraction rates)が増加すれば，人間の採水量(＝output)も水循環の標準図に加えられるだろう」とあり，まだ加えられていないことがわかるので不適である。

【2】(1)　イ　(2)　ア　(3)　ウ　(4)　ア　(5)　エ　(6)　ウ　(7)　エ　(8)　ア　(9)　ウ　(10)　イ

〈解説〉(1)　citeは「引用する」である。訳：彼の裁定(ruling)を証明するために，裁判官は法廷における似た事例を引用した。

(2)　ambiguousは「あいまいな」であり，"X escape me"は「Xが私の記憶にとまらない」という意味である。訳：彼のスピーチはあいまいすぎた。意味が全く記憶にとまらなかった。　(3)　plausibleは「もっともらしい」である。訳：彼の服はずぶ濡れだったので，小川に落ちたという彼の話はもっともらしかった。　(4)　inedibleは「食用に適さない，食べられない」である。訳：レストラン自体は美しく，サービスも素晴らしかったが，食べ物はひどかった。　(5)　"of one's volition"は「～の意志で」という意味である。"be coerced into ～ing"は「無理に～させられる」の意味。訳：政治家は無理に人に税を課しているのではない。むしろ彼らの意志でそうしているのだ。　(6)　strenuousは「非常に活発な，熱心な」である。訳：はじめに身体の検査を受けずに，ジョギングのような活発な運動を日常的に始めてはいけない。

(7)　enhanceは「(価値など)を高める」である。訳：新しいキッチンを入れることは，家の再販売価値を高める良い方法だと知られている。

(8)　"be confronted"は「(受身形で)たちはだかる」である。"often～firefighting"はdangersを後置修飾している。"keep O from ～ing"で「Oに～させない，Oが～できないようにする」という意味である。訳：消防活動でしばしば直面する危険のために，多くの人がその仕事に就くことをやめてしまう。　(9)　wallは「壁，障害」の意味である。訳：制服を着用することを選択制にしようという学校の計画は，PTAの反対という壁に直面した。　(10)　influentialは「影響のある，感化を及ぼすような」の意味である。訳：勧告ありがとうございました。仕事を得るのに参考になりました。

【3】正答例：日本の英語教育はEFLの環境にあり，生徒に意味のあるやりとりをさせるためには，生徒間の意味のある英語使用を奨励し，会話術や会話表現を教えることが重要である。また，流暢さやコミュニケーション術の習得には，失敗を恐れない精神の育成が必要である。(120字)

〈解説〉文章が短い割に字数は多いので，どの内容を削除するか考える。また，段落が2つあるので，それぞれを1文でまとめるつもりで答えるようにする。1段落目は，EFL環境について説明した"where students ～

can exist"や"Given the appropriate ～."の1文は必ずしも説明に必要な内容ではないので削除する。2段落目は"a new view"がどういうものかが"Rather, one that～."の1文に書かれているので，そちらの文を中心に内容をまとめればよい。

【4】(1)　正答例：おそらく会話について最も明白に言えることは，会話は協力的な相互活動であるということであろう。つまり，会話をしている者は，その話題について納得し，交互にその話題を発展させなければならない。また，その発言は明瞭で，関連性のある，誠実なものでなくてはならない。　(2)　正答例：人間は，進化によって，言語構造や言語処理能力の形成につながる生物学的基盤を得たが，まさにそれと同様に，このような協調的な社会的行動のための生物学的基盤も得たのだ。

〈解説〉(1)　設問となっている1文の構造としては，"the most obvious thing"が"it is a cooperative interaction"であるとし，"cooperative interaction"を「;」以下でさらに具体的に述べている。「;」以下には三箇所でmustが含まれており，それぞれが並列的に列挙されていることが分かる。"thing(s) to say about～"は「～について言えること」である。cooperativeは「協力的な」，"agree on～"は「～に賛成する」で，"take turns ～ing"は「順番に～する」である。contributionは「発言」(←「会話における貢献」から転じて)，intelligibleは「理解できる，明瞭な」，relevantは「関連のある」，truthfulは「誠実な，事実に即した」という意味である。　(2)　まず，Just as SV, so S'V'が，「ちょうどSVであるように，S'V'である」という意味であることに気付くことが重要である。human evolutionは「人間の進化」，"biological base(s)"は「生物学的基盤」という意味であり，直後の"underlying～processes"はこの"biological base(s)"を修飾する形容詞句である。underlieは「～の基礎となる」，shape(動詞)は「～を形成する」という意味で，linguistic structures and processesは「言語的構造と過程」という意味である。下線部(イ)に含まれるitは，前出の"human evolution"のことである。

【5】(1)　エ　(2)　カ　(3)　オ　(4)　ウ　(5)　ク

〈解説〉内容がやや抽象的だが，文法的に入りうる語を見極め，意味との整合性も考えながら答えるとよいだろう。(1)のwhereは，workを先行詞とする関係副詞である。"a constant work in progress, where we～."は，"a constant work in progress, and there we～."と置き換えられ，ここでのthereは"a constant work"のことを指している。また，(4)のwhatは関係代名詞で，先行詞を含んで「もの，こと」と訳すことが出来るものである。例えば，"That is what I would like to know."(それが，私の知りたいことです。)のように用いられる。全文訳は以下の通りである。「行動における道徳性は進歩途中の継続的な行いであり，その行いの中で(＝where)我々は行動の結果によりその意味を理解する。道徳的行動をさらに難しくするものは，行動により起こりうる(＝possible)結果を予想するのは容易ではないということ―つまり，一般的な人間の経験や性質から成る，より大きな集合(＝mosaic)の中で動く部分体(＝moving pieces)だということである。道徳的行動とは，行動を相互交流とみなし，できるだけ多くの異なったレベルにおいて私たちのすること(＝what we do)を理解し，そしてできるだけ多くの異なった視点(＝perspectives)から行動の結果について理解することを意味する。」

【6】(1)　カ　(2)　ウ　(3)　キ　(4)　エ

〈解説〉(1)は，Aが「地球温暖化についてのレポート書き終えた？」と聞いているので，「うん。ウェブでたくさん情報を見つけたんだ。」と答えているカが正解。(2)は，空欄2に対する応答として"The same goes for radio, television, and other information tools"(同じことがラジオ，テレビや他の情報ツールにも当てはまる)とあることから，選択肢を検討すればよい。選択肢ウのsomeは"some websites"のことで，Aはいくつかのウェブサイトは誤解を招きやすい(misleading)と注意を促しており，このことが"The same"であるとわかる。(3)，(4)については，Aの"Books and encyclopedias～."の発言から，情報源としての本や百科事典の利点についての話に話題が移っている。これを念頭に置き，対話として成立する2つの発言を選択肢から選びだす。old-fashionedは「時代遅れ」，captivateは「魅了する」，curiosityは「好奇心」という意味である。

【７】正答例：From now on, schools will be required to handle the changes in the industrial and employment structure as well as the demands in society and promote career education and vocational education based on the educational stages of development, to support students to build the foundation for their future and live independently.

〈解説〉以下では，正答例について文構造をわかりやすくするために句切れやかっこを入れてある。"From now on, schools will be required / to handle the changes in the industrial and employment structure (as well as the demands in society) / and promote career education and vocational education (based on the educational stages of development),/ to support students to build the foundation for their future / and live independently."「～にはすることが求められている」は"S will be required to V"で表す。ここでSは学校(schools)にあたるが，日本文から学校がすべきことは「対応する(＝handle)」「推進する(＝promote)」の2つである。一方で「生徒が～」に続く述語は「築く(＝build)」と「生きていく(＝live)」の2つである。産業・就業構造は"industrial and employment structure"で，キャリア教育・職業教育は"career education and vocational education"で表す。解答例では"as well as"を用いているが，andでつないでも問題ない。また，"to support～"の部分は"so that S can V"を用いて「SがVできるように」としてもよい。

【中学校】

【1】(1) ① 文字や符号 ② 語と語のつながり ③ その理由 ④ 体験したこと ⑤ 文と文のつながり (2) (a) 選択問題A あいさつ，自己紹介，電話での応答，買物，道案内，旅行，食事のうちから3つ 選択問題B 申し出る，約束する，意見を言う，賛成する，反対する，承諾する，断るのうちから3つ (b) ① 発音 ② コミュニケーション ③ 言語活動 ④ 用語 ⑤ 用法 ⑥ 活用 ⑦ 語順 ⑧ 修飾

〈解説〉(1) ここは全国的に頻出の箇所である。「聞くこと」「話すこと」「読むこと」「書くこと」のそれぞれについて5つの目標が掲げられており，概要をつかんでおくことが大切である。前指導要領から変更されている点について把握しておく必要があるが，詳細については指導要領の解説を参照のこと。 (2) (a) どちらも内容を覚えていないと答えづらい問題である。自分がよく覚えているほうを選んで解答するしかない。 (b) 全国的にこの「言語材料の取り扱い」は出題頻度がやや高めである。綴りを無視した音だけの指導や文法の解説に偏った指導，母語だけを用いた指導など，指導法が極端にならないよう注意を喚起する内容が中心となる。

【高等学校】

【1】(1) practical (2) intentions (3) deepening (4) fostering (5) attitude

〈解説〉新学習指導要領実施までまだ期間があるため，現行の指導要領についても出題される可能性を考えておかなければならない。日本語版では「外国語を通じて，言語や文化に対する理解を深め，積極的にコミュニケーションを図ろうとする態度の育成を図り，情報や相手の意向などを理解したり自分の考えなどを表現したりする実践的コミュニケーション能力を養う。」となっている(下線部は空欄箇所)。特に高校の採用試験において，英訳版について出題される傾向が高い。「第1款目標」は頻出箇所だが，このような記述式だと文言まで覚えていない

と解答しづらい。

【2】・個人的なコミュニケーションの場面・グループにおけるコミュニケーションの場面・多くの人を対象にしたコミュニケーションの場面

〈解説〉同年の中学校教員採用試験の問題でも言語の使用場面について記述する問題が出されている。この箇所を意識して熟読していなかった人にとっては，非常に解答が難しい問題である。こういった問題が出題されやすいようなので，できるだけ指導要領の文言を正確に記憶する必要がある。各個人にあった覚え方でできるだけ覚えてから試験に臨みたい。

【3】(1)　英語に触れる機会　　(2)　コミュニケーションの場面
(3)　英語で行うこと　　(4)　理解の程度に応じた英語

〈解説〉「原則英語で授業を行うこと」としたのは，新学習指導要領の変更点の目玉の1つである。そのためこの箇所は今後しばらく出題される可能性が非常に高い。高校は科目名も大幅に改訂されたが，ここに書いてある内容は各科目に共通する重要な内容である。是非覚えておきたい。

2010年度　実施問題

【中高共通】

【1】[リスニングテスト]

ただいまから，リスニングテストをはじめます。受審者は問題用紙(その1)の問題1を見なさい。これから読む英文の内容に関して5つの質問をします。それぞれの質問の後に読まれるa，b，c，dの4つの選択肢の中から，答えとして最も適切なものを1つ選び，記号で答えなさい。英文と質問，選択肢は，全体を通して2回読みます。聞きながらメモを取ってもかまいません。それでは始めます。

After working for years as an engineer in New York, Lee Harrison was ready for early retirement at age 49. On his modest pension and savings, such a dream would have been impossible in Manhattan. So after reading various guides on retiring to Latin Arnerica, Harrison moved to Ecuador, where the good life promised to cost a fraction of his former salary.

Harrison said he was enchanted by the country's pleasant climate and friendly residents. He recently paid 34,000 dollars for a three-bedroom house alongside a river in a picturesque village in the south of the country. The spacious home is very different from his small apartment in Manhattan, and he pays less than 10 dollars a year in property taxes. But not everything in Harrison's adopted home is cheaper. Electricity, for example, costs twice as much: 23 cents per kilowatt hour, compared with 12 cents in New York City. And although property taxes are low, so is infrastructure maintenance: roads and sidewalks, he said, are in poor repair.

With pensions decreasing and life expectancies growing, retirees like Harrison around the world are doing the math and concluding that moving to a lower-cost location will increase the chances of their money lasting longer than they do. Americans tend to migrate to Mexico and to Central and South America, where beachfront properties can be purchased for a small amount of the cost of similar residences in Florida and California. Many countries, like Costa Rica, now offer tax breaks to foreigners who decide to retire there.

A key consideration when measuring quality-of-life expectations against available income is health care. Costs might be covered by health insurance agreements between countries, although --- as Americans know -- not all national health care systems are free.

Even if many seniors wind up living luxuriously on less money, some people just don't settle well in a foreign culture. Language may be a issue. Unmet expectations are also a risk. To avoid the disappointment --- and the expense --- of a bad move, retirees are recommended to spend at least six months in the new location before committing.

Question

(1) According to the passage, which statement is true about Harrison?

(a) Harrison retired from his engineering job after he had worked for 49 years.

(b) Harrison thought it too early to retire when he reached the age of 49.

(c) Harrison worked as an engineer but felt ready to retire at 49 years old.

(d) Harrison wanted to stop working at 49 years old because he didn't like his job.

(2) Why did Harrison decide to move in to Ecuador?

(a) Because he loved the country's pleasant climate and friendly residents.

(b) Because he got a three-bedroom house for 200,000 dollars.

(c) Because he can rent a large house for less than ten dollars a year.

(d) Because infrastructure maintenance there are in good situation.

(3) How much costs more electricity in Ecuador than in New York city?

(a) Half as much.

(b) Twice as much.

(c) Three times as much.

(d) About the same.

(4) Why do Americans tend to migrate to Latin America?

(a) Because both pensions and life expectancies are increasing there.

(b) Because beachfront properties there are cheaper than in America.

(c) Because moving to a higher-cost location will make their money last longer.

(d) Because all the countries there offer tax breaks to foreigners who retire there.

(5) According to the passage, which statement is true?

(a) Seniors can't settle in foreign countries when they have a language issue.

(b) Seniors all can settle well in foreign countries on less money.

(c) Seniors can live comfortably because all national health care systems are free.

(d) Seniors should live in the new locations at least half a year before settling there.

[REPEAT]

これでリスニングテストを終わります。

(☆☆☆◎◎◎)

【2】次の各文の(　　　)にあてはまる最も適切な語を，ア～エから1つ選び，記号で答えなさい。

(1) Alan waited (　　　) for his turn, relaxing in an easy chair with his eyes closed.

ア impatiently　イ calmly　ウ warily　エ tensely

(2) He was the chief (　　　) of his uncle's will. After taxes, he was left with an inheritance of three million dollars.

ア beneficiary　イ pensioner　ウ exemption

エ contestant

(3) Joan was so abrupt with clients that her supervisor eventually put a letter

in her file citing her (　　　).

ア　enthusiasm　　イ　diligence　　ウ　patience　　エ　rudeness

(4)　After the chemical spill, we had to drink bottled water; the well water was no longer (　　　).

ア　potable　　イ　tenable　　ウ　viable　　エ　risible

(5)　The celebrity sued the magazine, claiming that the article (　　　) his character.

ア　implicated　　イ　deplored　　ウ　defamed

エ　whitewashed

(6)　Algebra I is a (　　　) for Algebra Ⅱ; it must be taken first.

ア　precursor　　イ　prerequisite　　ウ　sinecure　　エ　substitute

(7)　Fountains are (　　　) in Rome; you can hardly turn a corner without spotting one.

ア　vicarious　　イ　meticulous　　ウ　ubiquitous　　エ　insidious

(8)　Professor Martin spent his entire career as a teacher trying to (　　　) his students to appreciate the beauty of poetry.

ア　encourage　　イ　disrupt　　ウ　repeal　　エ　define

(9)　The navy scoured the area for over a month, but the (　　　) search turned up no clues.

ア　temporary　　イ　fruitful　　ウ　painstaking　　エ　present

(10)　I could not bear the woodpecker's (　　　) rhythm; the endless choppy beat aggravated my headache.

ア　melodic　　イ　crescendo　　ウ　harmonic　　エ　staccato

(☆☆☆☆◎◎◎)

【3】次の英文を読んで，その趣旨を120字以内の日本語で書きなさい。ただし，句読点も字数に入れること。

Writing has always been regarded as an important skill in the teaching and learning English as a foreign language (EFL). On the other hand, it stimulates thinking, compels students to concentrate and organize their ideas, and cultivates their ability to summarize, analyze, and criticize. On the other hand, it reinforces learning in, thinking in, and reflecting on the English language. Nevertheless, students find composing in English difficult because the writing process demands that they utilize many cognitive and linguistic strategies of which they are uncertain. Many students complain that they lack ideas and cannot think of anything interesting or significant enough to write. While most EFL teachers are often perplexed by these problems in their writing classes, they cannot find an efficient way to awaken students' imagination and set their minds working. At best, some teachers only adopt a product-based approach, focusing on exemplifying contrast and comparison, description, classification, and so on. Many teachers are not aware of the role of the brainstorming strategy or the value of strategy training in promoting students' learning skills.

(☆☆☆◎◎◎)

【4】次の英文を読んで，(1)・(2)の問いに答えなさい。

(ア) The Communicative Approach, which took hold in the 1980s and is currently dominant in language teaching, holds that since the primary purpose of language is communication, using language to communicate should be central in all classroom language instruction. This focus on language as communication brings renewed urgency to the teaching of pronunciation, since both empirical and anecdotal evidence indicates that there is a threshold level of pronunciation for non-native speakers of English; (イ) if they fall below, this threshold level, they will have oral communication problems no matter how excellent and extensive their control of English grammar and vocabulary might be.

(1) 下線部(ア)を日本語に直しなさい。

(2) 下線部(イ)をtheyの内容を明らかにして，日本語に直しなさい。

(☆☆☆◎◎◎)

【5】次の英文の(　1　)〜(　5　)にあてはまる最も適切な語句をア〜クから選び，記号で答えなさい。ただし，同じ語句は1回しか使えないものとする。なお，選択肢は文頭にくる語句も小文字にしてある。

Native speakers of English are a (　1　); there are far more non-native speakers in the world. (　2　), native speakers' standard or 'correct' English, in terms of its grammar and phonology, is not always useful or even appropriate in international contexts. (　3　), the norms for ENL (English as a Native Language) remain dominant, most notably for the assessment of oral proficiency, (　4　) global changes in the use of the language. Yet it is a major (　5　) in the use of international oral tests that the proficiency of non-native speakers is measured against unrealistic and irrelevant standards.

ア　despite　　イ　efficiency　　ウ　deficiency
エ　majority　　オ　minority　　カ　however
キ　in addition　　ク　due to

(☆☆☆◎◎◎)

【6】次の対話文の(　1　)〜(　5　)にあてはまる最も適切な英文を，ア〜クから選び，記号で答えなさい。ただし，同じ選択肢を2回使わないこと。

A:　I'm looking forward to this three-day weekend.
B:　Do you have any plans for it?
A:　Not concretely, but I want to get out of the city. Do you know some good places?
B:　(　　1　　)
A:　(　　2　　)
B:　Oh, yes it can. I'm sure a lot of people will try to leave the city this weekend.
A:　(　　3　　)
B:　(　　4　　)
A:　(　　5　　)

B： Libraries make a good retreat for me. To read books in a quiet place always refreshes me.

A： I didn't know you like reading so much.

ア It can't be that bad. イ How about going camping with your family? It will be fair this weekend. ウ Even so, wouldn't it be wonderful to visit a place I've never been to, just for a day? エ I think it's nice to visit some villages in the mountains full of fresh air. オ Not on this weekend. I would stay in the city if I were you. カ You should not leave the city. It'll probably be busy on the expressway. キ Well, do you know some good places in the city? ク That sounds nice. Can you tell me some good places to visit?

(☆☆☆◎◎◎)

【7】次の日本文を英語に直しなさい。

文化は，国民の心に活力を与え，生きる喜びをもたらし，潤いのある心豊かな生活を実現していく上で不可欠なものである。さらに，文化は経済活動において新たな需要や高い付加価値を生み出しており，文化と経済は密接に関連しあっていると考えられている。

(☆☆☆☆◎◎◎)

【中学校】

【1】新中学校学習指導要領(平成20年3月告示)「外国語」の内容について，次の(1)・(2)に答えなさい。

(1) 次の文は「第2　各言語の目標及び内容等　英語　1　目標」について述べたものである。(　①　)～(　④　)に当てはまる語句を書きなさい。

(1)　初歩的な英語を聞いて(　①　)などを理解できるようにする。

(2)　初歩的な英語を用いて(　②　)などを話すことができるようにする。

(3)　英語を読むことに慣れ親しみ，初歩的な英語を読んで(　③　)などを理解できるようにする。

(4)　英語で書くことに慣れ親しみ，初歩的な英語を用いて(　④　)などを書くことができるようにする。

(2)　「第2　各言語の目標及び内容等　英語　2　内容　(2)言語活動の取扱い」について，次の(a)・(b)の問いに答えなさい。

(a)　(A)・(B)のどちらか1つを選び，その記号を記入し，問いに答えなさい。

(A)　「[言語の使用場面の例]　b　生徒の身近な暮らしにかかわる場面」として3つ示されている中から2つ選び，書きなさい。

(B)　「[言語の働きの例]　e　相手の行動を促す」として3つ示されている中から2つ選び，書きなさい。

(b)　次の文章は各学年の指導に当たっての配慮事項である。(　①　)～(　⑧　)に当てはまる語句を書きなさい。

(ア)　第1学年における言語活動

小学校における外国語活動を通じて(　①　)を中心としたコミュニケーションに対する積極的な態度などの(　②　)が育成されることを踏まえ，身近な言語の使用場面や言語の働きに配慮した言語活動を行わせること。その際，(　③　)や身の回りの出来事などの中から(　④　)を用いてコミュニケーションを図れるような話題を取り上げること。

(イ)　第2学年における言語活動

第1学年の学習を基礎として，言語の使用場面や言語の働きを更に広げた言語活動を行わせること。その際，第1学年における学習内容を(　⑤　)指導し(　⑥　)を図るとともに，(　⑦　)を伝えたり，(　⑧　)について判断したりした内容などの中からコミュニケーションを図れるような話題を取り上げること。

(☆☆☆◎◎◎)

【高等学校】

【1】次の英文のうち，現行高等学校学習指導要領に示されている，「高等学校で新たに指導される文型や文法事項」を含むものはどれか。ア～コから3つ選び，記号で答えなさい。

ア　It is important for you to get up early in the morning.

イ　I want him to come to my house to join the meeting.

ウ　Homework must be done every day at home.

エ　Mr. Green doesn't know how to drive a car.

オ　He told me that he was interested in Japan and its culture.

カ　Do you know the name of the flower Judy has?

キ　Have you ever seen him get angry?

ク　Mike looked happy when he met one of his old friends.

ケ　Talking with Jiro made me happy.

コ　There are many books written in English in this library.

(☆☆☆◎◎◎)

【2】次のア～ウの文は，現行高等学校学習指導要領「外国語」の「第3款　各科目にわたる指導計画の作成と内容の取扱い」2の(1)の中で述べられている，教材について留意すべき3つの観点である。(　1　)～(　6　)に入る適切な語句を書きなさい。

ア　多様なものの見方や考え方を理解し，公正な(　1　)を養い豊かな(　2　)を育てるのに役立つこと。

イ　世界や我が国の生活や文化についての理解を深めるとともに，(　3　)や文化に対する関心を高め，これらを(　4　)態度を育てるのに役立つこと。

ウ　広い視野から(　5　)を深め，国際社会に生きる日本人としての自覚を高めるとともに，(　6　)の精神を養うのに役立つこと。

(☆☆☆◎◎◎)

【3】現行高等学校指導要領「外国語」について，次の(A)・(B)のどちらかを選び，問いに答えなさい。

(A)　「英語Ⅰ」の「2　内容」「(1)　言語活動」には，生徒が情報や考えなどの受け手や送り手になるように，具体的な言語の使用場面を設定した上で行う4つのコミュニケーション活動が示されている。そのうちの3つを書きなさい。

(B)　「オーラル・コミュニケーションⅠ」の「2　内容」「(1)　言語活動」には，生徒が情報や考えなどの受け手や送り手になるように，具体的な言語の使用場面を設定した上で行う4つのコミュニケーション活動が示されている。そのうちの3つを書きなさい。

(☆☆☆◎◎◎)

解答・解説

【中高共通】

【1】(1)　c　(2)　a　(3)　b　(4)　b　(5)　d

〈解説〉(1)　第1段落第1文参照。　(2)　第2段落第1文参照。　(3)　第2段落最後から2文目参照。　(4)　第3段落最後から2文目参照。　(5)　最終段落最終文参照。

【2】(1)　イ　(2)　ア　(3)　エ　(4)　ア　(5)　ウ　(6)　イ　(7)　ウ　(8)　ア　(9)　ウ　(10)　エ

〈解説〉(1)　ア「待ちきれずに」　イ「静かに」　ウ「用心して」　エ「張り詰めた様子で」　(2)　ア「受益者」　イ「年金受給者」　ウ「免除」　エ「出場者」　(3)　ア「熱中」　イ「勤勉」　ウ「忍

耐」 エ「無礼」 (4) ア「飲料に適した」 イ「持ちこたえられる」 ウ「実行可能な」 エ「笑える」 (5) ア「～を(犯罪などに)巻き込む」 イ「～を残念に思う」 ウ「中傷する」 エ「～をごまかす」 (6) ア「先駆者」 イ「前もって［あらかじめ］必要な」 ウ「閑職」 エ「代わりの人［物］，代用品」 (7) ア「身代わりの」 イ「極めて注意深い」 ウ「遍在する」 エ「こっそりたくらまれた」 (8) ア「勇気づける」 イ「～を分裂させる」 ウ「無効にする」 エ「定義する」 (9) ア「一時的な」 イ「有意義な」 ウ「骨が折れる」 エ「現在の」 (10) ア「メロディー［旋律］で構成される」 イ「クレッシェンド」 ウ「調和した」 エ「スタッカート奏法」

【3】(正答例) ライティングは英語の指導や学習においてだけでなく，思考力や分析力など，生徒の多くの能力を育てるのに重要である。学習者がライティングに困難を感じている現状を踏まえ，指導者は，それを打開する効果的な方策について考えなければならない。
〈解説〉解答参照。

【4】(1) (正答例) 1980年代に提唱され，現在言語教育の主流となっているコミュニカティブアプローチとは，言語の主たる目的は意思伝達であることから，意思伝達のために言語を使うことが全ての語学の授業の中心となるべきである，という考え方である。 (2) (正答例) もし英語を母国語としない人々が，英語の発音において初歩のレベルを下回ることになれば，彼らの英語の文法力や語彙力がどれほど卓越し，豊富であったとしても，口頭での意思伝達に困難が生じるであろう。
〈解説〉解答参照。

【5】(1)　オ　(2)　キ　(3)　カ　(4)　ア　(5)　ウ

〈解説〉(1)　; there ～ world. を参照　(2)　native ～ contexts. は英語の劣勢点を述べている。(3)　dominant, ～ proficiency, は英語の優勢点を述べている。(4)　despite ～「～にもかかわらず」　(5)　a ～ tests ＝同格の that 以降に述べられた内容

【6】(1)　カ　(2)　ア　(3)　ウ　(4)　オ　(5)　キ

〈解説〉(1)　カのleave the city はget out of the city の言い換えである。

(2)　アの It は It'll ～ expressway. で述べられた状況を指す。

(3)　ウのso は a ～ weekend. で述べられた状況を指す。(4)　オのNot on this weekend. はウの問いかけに否定的に答えたものではない。

(5)　次のBの発言で Libraries と提案している。

【7】(正答例)　Culture is indispensable for inspiring people, bringing joy to their lives, and allowing them to lead a rich and fulfilling life. Moreover, in the field of economic activities, culture creates new demand and high added value, so that it is considered to have close relevance to economy.

〈解説〉解答参照。

【中学校】

【1】(1)　①　話し手の意向　②　自分の考え　③　書き手の意向　④　自分の考え　(2)の(a)　(A)　家庭での生活・学校での学習や活動・地域の行事　の3つから2つ　(B)　質問する・依頼する・招待する　の3つから2つ　(2)の(b)　①　音声面　②　一定の素地　③　自分の気持ち　④　簡単な表現　⑤　繰り返して　⑥　定着　⑦　事実関係　⑧　物事

〈解説〉解答参照。

【高等学校】

【1】ウ　オ　キ

〈解説〉高等学校学習指導要領　第8節　外国語　第2款　第6　ライティング「[英語言語材料]　ア　文型　(ウ)主語＋動詞＋間接目的語＋直接目的語の文型のうち，直接目的語がhowなど＋to不定詞，whatなど及びthatで始まる節並びにif又はwhetherで始まる節である場合　(エ)主語＋動詞＋目的語＋補語の文型のうち，補語が現在分詞，過去分詞及び原形不定詞である場合　イ　文法事項　(カ)受け身のうち，助動詞＋受け身のもの」

【2】(1)　判断力　(2)　心情　(3)　言語　(4)　尊重する
(5)　国際理解　(6)　国際協調

〈解説〉解答参照。

【3】(A)　英語を聞いて，情報や話し手の意向などを理解したり，概要や要点をとらえたりする。　英語を読んで，情報や書き手の意向などを理解したり，概要や要点をとらえたりする。　聞いたり読んだりして得た情報や自分の考えなどについて，話し合ったり意見の交換をしたりする。　聞いたり読んだりして得た情報や自分の考えなどについて，整理して書く。　(B)　英語を聞いてその内容を理解するとともに，場面や目的に応じて適切に反応する。　関心のあることについて相手に質問したり，相手の質問に答えたりする。　情報や考えなどを，場面や目的に応じて適切に伝える。　聞いたり読んだりして得た情報や自分の考えなどをまとめ，発表する。また，発表されたものを理解する。

〈解説〉解答参照。

2009年度　実施問題

【中高共通】

【1】[リスニングテスト]

問題文及び5つの質問を聞き，各質問の後に読まれるa～dの4つの選択肢の中からその質問に対する答えとして最も適切なものを1つ選び，記号で答えなさい。

ただいまから，リスニングテストをはじめます。受審者は問題用紙(その1)の問題1を見なさい。これから読む英文の内容に関して5つの質問をします。a，b，c，dの4つの答えの中から最も適切なものを1つ選び，記号で答えなさい。英文を2回読んだ後，それぞれの質問を2回，選択肢を1回読みます。聞きながらメモを取ってもかまいません。それでは始めます。

Did you know that one person in 20 has had a fight with a next-door neighbour? That one driver in four admits to committing an act of road rage? That cases of "air rage" rose by 400 per cent between 1997 and 2000?

We appear to be living in an age of rage. Earlier this week there seems to have been an incidence of "queue rage" in a supermarket during which a man was punched — and later died. The death raises the whole issue of apparently random acts of violence that are often the product of momentary losses of self-control.

Anger, humankind's natural and healthy reaction to stressful situations, is increasingly being acted out via physical violence, even though we are richer, take more holidays and lead more comfortable lives than ever before. There are several theories as to why our society is becoming ever more angry. The fast pace at which we live our lives, "hurry sickness", for instance, has taught us to desire and demand instant satisfaction.

If something or someone delays us, we see it as a threat to our precious, finite time. There is also huge pressure to deliver at work in jobs that are increasingly insecure, competitive and strictly based on performance.

Dr Michael Sinclair, a consultant psychologist in London specialising in anger management, says that, generally, people who overreact to trivial events with violence are suffering from a central lack of confidence. The normal reaction, he says, when someone bumps into you is to think "that was a bit rude" and move on.

But angry people interpret everything as an insult to their already fragile egos. "Being bumped into will make the inadequate person feel even more inadequate," Sinclair explains. "It makes their feeling of insecurity worse.

Experts have said that in decades such as the 1960s and 1970s people tended to turn their frustration inwards, perhaps taking their anger out on their loved ones behind closed doors. The tendency now is to turn it outwards: to impose the problem on a complete stranger.

【REPEAT】

Question

(1) According to the passage, which statement is true? 【REPEAT】

(a) Twenty people often have a fight with their neighbors in their daily life.

(b) Twenty-five percent of drivers confess they have lost their temper while driving.

(c) The amount of violence in airplanes decreased from 1997 to 2000.

(d) The death rate due to human violence has remarkably been increasing these four years.

(2) What has the pace of our lives taught us? 【REPEAT】

(a) To desire and demand instant satisfaction.

(b) To become more angry.

(c) To take more holidays and lead more comfortable lives.

(d) To react to stressful situations via violence.

(3) If something or someone delays us, what do we think about it? 【REPEAT】

(a) It is a huge pressure at work.

(b) It is an insecure performance.

(c) It is a threat to our precious time.

(d) It is an increasingly competitive job.

(4) What do angry people think in general? 【REPEAT】

(a) Everything is a fragile ego.

(b) Everything has adequate explanations.

(c) Everything has a feeling of insecurity.

(d) Everything is a personal insult.

(5) According to experts, what is people's tendency now? 【REPEAT】

(a) People tend to turn their frustration inwards.

(b) People tend to turn their frustration outwards.

(c) People tend to take their anger out on their loved ones.

(d) People tend to take their anger behind closed doors.

これでリスニングテストを終わります。

(☆☆☆◎◎◎◎◎)

【2】次の各文の(　　)にあてはまる最も適切な語を，ア～エから1つ選び，記号で答えなさい。

(1) The singer, long past bet prime, loved the (　　) that her aging male admirers still showered on her.

ア testimony　イ flattery　ウ bribery　エ apathy

(2) I didn't have enough time to read the report thoroughly, so I just (　　) through it for the main points.

ア skimmed　イ smashed　ウ scraped　エ scribbled

(3) After a five-hour (　　), the medical examiner confirmed that the president had died of natural causes.

ア analogy　イ amenity　ウ anarchy　エ autopsy

(4) The volleyball team found itself in a (　　) position in the league, having lost five games in a row.

ア subtle　イ lofty　ウ precarious　エ prominent

(5) One of major problems with liver transplants is not just the difficulty of the operation but finding a donor whose organ is (　　) with the patient.

ア parallel　イ flexible　ウ uniform　エ compatible

(6) The clerk was unable to deal with the (　　) flow of orders, so she requested that the company assign three more workers to her section.

ア rational　イ improper　ウ ceaseless　エ intermittent

(7) The gymnasium was in an (　　) after the captain of the home team was sent off for arging with the referee.

ア uproar　イ upturn　ウ upside　エ uplift

(8) The movie star's condition could get worse at any time, so I want him kept under constant (　　).

ア inspection　イ preservation　ウ observation

エ investigation

(9) Would you please (　　) the ten-page report into a one-page summary for me?

ア concede　イ conduct　ウ constitute　エ condense

(10) As a member of this company, you are expected to (　　) to the rules of this handbook.

ア adhere　イ assure　ウ amend　エ adjourn

(☆☆☆☆◎◎◎◎◎)

【3】次の英文を読んで，その趣旨を120字以内の日本語で書きなさい。ただし，句読点も字数に入れること。

Most members of the language teaching profession realize that their students' learning potential increases when attitudes are positive and motivation runs high. The research into the connection between positive attitudes and successfully learning a second language supports this simple observation, although it is important to understand that many variables are involved because we are dealing with complex social and psychological aspects of human behavior. For example, students' ability to learn a second language can be influenced by their attitudes towards the target language, the target language speakers and their culture, the social value of learning the second language, and also the students' attitudes towards themselves as members of their own culture.

In addition, English as a Foreign Language (EFL) teachers should recognize that all students possess positive and negative attitudes in varying degrees, and that the negative one; can be changed by thoughtful instructional methods, such as using materials and activities that help students: achieve an "understanding and appreciation of the foreign culture".

(☆☆☆☆☆◎◎◎◎◎)

【４】次の英文を読んで，(1)・(2)の問いに答えなさい。

(ア)Regardless of the culture or the environment in which children develop, key aspects of their development include their curiositv and imaeination. By imitatine adults and talkina to straneers. children demonstrate their fascination with things that are beyond their realm of possibilities. Thus it is no surprise that superheroes are extremely popular amongst youth. (イ)As the popularity of superheroes increased, so did the various media forms through which the lives and adventures of superheroes were disseminated. Initially introduced primarily through comic books, superheroes were soon included in television shows and films. Movies such as X-Men and Spider Man have generated large box-office receipts and received a lot of media attention, and several other movies about superheroes have also made their way to the big screen.

(1)　下線部(ア)を日本語になおしなさい。

(2)　下線部(イ)を日本語になおしなさい。

(☆☆☆☆◎◎◎◎◎)

【5】次の英文の(1)～(6)にあてはまる最も適切な語をア～クから選び，記号で答えなさい。ただし，同じ語を2度使わないこと。

Issues surrounding (1) and child health encompass a wide range of aspects from health care services, health care systems, and public health to the social environment that surrounds women who are to carry and (2) children. In developing countries, especially the (3) developed countries, urgent attention is needed to improve the health of pregnant and nursing women, (4) infant mortality and illnesses, and (5) measures against HIV / AIDS and other sexually (6) diseases.

ア feminine　イ least　ウ transmitted　エ promote
オ most　カ nurture　キ reduce　ク matemal

(☆☆☆◎◎◎◎)

【6】次の対話文の(1)～(5)にあてはまる最も適切な英文を，ア～クから選び，記号で答えなさい。ただし，同じ選択肢を2度使わないこと。

A : I haven't seen you this week.
B : I went to Canada with my family for a week.
A : Oh, did you? I didn't know that.
B : (1)
A : (2)
B : (3)
A : Thank you very much. Did you have a good time there?
B : Yes, very much. I had a lot of interesting things to do. Have you ever been?
A : (4)
B : (5)
A : I'd like to go again someday.

ア I was impressed with the big and beautiful field, so I want to go again.
イ Actually I visited Canada in winter two years ago. It is very cold.

ウ　I'm afraid I have not received them yet.

エ　My brother showed me some pictures he took in Canada.

オ　Really? I sent you some beautiful picture cards from Toronto.

カ　That's true, but I enjoyed skiing with my family every day.

キ　No, I had a plan to spend my holidays there.

ク　I think you'll get them in a day or two.

(☆☆☆◎◎◎◎)

【中学校】

【1】次の文は，平成15年度に文部科学省が出した，「『英語が使える日本人』の育成のための行動計画」の「Ⅱ．英語教育改善のためのアクション」の項で，「英語の授業の改善」について書かれている部分である。Thus, を書き出しにして，下線部を英語になおしなさい。

「英語が使える」ようになるためには，文法や語彙などについての知識を持っているというだけではなく，実際にコミュニケーションを目的として英語を運用する能力が必要である。このため，英語の授業においては，文法訳読中心の指導や教員の一方的な授業ではなく，英語をコミュニケーションの手段として使用する活動を積み重ね，これを通して，語彙や文法などの習熟を図り，「聞く」「話す」「読む」「書く」のコミュニケーション能力の育成を図っていく指導の工夫が必要である。

(☆☆☆☆☆◎◎◎)

【2】中学校学習指導要領「外国語」について，次の(1)～(2)の問いに答えなさい。

(1)　次の文は「第1　目標」を英語で表したものである。(　①　)～(　③　)に当てはまる語句を英語で書きなさい。

To develop students' (　①　) such as listening and speaking, (　②　) of language and culture, and (　③　) toward communication through foreign languages.

(2) 「第2　各言語の目標及び内容等」について，次の(a)・(b)の問いに答えなさい。

(a) (A)・(B)のいずれか1つを選び，その記号を記入し，問いに答えなさい。

(A) 「2　内容」の「(2)言語活動の取扱い」において，「[言語の働きの例]　c　気持ちを伝えるもの」として示されている4つの例から2つ選び，日本語で書きなさい。

(B) 「2　内容」の「(3)言語材料」において，「イ　文字及び符号」として示されている2つのことを日本語で書きなさい。

(b) 次の文章は「3　指導計画の作成と内容の取扱い」の，教材の使用についての事項である。(　①　)～(　⑧　)に当てはまる語句を日本語で書きなさい。

教材は，英語での実践的コミュニケーション能力を育成するため，実際の言語の(　①　)や言語の働きに十分配慮したものを取り上げるものとする。その際，英語を使用している人々を中心とする(　②　)及び日本人の(　③　)，風俗習慣，物語，地理，歴史などに関するもののうちから，生徒の心身の発達段階及び興味・関心に即して(　④　)な題材を(　⑤　)をもたせて取り上げるものとし，次の観点に配慮する必要がある。

ア　(　⑥　)なものの見方や考え方を理解し，公正な判断力を養い豊かな心情を育てるのに役立つこと。

イ　世界や我が国の生活や文化についての理解を深めるとともに，言語や文化に対する関心を高め，これらを(　⑦　)する態度を育てるのに役立つこと。

ウ　広い視野から国際理解を深め，国際社会に生きる日本人としての自覚を高めるとともに，(　⑧　)の精神を養うのに役立つこと。

(☆☆☆☆☆◎◎◎◎◎)

【高等学校】

【1】次の文は，平成15年度に文部科学省が出した，「『英語が使える日本人』の育成のための行動計画」の「Ⅱ．英語教育改善のためのアクション」の項で，「英語の授業の改善」について書かれている箇所の冒頭の部分である。下の(1)，(2)の問いに答えなさい。

【目標】

「英語を使用する活動を積み重ねながらコミュニケーション能力の育成を図る」

○　英語の授業の大半は(　①　)行い，生徒や学生が英語でコミュニケーションを行う活動を多く取り入れる。

○　中・高等学校等の英語の授業で(　②　)や(　③　)などを積極的に取り入れる。

○　(ア)地域に英語教育に関する先進校を形成する。

「英語が使える」ようになるためには，文法や語彙などについての知識を持っているというだけではなく，実際にコミュニケーションを目的として英語を運用する能力が必要である。(イ)このため，英語の授業においては，文法訳読中心の指導や教員の一方的な授業ではなく，英語をコミュニケーションの手段として使用する活動を積み重ね，これを通して，語彙や文法などの習熟を図り，「聞く」「話す」「読む」「書く」のコミュニケーション能力の育成を図っていく指導の工夫が必要である。

(1)　文中の(　①　)～(　③　)に入る適切な語句を書きなさい。また，下線部(ア)の一環として，高等学校及び中等教育学校における先進的な英語教育を推進し，その成果の普及を図ることを目的に平成14年度から実施している研究指定校事業を何というか，答えなさい。

(2)　下線部(イ)を，Thus，を書き出しにして，英語になおしなさい。

(☆☆☆☆☆◎◎◎◎◎)

【2】次の文は，高等学校学習指導要領「外国語」の，「英語Ⅰ」と「英語Ⅱ」の目標である。(　1　)～(　6　)にあてはまる語句を書きなさい。

「英語Ⅰ」：(　1　)話題について，聞いたことや読んだことを理解し，(　2　)や考えなどを英語で話したり書いたりして伝える(　3　)能力を養うとともに，積極的に(　4　)を図ろうとする態度を育てる。

「英語Ⅱ」：(　5　)話題について，聞いたことや読んだことを理解し，(　2　)や考えなどを英語で話したり書いたりして伝える能力を(　6　)とともに，積極的に(　4　)を図ろうとする態度を育てる。

(☆☆☆☆◎◎◎◎◎)

【3】高等学校学習指導要領「外国語」について，次の(A)・(B)のいずれか1つを選び，問いに答えなさい。

(A)　「オーラルコミュニケーションⅠ」の「2　内容　(1)　言語活動」には，具体的な言語の使用場面を設定して行うコミュニケーション活動の例が4つ示されている。その内の2つを書きなさい。

(B)　「オーラルコミュニケーションⅡ」の「2　内容　(1)　言語活動」には，「オーラルコミュニケーションⅠ」に示すコミュニケーション活動に加えて行うコミュニケーション活動の例が4つ示されている。その内の2つを書きなさい。

(☆☆☆◎◎◎)

解答・解説

【中高共通】

【1】(1)　b　　(2)　a　　(3)　c　　(4)　d　　(5)　b

〈解説〉リスニング力を上達させるためには，日頃からテレビ・ラジオ・CDなどを利用して，英語に耳を慣らせておくことが大切である。このようなタイプのリスニング問題に対しては，TOEICや英語検定などの教材を使って準備しておきたい。問題と質問は2回読まれるので1回目で聞き取れなかった内容は2回目で聞き取れるように，また，選択肢は1回しか読まれないので，集中してメモをとりながら聞くようにすることが大切である。

【2】(1)　イ　(2)　ア　(3)　エ　(4)　ウ　(5)　エ　(6)　ウ　(7)　ア　(8)　ウ　(9)　エ　(10)　ア

〈解説〉空欄にあてはまる語の選択肢は動詞と名詞が中心である。1つの単語でも複数の意味を持つ語が少なくないので，意味を機械的に学習するだけでなく，日ごろからまとまった英文を読んだり，聞いたりすることが重要である。このような問題を解く際には，はじめに問題文を読んで，空欄に入る語の意味を推測して答えを選ぶようにできるとよい。以下は設問ごとの解説。(1)「盛りをとっくに過ぎている歌手は彼女の古い男性がまだ雨のように浴びせていた賞賛のお世辞がとても好きでした。」という意味なので，flattery「お世辞，おだて」が正解。shower on～「雨のように浴びせる(降らせる)」　(2)「レポートを徹底的に読むだけの十分な時間がなかったので，私は要点をつかむためにただそれをざっと読みました。」の意。　(3)「5時間の検死の後，監察医は社長が自然死だったことを確認しました。」の意。autopsy「検死」　(4)「リーグにおいてバレーボールチームが不安定な立場におり，・・・」precarious「不安定な，危うい」　(5)　compatible with～「～と適合(一致)した」　(6)「その社員は絶え間ない注文に対処できなかったので，彼女は会社がもう3人の労働者を彼女の部署に配属するよう要求しました。」ceaseless「絶え間ない，間断ない，不断の」

(7)　be in (an) uproar「大騒ぎをしている」　(8)　keep under constant observation「しょっちゅう観察し続ける」

(9)　condense…into～「…を～に簡略にする」　(10)　adhere to～「～に固執する」

【3】(正答例)　言語に対する学習者の意欲や態度が言語学習に与える影響は大きい。意欲や態度に影響を与えるとされる要因は多様だが，特に英語では，学習者の否定的な態度は教授法を熟考することにより改

善することが可能であることを指導者は認識すべきである。(114字)

〈解説〉この問題は，その趣旨を書くことを要求しているので，指定の字数内でいかに要点をまとめることができるかを問われている。英文の段落が2つあるので，1つ目の段落と２つ目の段落の要点をそれぞれまとめて書けるとよい。1つ目の段落では，第1文と第2文の内容をまとめる。第3文は，For example,…という出だしで単に例を述べているにすぎないので割愛してかまわない。

【4】(1)　(正答例)　子供の成長の決め手となるのは，好奇心と想像力であり，子供が育つ文化や環境とは関係ない。大人のまねをしたり，見知らぬ人に話しかけたりすることによって，子供は自分の可能性の領域を超えたものに，目に見えて惹かれていく。　(2)　(正答例)　スーパーヒーローたちの人気が高まると同時に，彼らの生きざまや冒険を人々に伝える様々なメディア媒体も増えてきた。

〈解説〉このような英文和訳の問題は，熟語や構文に注意して正確な日本語で解答できるようにしたい。そのためには，完成した文をもう1度読み直して，意味の通る日本語で書けているかを確認することが大切である。　(1)　regardless of～「～にかかわらず,関係なく，～を無視して」　(2)　As～, so…「～つれて，…になる」

【5】(1)　ク　(2)　カ　(3)　イ　(4)　キ　(5)　エ　(6)　ウ

〈解説〉まとまった英文の空欄にあてはまる語を選ぶ問題では，空欄の前後に注目し文脈全体で正解を選ぶことが大切である。このような問題の準備としては，日ごろから，教育問題や社会動向に関心を持ち，それらに関する英文を多く読むように心がけたい。全文訳：「母と子の健康の問題は，健康管理サービス，ヘルス・ケア・システム，および子供を持ち育てる女性をとり囲む社会環境に対する国民の健康まで，さまざまな局面を持っている。発展途上国，特に，後発発展途上国では，妊娠し育児をしている女性の健康を改善し，幼児死亡率と病気を減少させ，HIVやAIDSと他の性感染症に対する対策を促進させるため，緊急に注目されなければならない。」　(1)　feminine「女性の」と間違えやすいが，2行目後半にwomen who are to carry and (2) children.とあり，子供を持つ女性の意味が含まれているmaternal「母の」がふさわしい。　(2)　全文訳参照　(3)　the least developed countries「後発発展途上国」　(4)　infant mortality「幼児死亡率」　(5)　measureは「測定，測量」の意味があるが，measuresと複数になると，「(目的達成の手段としての)行動，処置，方策，対策，手段」という意味になる。　(6)　transmitは「〈物を〉送る，運ぶ」の意味があるが，病気の場合は「(人に)移す,伝染させる」という意味になる。

【6】(1)　オ　(2)　ウ　(3)　ク　(4)　イ　(5)　カ

〈解説〉このような対話文に対応するためには，日頃からテレビ・ラジオ・CDなどを利用して，対話文を聞いたり，対話文の内容を音読したりして，慣れておく必要がある。TOEICや英語検定などのリスニング教材を活用するなども効果的である。　(1)　I didn't know that.に対して，Really?...「本当に。カナダから絵葉書送ったのに。」と対応する。(2)　(1)の絵葉書を送ったことに対して，「まだ(絵葉書を)受け取ってないよ。」となる。　(3)　(2)の絵葉書を受け取っていないことに対して，「あと1～2日で受け取れると思うよ。」となる。　(4)　前に質問文Have you ever been? に対する返答で，「カナダには2年前の冬に訪問してとても寒かった。」　(5)　(4)のとても寒かったに対して，「そうだね，でも毎日家族とスキーを楽しんだよ。」となる。

【中学校】

【1】(正答例)　In English classes, instruction mainly based on grammar and translation or teacher-centered classes are not recommended. Through the repetition of activities making use of English as a means of communication, the learning of vocabulary and grammar should be enhanced, and communication abilities in “listening,” “speaking,” “reading,” and “writing,” should be fostered. Such techniques for instruction are necessary.

〈解説〉今回の出典は，文部科学省の「『英語が使える日本人』の育成のための行動計画」の1部であるが，日ごろから英語教育の社会動向に注目したい。「『英語が使える日本人』の育成のための戦略構想」，及び，「『英語が使える日本人』の育成のための行動計画」は，文部科学省のHPに掲載されている。さらに，「『英語が使える日本人』の育成のための行動計画」は英文も掲載されている。

【2】(1) ① basic practical communication ② abilities
③ deepening the understanding ④ fostering the positive attitude
(2) (a) (A) 礼を言う・苦情を言う・ほめる・謝る，の4つから2つ
(B) アルファベットの活字体の大文字及び小文字　終止符，疑問符，コンマ，引用符，感嘆符などの基本的な符号　(b) ① 使用場面
② 世界の人々 ③ 日常生活 ④ 適切 ⑤ 変化
⑥ 多様 ⑦ 尊重 ⑧ 国際協調

〈解説〉中学校学習指導要領の「外国語」は，文章がそのまま空欄補充問題として出題されたり，内容を詳しく尋ねる設問が出題されたりするので，詳しく内容を把握しておく必要がある。 (1)「第1　目標」は，日本語，英語版ともにしっかりと頭に入れておく。今回は英語による出題。 (2) (a)「第2　内容」について，中学校学習指導要領で示されている内容を問う問題。今回は「〔言語の使用場面の例〕」と「イ　文字及び符号」に関する出題であったが，どこを聞かれても解答できるようにしておく。 (b) 空欄補充問題。中学校学習指導要領で示されている内容を問う問題。(a)同様どこを聞かれても解答できるようにしておく。

【高等学校】

【1】(1)　①　英語を用いて　②　少人数指導　③　習熟度別指導
(ア)　スーパー・イングリッシュ・ランゲージ・ハイスクール(SELHi)
(2)　(正答例)　In English classes, instruction mainly based on grammar and translation or teacher-centered classes are not recommended. Through the repetition of activities making use of English as a means of communication, the learning of vocabulary and grammar should be enhanced, and communication abilities in "listening," "speaking," "reading," and "writing," should be fostered. Such techniques for instruction are necessary.

〈解説〉(1)　今回の出典は，文部科学省の「『英語が使える日本人』の育成のための行動計画」の一部であるが，日ごろから英語教育の社会動向に注目したい。「『英語が使える日本人』の育成のための戦略構想」，及び，「『英語が使える日本人』の育成のための行動計画」は，文部科学省のHPに掲載されている。　(2)「『英語が使える日本人』の育成のための行動計画」は英語版も作成されており，同じく文部科学省のHPで見ることができる。

【2】(1)　日常的な　(2)　情報　(3)　基礎的な　(4)　コミュニケーション　(5)　幅広い　(6)　更に伸ばす

〈解説〉高等学校学習指導要領の「外国語」は，文章がそのまま空欄補充問題として出題されるので，詳しく内容を把握しておく必要がある。英語版もあるので，こちらも目を通しておきたい。今回は「英語Ⅰ」，「英語Ⅱ」の目標についてであったが，全ての科目において知っておく必要がある。

【3】(A)　(正答例)　・英語を聞いてその内容を理解するとともに，場面や目的に応じて適切に反応する。　・関心のあることについて相手に質問したり，相手の質問に答えたりする。　・情報や考えなどを，場面や目的に応じて適切に伝える。　・聞いたり読んだりして得た情報や自分の考えなどをまとめ，発表する。また，発表されたものを理

解する。 (B) (正答例) ・スピーチなどまとまりのある話の概要や要点を聞き取り，それについて自分の考えなどをまとめる。 ・幅広い話題について情報や考えを整理し，効果的に発表する。 ・幅広い話題について，話し合ったり，討論したりする。 ・スキットなどを創作し，演じる。

〈解説〉高等学校学習指導要領の「外国語」は，空欄補充問題の他に，示されている内容に対して詳しく答えなければならない問題がある。今回は，具体的な言語の使用場面を設定して行うコミュニケーション活動の例について，指導要領に記載されている内容を答える問題であった。科目ごとに，1の目標，2の内容について，詳しく正確に理解しておく必要がある。

2008年度　実施問題

【中高共通】

【1】リスニングテスト

問題文及び5つの質問を聞き，各質問の後に読まれるa～dの4つの選択肢の中からその質問に対する答えとして最も適切なものを1つ選び，記号で答えなさい。

(台本)

ただいまから，リスニングテストを始めます。受審者は問題用紙(その1)の問題1を見なさい。これから読む英文の内容に関して5つの質問をします。a，b，c，dの4つの答えの中から最も適切なものを1つ選び，記号で答えなさい。英文を2回読んだ後，それぞれの質問を2回，選択肢を1回読みます。聞きながらメモを取ってもかまいません。それでは始めます。

On a September day in 1991, two Germans were climbing the mountains between Austria and Italy. High up on a mountain pass, they found the body of a man lying on the ice. At 3,200 meters, the ice is usually permanent, but that year had been exceptionally hot. The mountain ice had melted more than usual and the body had come to the surface. It was lying face downward with the skeleton in perfect condition, except for a large wound in his head. There was still skin on the bones and the remains of some clothes.

The hands were holding the wooden handle of an ax. On the feet there were very simple leather and cloth boots. Nearby was a pair of gloves made of tree bark and a holder for arrows.

Who was this man? How and when had he died? Everybody had a different answer to these questions. Perhaps it was the body of a soldier who died in World War I. In fact, several World War I soldiers had already been found in that area of the mountain. On the other hand, a Swiss woman believed it might be her father who had died in those mountains 20 years before and his body had never been found. Or some said it could have been one of the soldiers in the army of Frederick, Duke of Austria.

When Italian and Austrian scientists heard about the discovery, they rushed to the spot. They said the body couldn't possibly be the Swiss woman's father, because the articles were clearly from further back and the body had to be at least several centuries old. It required more data to prove this hypothesis. Though they both insisted on bringing the body down in their laboratories urgently, there was a problem to solve. As the body was lying exactly on the border between two countries, it took two days for diplomats to decide which country had the right to keep it. Finally they decided that it lay on Austrian ground. By that time the body was partly unfrozen and somewhat damaged.

After the close examination the Austrian scientists reached the amazing conclusions that the man died around 2,700 B.C. This was a very important discovery. It would teach them a great deal about this very distant period of European history. From the clothes and the tools they could learn about how men lived in those days.

【REPEAT】

Question

(1) Who found the frozen body?【REPEAT】

a. Two German climbers.

b. The Austrian scientists.

c. The soldiers in the army of Frederick.

d. The Swiss diplomats,

(2) Why did some people think the body had been a soldier in World War I?【REPEAT】

a. Because a pair of gloves made of tree bark and a holder for arrows were nearby.

b. Because there had been a famous fierce battle in the nearby place.

c. Because several bodies of the soldiers in World War I had already been found around there.

d. Because the remains of some clothes were similar to those of the military uniform.

(3) What conclusion did the Austrian scientists reach after the close examination?【REPEAT】

a. The man died about 20 years ago.

b. The man died about 1,900 years ago.

c. The man died about 2,700 years ago.

d. The man died about 4,700 years ago.

(4) What best describes the lifestyle of the period the frozen man lived in?【REPEAT】

a. The large wound in his head.

b. The footprints on the ground.

c. The skin left on the bones.

d. The clothes and the tools.

(5) According to the passage, which sentence is NOT correct?【REPEAT】

a. The body had been kept in good condition in the ice.

b. The body was lying on his face with the skeleton in perfect condition,

c. The Swiss woman believed her father had died in World War I

d. The argument for the right to keep the body lasted for two days.

これでリスニングテストを終わります。

(☆☆☆◎◎◎)

【2】次の各文の(　　)にあてはまる最も適切な語を，ア～エから1つ選び，記号で答えなさい。

(1) Before man's language became complex, some people believe that man's (　　) language derived from roars and shouts.

ア inseparable　イ intricate　ウ primitive　エ conscious

(2) Cathy bought her condominium in January but she won't take (　　) of it until March.

ア admission　イ connection　ウ obsession
エ possession

(3) Canadians have a reputation for being (　　) and polite when meeting new people.

ア reservation　イ reserved　ウ reservedly　エ reserving

(4) The pianist was already (　　) in his own country before becoming famous world wide.

ア renowned　イ intolerable　ウ beneficial　エ splendid

(5) Our original schedule was never (　　), in spite of a lack of funding, and we completed the project on time.

ア descended　イ dislodged　ウ devoted　エ delayed

(6) The measles virus reached (　　) proportions in this region last year, forcing many schools to close.

ア immortal　イ superficial　ウ epidemic
エ insignificant

(7) The claim of innocence was (　　) by the evidence.

ア suppressed　イ contradicted　ウ suspended
エ comprised

(8) The use of bills of exchange (　　) the risk in transporting money from one country to another.

ア obviates　イ disregards　ウ partakes　エ ventures

(9) Please show some (　　) and give generously to our fund for earthquake victims.

ア compensation　イ contention　ウ compassion
エ condemnation

(10) After two days in the desert without water, the campers were (　　) and in need of immediate medical attention.

ア evaporated　イ dismissed　ウ extinguished
エ dehydrated

(☆☆☆☆◎◎◎)

【3】次の英文を読んで，120字以内の日本語で要約しなさい。ただし，句読点も字数に入れること。

It is important to clarify what we mean by 'acquiring the rules' of a language. It means being able to apply the rules (in other words, to understand and use the language correctly); it does not necessarily mean knowing how to explain the rules (in other words, to talk about the language). All native speakers of English 'know' the difference between the present perfect and past tenses, in the sense that they use them correctly, but very few would be able to explain the difference; by contrast, some learners of English can explain the difference between the two tenses (they 'know' the rule) but they cannot use the tenses correctly.

It is, of course, applying the rules that is important in language learning; and in the case of our first language this is an entirely subconscious process. It may be that in learning a second language too the best way to acquire rules is subconsciously, by reading and listening to language we understand and by attempting to communicate in the language, rather than by consciously 'learning grammar'.

(☆☆☆◎◎◎)

【4】次の英文を読んで，(1)・(2)の問いに答えなさい。

In many dual-earner families, one parent has a work schedule that differs from the standard 8am to 5pm,daytime schedule. (ア)<u>Under the broad definition of shift work, which includes weekend work, 57.3% of dual-earner couples with a child have at least one spouse with a nonstandard work schedule</u>. (イ)<u>Having a nonstandard schedule may either facilitate the supervision of children and handling family responsibilities or complicate family life</u>. For many families trying to balance work and family, the issue may not just be how many hours parents are working per week but when those hours occur.

(1)　下線部(ア)を，shift workの意味を明確にして，日本語になおしなさい。

(2) 下線部(イ)を日本語になおしなさい。

(☆☆☆◎◎◎)

【5】次の英文の(1)～(6)にあてはまる最も適切な語を，ア～クから選び，記号で答えなさい。

We live in a globalizing world where (1) amounts of people, goods, money, and information move fast across borders. This has brought about many challenges, such as (2) diseases, large-scale natural disasters, and environmental degradation. These pose major threats to people's survival and are difficult for a single government or nation to resolve.

"Human security," a concept and a framework (3) in the fare of such circumstances, is one of the basic policies of the New ODA Charter. Human security focuses on people and communities, particularly on the poor and the (4). The core value of this framework lies in linking both the (5) approach, which seeks to improve the capacity of governments to protect and expand the rights and freedoms of their people, and the (6) approach, which aims at strengthening the capabilities of people and communities to take the lead in development.

ア bottom-up　イ top-down　ウ destroyed　エ apparent
オ vulnerable　カ infectious　キ massive　ク developed

(☆☆☆◎◎◎)

【6】次の対話文の(1)～(4)にあてはまる最も適切な英文を，ア～キの中から選び，記号で答えなさい。ただし，同じ選択肢を2度使わないこと。

A : I hear you're going to open a restaurant. Is that right?

B : Mm. That's right.

A : Well, good luck. I wouldn't like to do it.

B : Why not?

A : (　1　)

B : (　2　)

A : You also have to work when everyone else is enjoying themselves.

B : (　3　)

A : (　4　)

B : Well, I'll see. I want to be my own boss. Then you don't have to work for someone else.

A : I'll be your first customer.

ア　If you have a restaurant, you don't have to do the same thing every day.

イ　I think you're taking quite a risk.

ウ　Because I've wanted to work at a shop.

エ　It's true, but you don't have to get up so early in the morning.

オ　I like cooking and entertaining, so that's all right.

カ　It's something we've always wanted to do.

キ　If you run a restaurant, you have to work until late at night.

(☆☆◎◎◎)

【7】次の文を英語になおしなさい。

これからの社会を担っていく子どもたちに，学校・家庭・地域社会が一体となって，命の大切さや思いやる心，善悪の判断などの規範意識や公共心など，豊かな心の育成を図ることが求められている。

(☆☆☆◎◎◎◎)

【中学校】

【1】中学校学習指導要領「外国語」の「第2　各言語の目標及び内容等」について，次の(1)・(2)の問いに答えなさい。

(1)　次の文章は，「2　内容」の「(1)　言語活動」のうち，「ア　聞くこと」と「イ　話すこと」で，主として指導する事項である。(　①　)～(　⑧　)にあてはまる語句を書きなさい。

ア　聞くこと

(ア)　強勢，イントネーション，区切りなど基本的な英語の音声の特徴をとらえ，正しく(　①　)こと。

(イ)　自然な口調で話されたり読まれたりする英語を聞いて，具体的な内容や(　②　)を聞き取ること。

(ウ)　(　③　)や依頼などを聞いて適切に応じること。

(エ)　話し手に(　④　)などして内容を正しく理解すること。

イ　話すこと

(ア)　強勢，イントネーション，区切りなど基本的な英語の音声の特徴に慣れ，正しく(　⑤　)こと。

(イ)　自分の(　⑥　)や気持ちなどが聞き手に正しく伝わるように話すこと。

(ウ)　聞いたり読んだりしたことについて，(　⑦　)意見を述べ合ったりすること。

(エ)　(　⑧　)を用いるなどいろいろな工夫をして話が続くように話すこと。

(2)　次の(A)・(B)のいずれか1つを選び，その記号を記入し，問いに答えなさい。

(A)「2　内容」の「(2)言語活動の取扱い」において，「〔言語の働きの例〕a　考えを深めたり情報を伝えたりするもの」として5つ示されている中から4つ選び，日本語で書きなさい。

(B)「2　内容」の「(3)言語材料」において，「ア　音声」として5つ示されている中から4つ選び，日本語で書きなさい。

(☆☆☆◎◎◎◎◎)

【2】平成14年に国立教育政策研究所が出した「評価規準の作成，評価方法の工夫改善のための参考資料(中学校)」の中に，外国語の評価に関する4つの観点が示されている。その4つの観点を，英語で書きなさい。

(☆☆☆◎◎◎◎◎)

【高等学校】

【1】次の文は，高等学校学習指導要領「外国語」の「第3　英語Ⅰ」において，言語材料を扱ううえで配慮すべき事項を述べたものである。(①)～(④)に入る適切な語句を書きなさい。

(ア)　言語材料は，現代の(①)な英語によること。

(イ)　言語材料の(②)や(③)は必要最小限にとどめ，実際の場面でどのように使われるかを理解し，実際に(④)ことを重視すること。

(☆☆☆◎◎◎◎)

【2】平成16年に国立教育政策研究所が出した「評価規準の作成，評価方法の工夫改善のための参考資料(高等学校)」の中に，外国語の評価に関する4つの観点が示されている。その4つの観点を，英語で書きなさい。

(☆☆☆◎◎◎)

【3】高等学校学習指導要領「外国語」について，次の(A)・(B)のいずれか1つを選び,問いに答えなさい。

(A)　「オーラルコミュニケーションⅠ」の中の「言語活動の取扱い」の項には，コミュニケーション活動を効果的に行うために，指導上必要に応じて配慮すべきことが4つ示されている。その内の3つを書きなさい。

(B)　「英語Ⅰ」の中の「言語活動の取扱い」の項には，コミュニケーション活動を効果的に行うために，指導上必要に応じて配慮すべきことが4つ示されている。その内の3つを書きなさい。

(☆☆☆◎◎◎)

解答・解説

【中高共通】

【1】(1) a　(2) c　(3) d　(4) d　(5) c

〈解説〉英文は詳細まで聞き取るようにし，特に数字などの情報はメモしておく。質問は疑問詞や主語・時制に注意する。

【2】(1) ウ　(2) エ　(3) イ　(4) ア　(5) エ　(6) ウ　(7) イ　(8) ア　(9) ウ　(10) エ

〈解説〉(1) primitive language「原始言語」 inseparable「切り離せない」 intricate「複雑な」 conscious「意識的な」 (2) take possession of「占有する」 (3) reserved「控えめな」 reservedly「よそよそしく」 (4) renowned「高名な」 intolerable「耐えられない」 splendid「素晴らしい」 (5) descend「下りる」 dislodge「取り除く」 devote「専念する」 (6)「昨年この地域では麻疹ウイルスが流行伝染病となり，多くの学校が休校した」 (7) contradict「否認する」 suppress「抑える」 comprise「構成する」 (8)「為替手形の使用は一つの国から他の国へ現金を輸送する危険を未然に防ぐ」 (9) compassion「思いやり」 compensation「代償」 contention「競争」 condemnation「糾弾」 (10) dehydrated「脱水する」 evaporate「蒸発する」 dismiss「捨てる」

【3】言語の習得とは，文法を説明できるようになることではなく，それを理解して正確に使えるようになることである。ネイティブスピーカーが無意識に母語を習得するように，第二言語習得においても，文法を意識的に学ぶより言葉を使って無意識に習得する方がよい。

〈解説〉文の構造上，最初に問題定義をし，最後に結論が書かれていることが多い。要約には，例としてあげられている文は入れない。

【4】(1)　週末労働を含め時間帯の変更が可能な就労体系を広義に解釈すると，子どもが一人いる共働きの夫婦のうち，少なくとも片方の配偶者が標準時間外に仕事をしている割合は，57.3%にのぼる。

(2)　標準時間外に仕事を持てば，子どもの養育や家族としての責任が軽減されるかもしれないが，家族の生活に支障をきたすかもしれない。

〈解説〉(1)　broad definition「広い定義」　shift work「交替制の仕事」　dual-earner「共働きの」　spouse「配偶者」　(2)　facilitate「楽にする」　supervision「監督」　complicate「複雑にする」　either…or～「…かまたは～か」に注意する。

【5】(1)　キ　(2)　カ　(3)　ク　(4)　オ　(5)　イ　(6)　ア

〈解説〉(1)　massive amounts of「大量の」　(2)　infectious disease「感染症」　(3)　そのような状況に直面して「構築された」概念と体制。『人間の安全保障』は新しいODA憲章の基本方針の1つです。

(4)　the vulnerable「傷つけられやすい人々」　the poorと同じような意味の単語が入ると考えられる。　(5)「政府の能力を向上させる」ので，「上から下へ」のアプローチとなる。　(6)「人々や共同体の能力を強化する」ので，「下から上へ」のアプローチとなる。

【6】(1)　キ　(2)　エ　(3)　オ　(4)　イ

〈解説〉「レストランを開いたんだって。本当なの」「本当だよ」「がんばって。そう言いたくはないけど」「どうして」「もしレストランを経営したら，夜遅くまで働かなければならないでしょう」「そうだね，でも朝早く起きなくてもいいんだよ」「みんなが楽しんでいるときにも働かなければならないよ」「料理したりもてなしたりするのが好きだから，かまわないよ」「リスクを負っていると思うよ」「わかってる。自分で決定権を持ちたいんだ。誰かのために働く必要はない」「私が最初の客になるよ」

【７】It is important for the school, the home and the local community to work together to cultivate a rich mind in our children, who will be responsible for society in future. This includes encouraging understanding of the value of human life, consideration for others, awareness of social norms such as judgment between right and wrong, and a sense of public duty.

〈解説〉長い文章はそのままにせずに，意味のとぎれる箇所で短く区切る。関係詞や代名詞を用いて，区切った中でもつながりを持つように工夫する。日本語の意味を理解し，文の骨格を見つけ，修飾を考えていく手順を取ると書きやすい。

【中学校】

【１】(1) ① 聞き取る　② 大切な部分　③ 質問　④ 聞き返す　⑤ 発音する　⑥ 考え　⑦ 問答したり　⑧ つなぎ言葉　(2) (A) 意見を言う／説明する／報告する／発表する／描写する　(B) 現代の標準的な発音／語と語の連結による音変化／語，句，文における基本的な強勢／文における基本的なイントネーション／文における基本的な区切り

〈解説〉学習指導要領は，英文のものも含めて良く読み込んでおくこと。

【２】Interest, willingness and a positive attitude toward communicating in English / Ability to express themselves (oneself) in English / Ability to understand English / Knowledge and understanding of language and culture

〈解説〉評価の観点として，①関心・意欲・態度，②表現の能力，③理解の能力，④知識・理解と示されている。

【高等学校】

【1】① 標準的　② 分析　③ 説明　④ 活用する

〈解説〉学習指導要領は，英語で書かれたものも含めて，よく読み込んでおくこと。

【2】Interest, willingness and a positive attitude toward communicating in English / Ability to express themselves (oneself) in English / Ability to understand English / Knowledge and understanding of language and culture

〈解説〉評価の観点として，①関心・意欲・態度，②表現の能力，③理解の能力，④知識・理解と示されている。

【3】(A) ・リズムやイントネーションなど英語の音声的な特徴に注意しながら，発音すること。・コミュニケーション活動に必要となる基本的な文型や文法事項などを理解し，実際に活用すること。・繰り返しを求めたり，言い換えたりするときなどに必要となる表現を活用すること。・ジェスチャーなどの非言語的手段の役割を理解し，場面や目的に応じて効果的に用いること。 (B) ・リズムやイントネーションなど英語の音声的な特徴に注意しながら，発音すること。・コミュニケーション活動に必要となる基本的な文型や文法事項などを理解し，実際に活用すること。・まとまりのある文章を音読したり暗唱したりして，英語の文章の流れに慣れること。・ジェスチャーなどの非言語的手段の役割を理解し，場面や目的に応じて効果的に用いること。

〈解説〉各科目で目標・内容・言語活動・言語活動の取扱い・言語材料・内容の取扱いが異なるので，確認しておくこと。

2007年度　実施問題

【中高共通】

【1】問題文及び5つの質問を聞き，各質問の後に読まれるa～dの4つの選択肢の中からその質問に対する答えとして最も適切なものを選び，記号で答えなさい。

ただいまから，リスニングテストを始めます。受審者は問題用紙(その1)の問題1を見なさい。これから読む英文の内容に関して5つの質問をします。a，b，c，dの4つの答えの中から最も適切なものを1つ選び，記号で答えなさい。英文を2回読んだ後，それぞれの質問を2回，選択肢を1回読みます。聞きながらメモを取ってもかまいません。それでは始めます。

[英文]

When Christopher Columbus landed on America's shores in 1492, he encountered the native people. He promptly called them "Indians." Mistaken in his geography, he believed that he had reached India. There were over a million Indians inhabiting North America then. There are approximately 800,000 Indians today. And about 250,000 of them live on reservations.

The early settlers had a friendly relationship with Indians, who shared their knowledge of fishing, hunting, and farming with their uninvited guests.

Then antipathy developed between them. As early as 1745, Indian tribes merged to drive the French off their land. The French and Indian War did not end until 1763. The Indians had succeeded in destroying many of the Western settlements. The British, superficially submissive, promised that further migrations west would not extend beyond a specified boundary. However, there was no holding back ardent adventurers, who ignored the British agreement and blazed a trail westward.

Driven out of their lands and pushed west, or worse still, Indians were robbed of their property by the white people for a few cheap ornaments. Soon furious wars broke out, the Indians were doomed to surrender because they didn't have enough power or people. However in 1876 at Little Big Horn River in Montana, the Sioux tribes massacred General Custer's soldiers. It caused the whites to intensify their campaign against the Indians.

The battle at Wounded Knee, South Dakota, in 1890 destroyed the last hope for amity between Indians and whites. After that battle Indians were forced to live on reservations provided by the federal government.

Although the Bureau of Indian Affairs had operated since 1824 to guard the Indians' interests, Indians on reservations lead notoriously deprived lives. They have suffered from poverty, unemployment, high infant death rate, and deficient medical care. Recently some Indians have appealed to the courts and the American people to improve their living conditions.【REPEAT】

Question

(1) Approximately how many Indians live on reservations today?【REPEAT】

a 100,000 Indians.

b 250,000 Indians.

c 800,000 Indians.

d A million Indians.

(2) What did the early settlers in America think of Indians?【REPEAT】

a They thought the Indians were helpful.

b They thought the Indians were cruel.

c They thought the Indians were doomed to surrender.

d They thought the Indians were militant.

(3) What agreement did the British reach with the Indians?【REPEAT】

a An agreement to get the Indians' land.

b An agreement to pay the Indians an enormous amount of money for their land.

c An agreement to stop westward migration.

d An agreement to send adventurers across the continent.

(4) What happened to the Indians at Little Big Horn River? 【REPEAT】

a They were massacred.

b They were defeated.

c They were obliged to retreat.

d They won a battle against whites.

(5) Which sentence is NOT correct according to the passage? 【REPEAT】

a The French and Indian war ended quickly.

b The last hope for peace was lost at the battle at Wounded Knee.

c The Bureau of Indian Affairs was formed to guard the Indians' interests.

d The Indians have recently begun to stand up for their rights.

これでリスニングテストを終わります。

(☆☆☆◎◎◎)

【2】次の(1)～(10)の各文の(　　　)にあてはまる最も適切な語を，ア～エから1つ選び，記号で答えなさい。

(1) "Bill is always talking through his (　　　)," said Fred. "Don't pay any attention to his bragging."

ア hat　イ head　ウ glasses　エ lips

(2) He still can't get the (　　　) of English pronunciation though he's lived in the US for five years.

ア ability　イ hang　ウ space　エ mark

(3) After a few hours the police (　　　) to stop the rioting.

ア interpreted　イ intersected　ウ interlocked

エ intervened

(4) No ship could leave port in such (　　　) weather.

ア appalling　イ despotic　ウ amicable　エ moderate

(5) The beefsteak will look better if you (　　　) it with vegetables.

ア garnish　イ garner　ウ conclude　エ conserve

(6) They say that the accident was caused by the driver's (　　　).

ア aspiration　イ negligence　ウ indulgence

エ　conspiracy

(7)　We are all (　　　) towards him when we speak to him.

ア　respectable　　イ　respecting　　ウ　respectful

エ　respective

(8)　Traffic signs should be (　　　) enough for everybody to notice.

ア　artificial　　イ　decorative　　ウ　conspicuous　　エ　obscure

(9)　Recently the ruins of an ancient palace were (　　　).

ア　deserted　　イ　excavated　　ウ　mingled　　エ　deterred

(10)　Some members supported the second resolution and spoke in (　　　) of it.

ア　sake　　イ　change　　ウ　opposition　　エ　favor

(☆☆☆◎◎◎)

【3】次の英文を読んで，120字以内の日本語で要約しなさい。(ただし，句読点も字数に入れること。)

Although English is not the language with the largest number of native or 'first' language speakers, it has become a lingua franca. A lingua franca can be defined as a language widely adopted for communication between two speakers whose native languages are different from each other's and where one or both speakers are using it as a 'second' language. Many people living in the European Union, for example, frequently operate in English as well as their own languages (where these are different) , and the economic and cultural influence of the United States has led to increased English use in many areas of the globe. Like Latin in Europe in the Middle Ages, English seems to be one of the main languages of international communication, and even people who are not speakers of English often know words such as bank, chocolate, computer, hamburger, hospital, hot dog, hotel, piano, radio, taxi, telephone, television, university and walkman. Many of these words have themselves been borrowed by English from other languages of course.

(☆☆☆◎◎◎)

【4】次の英文を読んで，(1)・(2)の問いに答えなさい。

Members of all groups exhibit certain regularities in their patterns of interaction. (ア)A close look at these patterns reveals that they often involve behavior which is considered desirable by group members. Further, they often involve behavior in which members exert pressures upon one another to conform to some recognized standard. Such regularities in group behavior have been explained in terms of social norms. A social norm is an expectation shared by group members which specifies behavior that is considered appropriate for a given situation. (イ)In this context behavior is broadly conceived to include not only overt behavior, but also verbal behavior associated with an individual's perceptions, thoughts, or feelings.

(1) 下線部(ア)を日本語になおしなさい。

(2) 下線部(イ)を日本語になおしなさい。

(☆☆☆◎◎◎)

【5】次の英文の(　1　)～(　6　)にあてはまる最も適切な語をア～クから選び，記号で答えなさい。

Health food gained popularity when people began to think more seriously about their physical (　1　). The very term health food is (　2　) because it implies that there is also "unhealthy" food. Health food is fresh, natural, unprocessed food. It does not contain (　3　) to make it (　4　) longer or (　5　) to make it taste or look better. Most health food enthusiasts are vegetarians. They eat no meat; they prefer to get their essential (　6　) from other sources, such as beans, cheese, and eggs.

ア ironic　イ vitamins　ウ preservatives　エ chemicals
オ well-being　カ exercise　キ last　ク proteins

(☆☆☆◎◎◎)

【6】次の対話文の(　1　)～(　5　)にあてはまる最も適切な英文を，ア～クの中から選び，記号で答えなさい。(ただし，選択肢を2度使わないこと。)

A : You're England's youngest football manager, Johnny. How old are you?

B : Thirty-five.

A : (　1　)

B : (　2　)

A : (　3　)

B : Seven years.

A : What was your first club?

B : (　4　)

A : (　5　)

B : Well, I went to America to play for the Los Angeles Dynamos next.

ア　When did you start to play for the club？

イ　I've been manager for five years, but I played for the club before that.

ウ　Newcastle United, and I left that club in 1990.

エ　How long have you been the manager of Birmingham City?

オ　You played for the club so long, didn't you?

カ　In Scotland, but my family moved to New castle when I was five.

キ　Then, did you come to play for Birmingham City?

ク　How long did you play for Birmingham?

(☆☆☆◎◎◎)

【7】次の文を英語になおしなさい。

「生きる力」は「確かな学力」,「豊かな人間性」,「健やかな体」から構成され,これらの要素は独立して機能するのではなく,様々なかたちで複雑に作用し合っているのです。

(☆☆☆◎◎◎)

【中学校】

【1】中学校学習指導要領「外国語」の「第2　各言語の目標及び内容等」について，次の(1)～(3)の問いに答えなさい。

(1)　「2　内容」の「(1)　言語活動」で領域別に示されている主として指導する事項について，「読むこと」,「書くこと」のどちらかの領域を選び，主として指導する事項を2つ，日本語で書きなさい。

(2)　次の(A)・(B)のいずれか1つを選び，問いに答えなさい。

(A)　「2　内容」の「(2)　言語活動の取扱い」において「〔言語の使用場面の例〕a　特有の表現がよく使われる場面」として7つ示されている中から3つ選び，日本語で書きなさい。

(B)　「2　内容」の「(4)　言語材料の取扱い」において，理解の段階にとどめることとされている3つの文法事項の例文を，英語で書きなさい。

(3)　次のア～エは,「3　指導計画の作成と内容の取扱い」の，指導計画の作成に当たって配慮するべき事項である。(　①　)～(　⑧　)にあてはまる語句を書きなさい。

ア　各学校においては，生徒の実態や地域の実情に応じて，(　①　)の目標を適切に定め，(　②　)を通して英語の目標の実現を図るようにすること。

イ　各学年とも，2の「(1)言語活動」のうち，特に(　③　)及び(　④　)の言語活動に重点をおいて指導すること。

ウ　2の「(3)言語材料」については，(　⑤　)に応じて平易なものから難しいものへと段階的に指導するとともに，理解の段階にとどめたり(　⑥　)の段階まで高めたりするなどして効果的に指導すること。

エ　音声指導に当たっては，(　③　)及び(　④　)を重視する観点から(　⑦　)などを通して2の(3)の「ア音声」に示された言語材料を継続して指導すること。

また，音声指導の補助として，必要に応じて(　⑧　)を用いて指導することもできること。

(☆☆☆◎◎◎)

【高等学校】

【1】次の文は，高等学校学習指導要領「外国語」の「第1款　目標」である。(　1　)～(　6　)に入る適切な語句を書きなさい。

外国語を通じて，言語や(　1　)に対する理解を深め，積極的に(　2　)を図ろうとする(　3　)を図り，(　4　)や相手の意向などを理解したり(　5　)などを表現したりする(　6　)を養う。

(☆☆☆◎◎◎)

【2】高等学校学習指導要領「外国語」の[言語の使用場面の例]の中で，グループにおけるコミュニケーションの場面としてあげられている例のうち，4つを英語で書きなさい。

(☆☆☆◎◎◎)

【3】高等学校学習指導要領「外国語」について，次の(A)・(B)のいずれか1つを選び，問いに答えなさい。

(A)　「オーラル・コミュニケーションⅠ」において，中学校における音声によるコミュニケーション能力を重視した指導を踏まえて内容をどのように取り扱うべきか，書きなさい。

(B)　「英語Ⅰ」において，中学校における音声によるコミュニケーション能力を重視した指導を踏まえて内容をどのように取り扱うべきか，書きなさい。

(☆☆☆◎◎◎)

解答・解説

【中高共通】

【1】(1) b　(2) a　(3) c　(4) d　(5) a

〈解説〉(1)は注意しないと間違いやすい。reservationを「予約」としか解せないようではかなり混乱するはずである。ここでは「居留地」である。(2)はfriendly relationshipが聞こえれば選べる。(3)はpromised以下が重要である，(4)はmassacredがわかれば大丈夫である。(5)は原稿では触れられていない。

【2】(1) ア　(2) イ　(3) エ　(4) ア　(5) ア　(6) イ　(7) ウ　(8) ウ　(9) イ　(10) エ

〈解説〉(1)は「くだらないことをいう」，(2)は「コツをつかむ」，(3)は「干渉する」，(4)は「ショックを与えるような」，(5)は「付け合わせで飾る」，(6)は「不注意」，(7)は「尊敬すべき」，(8)は「目立つ」，(9)は「発掘された」，(10)は「～を支持して」である。

【3】英語は母語や第一言語の異なる人々にも用いられる国際語である。EUでは母語のように使われ，世界各地でも，合衆国の経済的，文化的影響を受け，より多く使われるようになっている。英語を話さない人々でも知っている単語であり，その中には外来語も多い。(120字)

〈解説〉lingua franca「国際語」をもし知らなければかなりの基礎学力不足である。指定語数が英文に対してそれほど少なくはないので，全訳するつもりで訳語を書いていき，明らかに瑣末的だと思われることを省くという方針で解答を作成するとよい。

【4】(1)　これらの傾向を詳しく見ると，それらは集団に属する人々によって望ましいと考えられる行動を伴っていることがよくあるということが明らかとなった。　(2)　この文脈において，行動とは顕在行動だけではなく，個人の知覚や思考，あるいは感情と結びついた言語行

動も含むものとおおむね考えられる。

〈解説〉いずれの箇所も下線部のみ読んでも正確に訳すことができる問題である。出題者はなぜその前後の英文を示したかったのか理解に苦しむ。前後の英文を示しているのであるから，代名詞はそれが指す具体的内容を示しながら訳しなさい，というような指示があってもよさそうである。たとえば，(1)の「それら」とは何か考えていただきたい。ここではthese patternsである。

【5】(1)　オ　(2)　ア　(3)　ウ　(4)　キ　(5)　エ　(6)　ク

〈解説〉「(品質が)持つ」のlastがピンとこないかもしれないくらいであると思われる。保存料とは何か，また，味や見かけをよくするものといえばどういったものかなど，少し考えれば容易に正答に至ることができる非常にやさしい問題である。

【6】(1)　エ　(2)　イ　(3)　ク　(4)　ウ　(5)　キ

〈解説〉サッカーチームのマネジャー(おそらく社長か何か経営者の立場の方)へのインタビューであることは最初のやりとりですぐに理解できる。基本的にAは質問するはずであり，Bは答えるはずである。選択肢を質問と回答に分類してから取りかかると答えやすい。

【7】A “zest for living” consists of “solid academic prowess,” “a well-rounded character,” and “a healthy body.” These elements do not function independently but intricately affect one another.

〈解説〉学習指導要領の英語版に目を通してあってカギ括弧で囲まれているような語句の英訳がスムーズに書ければあとは簡単である。もしそのような語句の定訳を知らなければ，その場で自分なりに意味を考えて訳せばそれほど減点されるとは思えない。

【中学校】

【1】(1)　読むこと：(ア)　文字や符号を識別し，正しく読むこと。(イ)　書かれた内容を考えながら黙読したり，その内容が表現されるように音読すること。　(ウ)　物語や説明文などのあらすじや大切な部分を読み取ること。　(エ)　伝言や手紙などから書き手の意向を理解し，適切に応じること。のうち2つ答えればよい。　書くこと：(ア)　文字や符号を識別し，語と語の区切りなどに注意をして正しく書くこと。　(イ)　聞いたり読んだりしたことについてメモをとったり，感想や意見などを書いたりすること。　(ウ)　自分の考えや気持ちなどが読み手に正しく伝わるように書くこと。　(エ)　伝言や手紙などで読み手に自分の意向が正しく伝わるように書くこと。のうち2つ答えればよい。　(2)　(A)　あいさつ，自己紹介，電話での応答，買い物，道案内，旅行，食事のうち3つ答えればよい。　(B)　I know what color hi likes the best.　I don't know how to play the drum.　I know the man who worked hard for the people in Asia.　(3)　①　学年ごと　②　3学年間　③　聞くこと　④　話すこと　⑤　学習段階　⑥　表現　⑦　発音練習　⑧　発音表記

〈解説〉学習指導要領を熟読し理解するしかない。ここでは(2)(B)のみ解説する。つぎのようなものが対象ということを理解し，この例文を挙げればよい。(ア)　[主語＋動詞＋目的語]の文型のうち主語＋動詞＋whatなどで始まる節，(イ)　[主語＋動詞＋間接目的語＋直接目的語]の文型のうち主語＋動詞＋間接目的語＋how(など)to不定詞，(ウ)関係代名詞のうち，主格のthat，which，who及び目的格のthat，whichの制限的用法の基本的なものである。

【高等学校】

【1】(1)　文化　(2)　コミュニケーション　(3)　態度の育成
(4)　情報　(5)　自分の考え　(6)　実践的コミュニケーション能力

〈解説〉学習指導要領のなかでも目標は全体を網羅するものである。暗記するほどに読み込んでおく必要がある。

【2】recitations, speeches, presentations, role-plays, discussions, debates のうち4つ答えればよい。

〈解説〉学習指導要領を読んでおけばよい。ただ英語で書きなさいというのが少し意地悪ではある。英語版を見るといずれも複数形であり，ここでも複数形で答えた方が無難ではある。ただし，単数形で答えたからといって減点まではされないと考えられる。

【3】(A)　(中学校のおける音声によるコミュニケーション能力を重視する指導を踏まえ,)話題や対話の相手を広げたコミュニケーション活動を行いながら，中学校における基礎的な学習事項を整理し，習熟を図るものとする。　(B)　(中学校のおける音声によるコミュニケーション能力を重視する指導を踏まえ,)聞くこと及び話すことの活動を多く取り入れながら，読むこと及び書くことを含めた四つの領域の言語活動を総合的，有機的に関連させて指導するものとする。

〈解説〉学習指導要領を読んでおけばよい。数語で終わる解答ではないので，多少語句が異なっても趣旨が合致していれば問題ないと考えられる。学習指導要領が暗記しにくいとお考えの方は，自分なりのノートを作ってまとめるとよい。内容もよく頭に入るし，繰り返しているうちに覚えてしまうものである。

2006年度　実施問題

【中高共通】

【1】問題文及び5つの質問を聞き，各質問の後に読まれるa～dの4つの選択肢の中からその質問に対する答えとして最も適切なものを選び，記号で答えなさい。

ただいまから，リスニングテストを始めます。受審者は問題用紙(その1)の問題1を見なさい。

これから読む英文の内容に関して5つの質問をします。a, b, c, dの4つの答えの中から最も適切なものを1つ選び，記号で答えなさい。問題文と質問の英文はそれぞれ2回読みます。聞きながらメモを取ってもかまいません。それでは始めます。

In Japan, more than 4.17 million young people are characterized by the government as "freeters "---those in the 15-34 age range without steady jobs. A Cabinet Office White Paper on the National Lifestyle found that just one in five of all Japanese in that age range are working as freeters. While more than 70 percent of the freeters wish to eventually be hired as full-time employees, more companies have been cutting back on expenses, letting full-time employees go and hiring temporary employees.

Full-time employees have benefits like bonuses, social insurance and pension plans. While more freeters are expected in the future, a report warns that their growing numbers will lead to a social anxiety which will badly effect Japan's financial standing. An institute did research on the difference of average life-time wages earned by freeters and full-timers, assuming each group maintains the same working style from ages 19 to 60. According to the research, full-timers earn a lifetime wage of 215 million yen. Freeters, though, earn a lifetime wage of 52 million yen. According to the report, the number of freeters will likely reach 4.76 million by 2010.

"Sooner or later, it will hit the Japanese economy, " says an economist.

"The problem would be the majority of the freeters who would continue working as cheap, casual labor, in which they have little opportunity to develop their professional skills." To improve this situation, the report stresses that society m just find ways to encourage young people to be part of the salary system. This would guarantee stability of the national tax base and payments into the insurance and pension programs. Part of the measures introduced by the government to lower the rate of freeters includes giving young students an opportunity to have some real working experience.

Employers are also expected to establish systems which would encourage their workers---full-timers or freeters---to develop motivation as well as professional skills. There should be an employment system that allows freeters to develop professional skills. Also, the difference of benefits and salaries between full-timers and freeters should be reduced.

[REPEAT]

Question

(1) What is the definition of "freeter"? [REPEAT]

a Young people without working.

b Young people without steady jobs.

c Young people without social insurance.

d Young people without professional skills.

(2) What is a possible negative effect if the number of freeters increases? [REPEAT]

a More companies will cut back on expenses.

b Full-timers will lose benefits like bonuses, social insurance and pension plans.

c A social anxiety will effect Japan's financial standing.

d Full-timers will lose motivation as well as professional skills.

(3) What is the difference between average lifetime wages earned by freeters and full-timers? [REPEAT]

a Full-timers earn twice as much as freeters.

b Full-timers earn three times as much as freeters.

c Full-timers earn four times as much as freeters.

d Full-timers earn five times as much as freeters.

(4) What would be the problem if freeters continue working as cheap casual labor? [REPEAT]

a They have more free time.

b They don't pay tax.

c They can't find a job they want to do.

d They have little opportunity to develop their professional skills.

(5) Which sentence is NOT correct according to the passage? [REPEAT]

a Society must find ways to encourage young people to be part of the salary system.

b The government has introduced no measures to lower the rate of freeters yet.

c There should be an employment system that allows freeters to develop professional skills.

d The difference of benefits and salaries between full-timers and freeters should be reduced.

これでリスニングテストを終わります。

(☆☆☆☆◎◎◎◎◎)

【2】次の(1)～(10)の各文の(　　)に当てはまる最も適切な語または語句を，ア～エから1つ選び，記号で答えなさい。

(1) Students will be (　　) for exceeding the time limit in their speech. They will lose one point for every minute over the limit.

ア penalized　イ criticized　ウ accused

エ condemned

(2) A : What will you do while you're waiting for me to come out of the hairdresser's?

B : Oh, I'll just go to that bookstore over there and (　　) through the magazines.

ア　graze　　イ　browse　　ウ　dip　　エ　hop

(3)　The teacher arranged the dates of famous inventions in (　　) order so that the students could see the developments in human history.

ア　timely　　イ　random　　ウ　spontaneous

エ　chronological

(4)　The professor lost his notes just before his speech, so he had to (　　) on the spot.

ア　memorize　　イ　supervise　　ウ improvise　　エ　authorize

(5)　When my co-worker get into arguments, I try to avoid taking (　　). It's safer to stay neutral.

ア　angles　　イ　turns　　ウ　sides　　エ　places

(6)　After graduating from university, James kept all his old textbooks, believing they would (　　) someday.

ア　be a handful　　イ　fall on hard times

ウ　come in handy　　エ　comedown on

(7)　I only said it as a joke, but he took my words (　　) and got very upset.

ア　decently　　イ　literally　　ウ　typically　　エ　promptly

(8)　The doctor wrote a (　　) for some medicine for Jack to take while his leg was healing.

ア　depiction　　イ　description　　ウ　prescription

エ　subscription

(9)　I will always (　　) the memory of the wonderful time we had together on our vacation.

ア　cherish　　イ　diminish　　ウ　perish　　エ　polish

(10)　The hotel had a variety of (　　), including two restaurants, and a hot spring.

ア　borders　　イ　facilities　　ウ utensils　　エ　ingredients

(☆☆☆☆◎◎◎◎◎)

【3】次の英文を読んで，その趣旨を100字以内の日本語で書きなさい。ただし，句読点も字数に入れること。

In deciding how to approach the teaching and learning of English we can divide classroom activities into two broad categories: those that give students language input, and those which encourage them to produce language output. Whether acquisition or conscious learning is taking place there will be stages at which the student is receiving language — language is in some way being 'put into' the students (though they will decide whether or not they want to receive it). But exposing students to language input is not enough: we also need to provide opportunities for them to activate this knowledge, for it is only when students are producing language that they can select from the input they have received. Language production allows students to rehearse language use in classroom conditions while receiving feedback (from the teachers, from other students and from themselves) which allows them to adjust their perceptions of the language input they have received.

(☆☆☆☆◎◎◎◎◎)

【4】次の英文を読んで，(1)・(2)の問いに答えなさい。

(ア) <u>Parents, educators, and others have often expressed concern about the high proportion of crime and violence in mass media and about its effects on children, particularly the possibility that it may contribute to juvenile delinquency.</u> Periodically, leading public figures question its impact, and Congress has conducted a number of inquiries over the years. (イ) <u>Contemporary discussions parallel earlier ones indicting older media such as movies and comic books.</u>

(1) 下線部(ア)を日本語になおしなさい。

(2) "Contemporary discussions"の内容を明らかにして，下線部(イ)を日本語になおしなさい。

(☆☆☆☆◎◎◎◎)

【5】次の英文の(　1　)～(　6　)に当てはまる最も適切な語をア～クから選び，記号で答えなさい。ただし，文頭に来る語もすべて小文字にしてある。

In the 1950s and 1960s, blacks fought to gain fair (　1　), and they now have legal (　2　)in housing, education and employment. Because their neighborhoods are (　3　), many blacks feel that educational opportunities are not (　4　) for their children. (　5　) children from one neighborhood to another is one solution to (　6　) in education. Naturally, all parents want the best possible education for their children.

ア	adequate	イ	busing	ウ	enlightenment
エ	inequality	オ	poor	カ	protection
キ	segregated	ク	treatment		

(☆☆☆☆◎◎◎◎)

【6】次の対話文の(　1　)～(　5　)に当てはまる最も適切なものを，ア～エから1つ選び，記号で答えなさい。

A : Your house is very (　1　) to work, isn't it?

B : Yes, it is. I always walk to work －even (　2　)!

A : I usually take the bus. It takes so long!

B : How long does it take?

A : Oh, it takes about 20 minutes.

B : That is a long time. Well, have some cake.

A : (Taking a bite of some cake) This is delicious! (　3　)

B : Yes, I usually bake something at the weekend. I like having sweets in the house.

A : You're a wonderful cook!

B : Thank you, it's nothing really.

A : (　4　) I'm just hopeless. My husband, David, usually does all the cooking.

B : Do you often go out to eat?

A : Yes, when he doesn't have time to cook, we go out to eat somewhere.

B : (　5　)

A : Too many! You can eat at a different restaurant every day.

(1) ア　wide　　イ　comfortable
　　ウ　close　　エ　inconvenient

(2) ア　when it will rain　　イ　when it rains
　　ウ　if it rained　　エ　if it will rain

(3) ア　Who baked this cake?
　　イ　When do you bake all of your own cakes?
　　ウ　Do you bake all of your own cakes?
　　エ　Can I tell you how to bake this cake?

(4) ア　I'm good at cooking too.
　　イ　I never cook.
　　ウ　I usually cook for my family.
　　エ　I like cooking too.

(5) ア　You will cook for him when he is busy.
　　イ　You can have many chances to cook.
　　ウ　I seldom go out to eat at the restaurants.
　　エ　There are some wonderful restaurants in the city.

(☆☆☆◎◎◎◎◎)

【7】次の文を英語になおしなさい。

蒸し暑い夏の日の夕方，窓を開けるとどこからともなく笛や太鼓の音が聞こえてくる。毎年この時期になると，「よしこの」のリズムに心が躍るのである。

(☆☆☆☆◎◎◎◎◎)

【中学校】

【1】中学校学習指導要領「外国語」について，次の(1)・(2)の問いに答えなさい。

(1)　次の各文章は，「言語活動の取扱い」の「学習段階を考慮した指導上の配慮事項」である。(　①　)～(　⑧　)に当てはまる語句を書きなさい。

(ア)　第1学年における言語活動

英語を初めて学習することに配慮し，(　①　)に対する(　②　)な態度の育成を重視するとともに，身近な言語の使用場面や言語の働きに配慮した言語活動を行わせること。その際，自分の(　③　)や身の回りの(　④　)などの中から簡単な表現を用いてコミュニケーションを図れるような話題を取り上げること。

(イ)　第2学年における言語活動

第1学年の学習を基礎として，言語の使用場面や言語の働きを更に広げた言語活動を行わせること。その際，第1学年に加え，特に，(　⑤　)を伝えたり，物事について(　⑥　)したりした内容などの中からコミュニケーションを図れるような話題を取り上げること。

(ウ)　第3学年における言語活動

第2学年の学習を基礎として，言語の使用場面や言語の働きを一層広げた言語活動を行わせること。その際，第2学年に加え，特に，様々な(　⑦　)や(　⑧　)などの中からコミュニケーションが図れるような話題を取り上げること。

(2)　「各言語の目標及び内容等」の「目標」で，4領域別に示された目標から2領域を選び，日本語で書きなさい。

(☆☆☆☆◎◎◎◎◎)

【2】次の(A)・(B)のいずれか1つを選び，問いに答えなさい。

(A)　教育効果を高めるものの一つとして教育機器の有効活用があるが，英語の授業における効果的な活用法を3つ，英語で書きなさい。

(B)　生徒が広い視野から国際理解を深めるために，英語の授業において教師が配慮すべきことを3つ，英語で書きなさい。

(☆☆☆☆◎◎◎◎◎)

【高等学校】

【1】次の文は，高等学校学習指導要領「外国語」の「第3款　各科目にわたる指導計画の作成と内容の取扱い」において，内容の取扱いにあたって配慮する事項を述べたものである。(　1　)~(　6　)に入る適切な語句を書きなさい。

各科目の指導に当たっては，(　1　)や指導体制を工夫し，(　2　)やペア・ワーク，グループ・ワークなどを適宜取り入れたり，(　3　)や，LL，コンピュータ，情報通信ネットワークなどを指導に生かしたりすること。また，(　4　)などの協力を得て行う授業を積極的に取り入れ，生徒の(　5　)を育成するとともに，(　6　)を深めるようにすること。

(☆☆☆☆◎◎◎◎◎)

【2】高等学校学習指導要領「外国語」で「言語の働きの例」としてあげられている5項目のうち4項目を書きなさい。

(☆☆☆☆◎◎◎◎◎)

【3】高等学校学習指導要領「外国語」について，次の(A)・(B)のいずれか1つを選び，問いに答えなさい。

(A)　「オーラル・コミュニケーションI」の目標を<u>英語で書きなさい</u>。

(B)　「英語I」の目標を<u>英語で書きなさい</u>。

(☆☆☆☆◎◎◎◎◎)

解答・解説

【中高共通】

【1】(1)　b　(2)　c　(3)　c　(4)　d　(5)　b

〈解説〉リスニングに当たっては，話題の中心に注意して聞き取るようにする。Freetersに関してそれぞれ次のことについて述べている。質問と解答の内容はそれぞれ次の通りである。
(1)　質問「フリーターはどのように定義されていますか」　放送文の，those in the 15-34 age range without steady jobsから，「定職に就かない若者」とする。　(2)　質問「フリーターの数が増えると，どんなマイナス面のことが生じますか」　放送文の，their growing numbers will lead to a social anxiety which will badly effect Japan's financial standingから，「社会不安が日本の財政的な地位に影響を及ぼす」とする。　(3)　質問「フリーターと正規の労働者が得る生涯賃金はどのくらいの違いがありますか」　放送文の，full- timers earn a lifetime wage of 215 million yen. Freeters, though, earn a lifetime wage of 52 million yenから，「正規労働者はフリーターの四倍の収入がある」とする。　(4)　質問「フリーターが低賃金労働を続けると，どのような問題が生ずるだろうか」　放送文の，The problem would be the majority of the freeters who would continue working as cheap, casual labor, in which they have little opportunity to develop their professional skillsから，「専門的な技能を伸ばす機会がほとんどなくなる」とする。　(5)　質問「本文の内容から，述べていないことは次のどれですか」　放送文の，Part of the measures introduced by the government to lower the rate of freeters includes giving young students an opportunity to have some real working experienceから，「政府はこれまで，フリーターになる率を下げるためになんら方策を講じてこなかった」とする。

【2】(1)　ア　(2)　イ　(3)　エ　(4)　ウ　(5)　ウ　(6)　ウ　(7)　イ　(8)　ウ　(9)　ア　(10)　イ

〈解説〉(1)「時間を超過すると減点される」の意である。　(2)「本屋で雑誌を立ち読みする」の意である。　(3)「年代順に有名な発明を並べた」の意である。　(4)「教授はその場で講義を構築しなければならなかった」の意である。　(5)「いずれか一方の肩を持つことを避けなければならなかった」の意である。　(6)「いつか役立つと信じて」の意である。　(7)「そのまま受け取って，大変がっかりした」の意である。

(8)「ジャックに薬の処方箋を書いてくれた」の意である。 (9)「素晴らしいときの思い出を大事にする」の意である。 (10)「そのホテルにはいろいろな設備があった」の意である。

【3】英語の授業では生徒に知識を与えるインプットだけでなく，その知識を活用するアウトプットの機会も必要である。教室でフィードバックしながら言語を使用することによって，言語に対する理解を深めることができる。(100字)

〈解説〉趣旨をまとめるに当たって，次のようにポイントとなる箇所を挙げてまとめるようにすることである。 those that give students language input：「知識を与えるインプット」。those which encourage them to produce language output：「知識を活用するアウトプット」。 we also need to provide opportunities for them to activate this knowledge：「その知識を活用する必要がある」。Language production allows students to rehearse language use in classroom conditions while receiving feedback,：「教室でフィードバックしながら言語を使うようにする」。which allows them to adjust their perceptions of the language input they have received「学習した言語を理解するようにする」

【4】(1) 親や教育関係者その他の人たちは，マスメディアのかなりの割合を占める犯罪や暴力と，それらの子どもたちへの影響，特にそれらが青少年非行の一因になる可能性についての懸念をたびたび表明してきた。 (2) マスメディアの犯罪や暴力シーンが青少年非行につながるという今の議論は，映画や漫画本のような昔からのメディアを非難したかつての議論と類似している。

〈解説〉(1) have often expressed concern：「たびたび懸念を表明してきた」。～aboutは，the high proportion of crime and violence in mass media and about its effects on children, particularly the possibility ～とつながり，「かなりの割合を占める犯罪，それらの子どもへの影響，特にそれが青少年非行の一因になる可能性について」となることに留意する。

(2) Contemporaryは，前文の内容を受け，「マスメディアの犯罪や暴力シーンが青少年非行につながるという」となることに留意する。parallel＝is similarである。earlier onesは，「かっての議論」である。indicating older media「昔からのメディアを非難した」である。

【5】(1)　ク　(2)　カ　(3)　キ　(4)　ア　(5)　イ　(6)　エ

〈解説〉それぞれ次の意味である。(1)「公平な扱い」　(2)「法的な保護」　(3)「差別されている」　(4)「適切な」　(5)「一方の地域から他の地域にバスで通学する生徒」　(6)「教育の不平等」

【6】(1)　ウ　(2)　イ　(3)　ウ　(4)　イ　(5)　エ

〈解説〉それぞれAとBとの会話の流れから判断するようにする。

(1)　B : Yes, it is. I always walk to work.の対話文から，「お宅は勤務地にはとても近い」とする。　(2)　同じくBとの対話から，「雨が降っても」とする。副詞節when it rainsとなる。　(3)　B : Yes, I usually bake something at the weekendの対話文から，「ケーキはすべてあなたが焼くんですか」とする。　(4)　B : Thank you, it's nothing really .の対話文から，否定の意味の「私は料理しないの」とする。　(5)　A : we go out to eat somewhere.や，A : Too many～ の対話文から，「町には格好のレストランがあるから」とする。

【7】When I open the window on a muggy [hot and humid, sultry] evening in summer, I hear the sound of (Japanese) flutes and drums from nowhere. Every year around this time, I get excited a [by] the rhythm of "Yoshikono."

〈解説〉日本のある地域の状況を伝える含蓄のある文である。日本語を解さない外国人にこれを伝え理解してもらうつもりで英語で述べてみるような手法で取りかかってみるとよい。

先ず，「窓を開けると」When I open the window，で書き出すようにする。「蒸し暑い夏の日の夕方」は，on a muggy evening in summerと表す。「聞こえてくる」は，主語を明確にして，I hearとする。「どこからとなくもなく笛や太鼓の音」は，the sound of (Japanese) flutes and drums from nowhereで表す。「毎年この時期になると」は，Every year around this yearとして表現する。「心が躍る」は，主語を明確にして，I get excitedである。「『よしこの』のリズム」は，地元特有の名称なので，the rhythm of “Yoshikono” のように表現する。

【中学校】

【1】(1) ① コミュニケーション ② 積極的 ③ 気持ち ④ できごと ⑤ 事実関係 ⑥ 判断 ⑦ 考え ⑧ 意見
(2) 次のうちから二つの事項を解答する。「聞くこと」英語を聞くことに慣れ親しみ，初歩的な英語を聞いて話し手の意向などを理解できるようにすること。「話すこと」英語で話すことに慣れ親しみ，初歩的な英語を用いて自分の考えなどを話すことができるようにすること。「読むこと」英語を読むことに慣れ親しみ，初歩的な英語を読んで書き手の意向などを理解できるようにすること。「書くこと」英語を書くことに慣れ親しみ，初歩的な英語を用いて自分の考えなどを書くことができるようにすること。

〈解説〉(1) 中学校学習指導要領 第9節 第2各言語の目標及び内容等 2内容 「言語活動の取り扱い」の「学習段階を考慮した指導上の配慮事項」に関する事柄である。中学校における「英語の学習を通して，日常的な会話や簡単な情報の交換などができるような実践的なコミュニケーション能力の基礎を養うことをねらいとして」言語活動についての考え方の下に，周知して実際の指導にも当たれるようにしておくことが大切である。 (2) 同じく学習指導要領 英語 目標について述べるようにする。「聞くこと」では，単に英語を聞いて文の表面的な意味を理解するだけでなく，話し手の意向などを理解することを重視している。「話すこと」では，与えられた文を機械的に繰り返すことだけでなく，自分の考えなどを話すことができることを重視している。「読むこと」では，単に英語を読んで表面的に文の意味を理解するにとどまらず，書き手の意向などを理解することを重視している。「書くこと」では，与えられた語や文を書き写すことができるだけでなく，自分の考えなどを書くことができることを重視している。

【2】(A)　①　Using a CD player, students can enjoy listening to many English songs.　②　The projector or OHP can be used for Show and Tell activities.　③　Using VTR or DVD, teachers can introduce various English movies to the students.　④　Teachers and students can access a lot of information and material for the classes on the Internet.　⑤　Students can exchange E-mails with other students inside or outside Japan.　などから3つ　(B)　①　Students will be free from prejudice and stereotypes against other peoples and races.　②　Students will understand Japan and Japanese culture through understanding other countries and their cultures.　③　Teachers will make opportunities for the students to introduce Japanese culture and our way of life to foreign people.　④　Students will recognize a variety of cultures, traditions, and ways of life and respect them.
⑤　Students will understand they are part of the world and try to cooperate with people in other countries.　などから3つ

〈解説〉英語の授業に次のような方法で教育機器の活用を図り，教育効果を高めるようにする。
(A)　①　CDプレイヤーを使って，生徒が英語の歌を聞く機会を多く持つようにする。　③　VTRやDVDを使って，教師が生徒に映画を見せ外国のことを知るようにする。　⑤　生徒が日本内外の生徒とE-mailで交流できるようにする。　(B)　①　生徒が外国あるいは外国人に偏見を持たないようにする。　②　他の国や文化を知ることによって，日本及び文化をよく理解するようにする。　③　教師が，外国人に生徒が日本文化や生活方法について紹介する機会をもつ。

【高等学校】

【1】(1)　指導方法　(2)　ティーム・ティーチング　(3)　視聴覚教材
(4)　ネイティブ・スピーカー　(5)　コミュニケーション能力
(6)　国際理解

〈解説〉現行学習指導要領では，実践的なコミュニケーション能力の育成を重要な目標として挙げている。指導に当たっては，この目標の達成に向けて，生徒の能力・適性や興味・関心に応じて指導法や指導体制を様々に工夫することが求められている。実践的コミュニケーション能力を育成するためには，外国語の知識を増やすだけでなく，それを実際の場面で使うことを指導することが大切である。

【2】① 人との関係を円滑にする　② 気持ちを伝える　③ 情報を伝える　④ 考えや意図を伝える

〈解説〉① 人との関係を円滑にする言語の働きは，コミュニケーションを開始し，維持する働きであり，言語の使用場面と言語材料との関連で更に発展させる。 ② 気持ちを伝える働きについては，言語の使用場面と言語材料との関連で，「歓迎する」「祝う」「満足する」なども併せて指導する。 ③ 情報を伝える働きについては，更に発展させて指導する。 ④ 考えや意図を伝える働きについては，「推論する」「仮定する」「説得する」も加えて指導する。なお，五項目の最後は，「相手の行動を促す」である。

【3】(A) To further develop students' abilities to organize, present and discuss information, ideas, etc. in English, and to foster a positive attitude toward communication through dealing with a wide variety of topics. (B) To develop students' basic abilities to understand what they listen to or read and to convey information, ideas, and to foster a positive attitude toward communication through dealing with everyday topics.

〈解説〉「オーラルコミュニケーションI」は，「英語I」と同様に必履修科目である。中学校の学習を踏まえつつ，日常生活の身近な話題について，英語を聞いたり話したりして，情報や考えなどを理解し，伝える基礎的な能力を養うとともに，積極的にコミュニケーションを図ることを目的にしている。そのために，高等学校の英語指導に当たっては，内容を十分に理解し，実際の指導に生かせるようにすることが大切である。英語版は，文部科学省のホームページに示してある。英語でも表現できるようにし，日本における「実践的なコミュニケーション能力の育成」について，外国の英語教育指導者とも，語り合える責務を果たせる指導者として英語教育に当たることが大切である。

2005年度　実施問題

【中高共通】

【1】リスニングテスト

問題文及び5つの質問の英文を聞き，その質問に対する答えとして最も適切なものを，各質問の後に示されるa～dの4つの選択肢の中から選び，記号で答えなさい。

ただいまから，リスニングテストを始めます。受審者は問題用紙（その1）の問題1を見なさい。

これから読む英文の内容に関して5つの質問をします。a，b，c，dの4つの答えの中から最も適切なものを1つ選び，記号で答えなさい。問題文と質問の英文はそれぞれ2回読みます。聞きながらメモを取ってもかまいません。それでは始めます。

The Olympic Games originated in 776 B. C. in Olympia, a small town in Greece. Participants in the first Olympiad are said to have run a 200-yard race, but as the Games were held every four years, they expanded in scope. Only Greek amateurs were allowed to participate in this festival in honor of the god Zeus. The event became a religious, patriotic, and athletic occasion, and the winners were honored with wreaths and special privileges. There was a profound change in the nature of the Games under the Roman emperors. After they became professional circuses and carnivals, they were banned in 394 A. D. by Emperor Theodosius.

The modern Olympic Games began in Athens in 1896 as a result of the initiative of Baron Pierre de Coubertin. He was a French educator, and his desire was to promote international understanding through athletics. Nine nations participated in the first Games, while over 100 nations currently compete.

Political and racial controversy, however, has influenced the Olympic Games in our epoch. In 1936 Hitler, whose country hosted the Games, insulted Jesse Owens, a black American runner, by refusing to congratulate him on his great deed of having won four gold medals. In the 1972 Munich Games, the world was shocked by the horrible murder of eleven Israeli athletes by Arab terrorists. The next Olympic Games in Montreal were boycotted by African nations; in addition, Taiwan withdrew. In 1980, because the Soviet Union invaded Afghanistan, sixty-two nations refused to participate in the Games in Moscow and caused great disappointment to their athletes. The consensus among those nations was that their refusal would protest the Soviet invasion of Afghanistan.

In 2004, the Olympic Games will return to Athens. We really hope political controversy and war will never hinder the Games.

Question

［REPEAT］

(1) What was the purpose of the first Olympic Games? ［REPEAT］

a They were held for political reasons.

b They were held as an international competition.

c They were held as a religious festival.

d They were held as a professional athletes' competition.

(2) How long did the ancient Olympic Games continue? ［REPEAT］

a For about 200 years.

b For about 400 years.

c For about 800 years.

d For about 1200 years.

(3) What was the purpose of the modern Olympic Games? ［REPEAT］

a To give amateur athletes a chance to participate.

b To promote international understanding through athletics.

c To promote patriotic emotion.

d To solve political controversy.

(4) What was the reason why Hitler refused to congratulate Jesse Owens? ［REPEAT］

a　National pride.

b　Jealousy.

c　Personal preference.

d　Racial discrimination.

(5)　Which sentence is NOT correct according to the passage? [REPEAT]

a　In ancient time, only Greek amateurs were allowed to participate in Olympic Games.

b　More than 100 nations took part in the first modern Olympic Games.

c　In the 1972 Munich Games, eleven Israeli athletes were killed by Arab terrorists.

d　In the 1980 Moscow Games, 62 nations boycotted the games to protest the Soviet invasion of Afghanistan.

これでリスニングテストを終わります。

(☆☆☆◎◎◎)

【2】次の(1)～(10)の各文の（　　）に入れるのに最も適切なものを，ア～エから1つ選び，記号で答えなさい。

(1)　Scientists have found that classical music can（　　）plants to grow faster and larger.

ア　insulate　　イ　stimulate　　ウ　provoke　　エ　wither

(2)　The bright light from the movie screen was so（　　）that many of the children began to get headaches.

ア　delicate　　イ　feeble　　ウ　intense　　エ　passionate

(3)　Company policy is to keep all personal data（　　）. We never disclose customer information without permission.

ア　confidential　　イ　conceptual　　ウ　comprehensive

エ　conditional

(4)　The government（　　）provided the extra money needed to keep the local bus service running.

ア　clemency　　イ　fallacy　　ウ　insolvency　　エ　subsidy

(5) The young designer was very proud to have had a (　　) in the production of such a wonderful play.

ア foot　イ hand　ウ mouth　エ thumb

(6) If you can't state exactly what the repairs will cost, can you give us an (　　) figure to go on?

ア expended　イ enormous　ウ irrelevant

エ approximate

(7) When you travel in the United States, you need to be able to understand such (　　) of measure as miles, pounds, and gallons.

ア marks　イ units　ウ digits　エ tools

(8) This patient's condition could worsen at any time, so I want her kept under constant (　　).

ア inspection　イ investigation　ウ observation

エ preservation

(9) I don't understand why you're so upset over something so (　　). Who cares what color my necktie is?

ア feasible　イ sensitive　ウ vital　エ trivial

(10) We were very happy to help you. Please don't feel (　　) to repay us.

ア obliged　イ gratified　ウ impaired　エ restrained

(☆☆☆◎◎◎)

【3】次の英文を読んで，その趣旨を100字以内の日本語で書きなさい。ただし，句読点も字数に入れること。

In order to be able to "make use of English", it is necessary not only to have a knowledge of grammar and vocabulary but also the ability to use English for the purpose of actual communication. Thus, in English classes, instruction mainly based on grammar and translation or teacher-centered classes are not recommended. Through the repetition of activities making use of English as a means of communication, the learning of vocabulary and grammar should be enhanced, and communication abilities in "listening," "speaking," "reading," and "writing" should be fostered. Such techniques for instruction are necessary.

To carry out such instruction effectively, it is important for teachers to establish many situations where students can communicate with each other in English and routinely to conduct classes principally in English. Through such opportunities, learners can experience the fulfillment of expressing themselves and understanding others, and feel the joy of learning English. Furthermore, it is also important to devise creative teaching methods so that learners can become interested in the importance and necessity of acquiring English, which can broaden the student's world and possibilities.

(☆☆☆◎◎◎)

【4】次の英文を読んで，下線部(1)・(2)を日本語になおしなさい。

(1) The world does not come to us as a given, fully formed and waiting to be perceived; rather, it is an achievement that must be constructed by active process. The world becomes objectivized by grades. In the course of this process, the object is transformed through various states, accompanied by different forms of awareness and affective bonds, toward the final exteriorized or "projected" image. This image is the goal of perception. (2) We may say that perception strives toward the realization of models in the abstract that can be taken for external things.

(☆☆☆◎◎◎)

【5】次の英文の（　1　）～（　6　）にあてはまる最も適切なものをア～クから選び，記号で答えなさい。（ただし，同じ選択肢を2度用いてはいけない。）

Wisdom, as usual, lies somewhere between compulsion and revulsion. The first sensible step is to acknowledge that measurement is a means, not an（　1　）in itself.

Precise measurement is an indispensable part of the larger（　2　）of understanding ourselves and our universe. The knowledge so acquired is not a useless ornament of the educated (3) ; it sets policy, guides action, and supports decision in every (4) it touches. But not all measurements are equally valuable. Measurements made without a supporting context of theory or practical (5) seldom justify the time and money spent on them. To make measurements without knowing (6) is like buying petrol without owning a car.

ア realm	イ beginning	ウ application	エ end
オ enterprise	カ mind	キ why	ク education

(☆☆☆◎◎◎)

【6】次の対話文の（　　）にあてはまる最も適切なものを，ア～クの中から選び，記号で答えなさい。(ただし，同じ選択肢を2度使ってはいけない。)

〔Lance Jones is having a job interview with a TV station.〕

A: OK, Lance, let's talk about your education and experience.

B: Yes, certainly.

A: (1)

B: That's right, I majored in Broadcasting.

A: Right. How was the course?

B: It was an excellent course. I learned a lot.

A: And what was your first job after graduation?

B: (2)

A: Did you enjoy it?

B: Yes, it was a great first job. (3)

A: And after a year, you were promoted, and became a news presenter?

B: That's right. (4)

A: And now you're with CTV in Springfield?

B: Yes, I'm working for CTV as a freelance reporter.
(5)

A: I see, and what would you like to do for us?

B: I'd like to work as a presenter and a reporter.

ア　I got a lot of reporting experience.

イ　I do a lot of live reports.

ウ　You have a lot of experiences of reporting.

エ　I worked on the seven o'clock newscast.

オ　I was a reporter for the Journal in Chicago.

カ　What did you major in?

キ　You graduated from East State University in 1996?

ク　What university did you graduated from?

(☆☆☆◎◎◎)

【7】次の文の下線部を英語になおしなさい。

21世紀を迎えて，日本に対する国際的期待は一層強まり，我が国が国際的に果たすべき役割も，ますます重要度が増してきている。特に，我が国としては，各分野における国際交流や広報活動を通じて諸外国との間の相互理解を増進し，相互信頼に基づいた友好関係を築いていくことが極めて重要である。

(☆☆☆◎◎◎)

【中学校】

【1】中学校学習指導要領「外国語」について，次の(1)・(2)の問いに答えなさい。

(1)　次の文は，内容の取扱いにおいて，題材を選定するうえで配慮すべき観点を述べたものです。①～⑧にあてはまる言葉を書きなさい。

ア　多様なものの見方や（　①　）を理解し，公正な（　②　）を養い豊かな（　③　）を育てるのに役立つこと。

イ　世界や我が国の（　④　）や文化についての理解を深めるとともに，（　⑤　）や文化に対する関心を高め，これらを（　⑥　）する態度を育てるのに役立つこと。

ウ　広い視野から（　⑦　）を深め，国際社会に生きる（　⑧　）としての自覚を高めるとともに，国際協調の精神を養うのに役立つこと。

(2)　「第2　各言語の目標及び内容等」に，言語活動の取扱いにおける3年間を通じた全体的な配慮事項が述べられているが，その主なものを3つ日本語で書きなさい。

(☆☆☆◎◎◎)

【2】次の(a)・(b)のいずれかを選択し，答えなさい。

(a)　外国語指導助手（ALT）とのティーム・ティーチングを行うことによるメリットの主なものを3つ英語で書きなさい。

(b)　英語のコミュニケーション能力を高める工夫のひとつとして，グループワークがあるが，授業の中でグループワークを行う際に，教師が配慮すべき事柄を3つ，英語で書きなさい。

(☆☆☆◎◎◎)

【高等学校】

【1】次の文は，新高等学校学習指導要領「外国語」の「各科目にわたる指導計画の作成と内容の取扱い」において，題材を取り上げるうえで留意すべき観点を述べたものである。（　①　）～（　⑧　）に入る適切な語句を書きなさい。

ア　多様なものの見方や（　①　）を理解し，公正な（　②　）を養い豊かな（　③　）を育てるのに役立つこと。

イ　世界や我が国の（　④　）や文化についての理解を深めるとともに，（　⑤　）や文化に対する関心を高め，これらを（　⑥　）する態度を育てるのに役立つこと。

ウ　広い視野から（　⑦　）を深め，国際社会に生きる（　⑧　）としての自覚を高めるとともに，国際協調の精神を養うのに役立つこと。

(☆☆☆◎◎◎)

【2】生徒のコミュニケーション能力を高める工夫のひとつとして，グループワークがあるが，授業の中でグループワークを行う際に，教師が配慮すべき事柄を3つ，英語で書きなさい。

(☆☆☆◎◎◎)

【3】次の(A)・(B)のいずれか1つを選び，日本語で答えなさい。

なお，解答用紙の所定欄に，選択した問題を記号(A)または(B)で記しなさい。

選択問題

(A)　新学習指導要領「オーラル・コミュニケーションⅠ」の目標を達成するためにどのようなコミュニケーション活動を行うべきか，3つ書きなさい。

(B)　新学習指導要領「英語Ⅰ」の目標を達成するためにどのようなコミュニケーション活動を行うべきか，3つ書きなさい。

(☆☆☆◎◎◎)

解答・解説

【中高共通】

【1】(1)　c　(2)　d　(3)　b　(4)　d　(5)　b

〈解説〉(1)「最初のオリンピックの目的は何でしたか」　第3文で，オリンピックに参加したのはin honor of the god Zeus（ゼウス神に敬意を表して）であると述べ，さらに，続く第4文で，The event became a religious,…occasion（この大会は，宗教的…な行事となった）とあるので，cの「宗教的な祭典として開催された」が正解である。

(2)「古代オリンピックは，どれだけの期間続きましたか」　第1文で，紀元前776年に始まり，第6文で西暦394年に禁止されたとあるので，1,170年続いたことになる。したがって，正解は，dの「約1,200年間」

である。英語と日本語では，位取りが3桁か4桁かの違いがあるので，数字の聞き取りは難しい。その意味で，これは難問に入るだろう。
(3)「近代オリンピックの目的は何でしたか」　第2パラグラフの第2文で，近代オリンピックの創始者の願いは，to promote international understanding through athletics（運動競技を通じて，国際理解を増進すること）であると述べているので，そのものずばりが選択肢となっているbが正解である。ちなみに，選択肢にも挙がっているpromote…understanding throughは，第7問で，「を通じて，…理解を増進し」の部分を英訳する際に使える。それに気がつくだけの余裕がある受験生は，合格しているだろう。　(4)「ヒットラーがジェシー・オーウェンにお祝いの言葉をかけなかった理由は何ですか」　第3パラグラフの冒頭で，racial controversy（人種にまつわる論争）がオリンピックに影響を及ぼしたことについて触れ，続く次の文で，その一例としてヒットラーの行為が引き合いに出されている。さらに，オーウェンが黒人であることに，特に言及されていることから，正解は，dの「人種差別」である。　(5)「本文の内容から考えて，正しくない文はどれですか」　第2パラグラフの第3文に，最初の（近代）オリンピックには，9カ国が参加したとあるので，本文の内容に一致しないのは，bの「100を超える国々が，第1回の近代オリンピックに参加した」である。

【2】(1)　イ　(2)　ウ　(3)　ア　(4)　エ　(5)　イ　(6)　エ　(7)　イ　(8)　ウ　(9)　エ　(10)　ア

〈解説〉(1)　クラシック音楽をかけると，植物は，成長が早くなるだけでなく，大きさも増すことに，科学者は気づいていた。V＋O＋to do～で，「Oが～するのを促進する」の意味を表す動詞を探す。選択肢中にはないが，この意味では，encourageも使える。　(2)　映画のスクリーンから反射する明るい光が非常に強烈だったので，子供の多くが，頭痛を訴えだした。　(3)　会社の方針として，個人情報はすべて秘密にすることになっている。顧客の情報を許可なく開示することは決してない。　(4)　政府の補助金が支出されたので，近距離バスの運行の維持に必要な資金が臨時に入った。　(5)　その若いデザイナーは，こんなに素晴らしい芝居の製作に参加できたことを非常に誇りに思った。have a hand in～で「～に関与する・～に影響を与える」を意味する　(6)　修理費の額が正確に言えないのなら，だいたいの目安でいいから数字を言ってくれない。ちなみに，to go onは，「手がかりになる，判断材料となる」の意味で，figureを修飾している。　(7)　アメリカを旅行するときは，マイル，ポンド，ガロンといった度量衡の単位を理解できることが必要だ。　(8)　この患者の病気はいつ悪くなるか分からないので，いっときも目を離さないでください。under observationで，「観察下に置かれた状態で」を表す。　(9)　どうしてそんなつまらないことを気にするのか分からない。誰も僕のネクタイの色なんか気にしないよ。ちなみに，Who cares以下は，「誰が…を気にしよう(いや，誰も気にしない)」を表す修辞疑問文。　(10)　お役に立てて非常に嬉しかった。お礼の心配などしないでください（＜お礼をしなければいけないと思わないでください)。

【3】(例) 英語の授業において実践的コミュニケーション能力を育成するためには，主に英語で授業を行いながら，生徒が英語でコミュニケーションを行う場面を多く設定し，生徒に興味や関心をもたせる指導法の工夫が重要である。

〈解説〉第2パラグラフから見ると要点が見えやすいだろう。趣旨とは「重要な点」を表すので，It is importantで始まる文をチェックすると，It is important for teachers　①　to establish many situations where students can communicate with each other in English（生徒がお互いに英語を使ってコミュニケーションを行うことができる状況を数多く設定する）　②　routinely to conduct classes principally in English（主に英語を使って，授業を行う回数を多くする）　*routinely＝very often *principally＝mainly　③　to devise creative teaching methods so that learners become interested in the importance and necessity of acquiring English（英語を身につけることが重要であるだけでなく，必要でもあることに学習者が関

心を持つように創造的な指導法を考案する）となる。次に第2パラグラフの冒頭を見ると，「こうした指導を効果的に行うには」とあり，①～③は，その目的を達成するための方策である。ここでようやく，第1パラグラフを見ると，出だしは，「『英語を使いこなす』ことができるようになるには」と，一般論で始まっているが，第2段落の冒頭と突合せると，「生徒が『英語を使いこなす』ことができるように教師が指導するには」と読まなければいけないことが分かる。しかも，『英語を使いこなす』が引用符付きなので，特別な意味で使われている。そこで，筆者がどのような意味で『英語を使いこなす』ことを考えているのか，第1パラグラフを見ると，the ability to use English for the purpose of actual communicationとあることから，『実際の場面で人とコミュニケーションできる』ことを指して使っていることが分かる。

すると，第一段落では，「実践的コミュニケーション」の必要性を説き，それを達成するための必要な方策として①～③を挙げていると考えることができる。

【4】(1)　世界は決して，ある与えられたもの，完全に形づくられたもの，そして知覚されることを待つばかりのものとして，われわれの所へやって来るのではない。それはむしろ，獲得されるものなのであって，能動的な過程によって形成されなければならないのである。

(2)　知覚とは，外的な事物として捉え得る抽象的なモデルを現実化の方向に向かわせるものであるといえよう。

〈解説〉(1)　The world does not come to as X; rather, it is an achievement Y.としてみると分かるように，not A but Bの構文が使われている。Xについてみると，givenにaが付いていることから分かるように，品詞は，名詞で，an established situation（COED）を意味する。後に続く，fully formed and waiting to be perceivedは，a givenについて補足説明をしている—a given, which is fully…perceived（すでに確立した存在で，形が完全であり，あとはただ人間が見つけてくれるのを待っているばかりである（存在））と考えてみるとよいだろう。fully…perceivedを脇におくと，「世界は，すでに確立した存在として人間の前に姿を現すのではなく，an achievementである」と読める。not A but Bの対比関係を基にan achievementの意味を考えると，something to be achievedであると推定することができる。つまり，世界とは，「すでに確立している存在」ではなく，「これから未来において獲得されるべき存在」であると筆者は考えているのである。a（n）＋名詞＋制限的関係節という構造では，制限的関係節が「新情報」を表すことが多く，その場合，日本語の処理では，模範解答にあるように，a（n）＋名詞でいったん切って，訳し下げてよい。　(2)　realizing models in the abstract（[抽象的な/理論上の]モデルを実現すること）としてみるとはっきりするように，ofは，意味上，目的語を導いている。thatの先行詞はmodelsである。これは，take models in the abstract for external things（＝believe that models in the abstract are external things：［抽象的な/理論上の］モデルが，われわれの外側に存在する事物と同じである，つまり，われわれの外側に存在する事物を表すと考える）を受身にした文が基になっている。

【5】(1)　エ　　(2)　オ　　(3)　カ　　(4)　ア　　(5)　ウ　　(6)　キ

〈解説〉(1)　B, not Aは，not A but Bの変形で，両者に対比が存在することを示している。ことわざに，The end justifies the means.（目的は手段を正当化する）があるように，meansと対になるendが正解である。

(2)　次の一文は，The knowledge so acquired（このようにして獲得された知識）で始まるので，(2)には，understanding ourselves and our universe（人間とその宇宙についての理解）を希求する意味と関係する名詞が入る。そこから，「企て・計画」を表すenterpriseが正解となる。

(3)　空所の直前のeducatedは「教育を受けた・学識のある」を意味するので，後には，人と関係する名詞が入る。したがって，知性面から見た「人」を表すmindが正解となる。　(4)　inは，make progress in（～の点で上達する）のように「～の点で」を表すことがある。同様に，support decision（-making）inで，「～の点で決断を下すのを支援する」を意味すると予測できる。そこで，決断の対象と関係する名詞を選択肢中に探すと，realm（領域）以外にないので，これが正解となる。(5) 意味上，theoryは，practiceの他に，applicationとも対をなす。たとえば，theoretical linguistics（理論言語学）に対して，applied linguistics（応用言語学）がある。したがって，空所には，applicationが入り，practical applicationで「実際面への応用＞実用化」を表す。 (6) likeは，making measurements: without knowing X＝buying petrol: without owing a carの関係が成立することを表す。すると，ガソリンを買ってもその使い道となる車がなければ無駄になるので，そこから同様の関係を推定すると，測定をしても，その理由や目的がなければ無駄になると判断できる。したがって，(6) には，why you make measurementsから，先行文脈－この場合，主語—の情報を基に復元可能なyou make measurementsを差し引いた，whyの1語が入る。

【6】(1) キ　(2) オ　(3) ア　(4) エ　(5) イ

〈解説〉Aは，冒頭でyour education and experienceと切り出しているので，学歴の話題が先で，職歴が後に来ると予測される。実際，(2)の直前で，And what was your first job after graduation?と発言していることから，(1)がeducationに関係し，(2)～(5)はexperienceに関係することが分かる。これと選択肢を見比べると，カ～クのうちの1つがeducationに関係する(1)に入り，ア～オの5つの選択肢のうちの4つが，残りの空所に入ることも分かる。 (2)～(5)は，すべてBの発言で，自己の職歴について発言していると考えられるので，Youで始まるウが排除される。また，ア・エ・オが過去時制であるのに対して，イのみが現在時制で，現在の仕事について触れている。(5)の前で，Aが，And now you're with CTV…と発言していることから，(5)には，自動的にイが入る。

今度は，意味に着目して考えると，(1)の後で，Bは，That's right,…と答えているので，Aは，疑問詞付き疑問文を使って質問したのではないことが分かる。したがって，キが入る。

残りを解答するに当たっては，reporterとnews presenterとで，後者の地位が上であることは知らなくてもよい。(4)の前で，AがAnd after a year, you were promotedと発言していることから，(2)と(3)は，大学卒業後に1年間従事した仕事に関係する表現が入る。選択肢を見ると，アとオが，語の一部にreportを共通に含むことから，機械的に，(4)にはエが入る。(2)は，first jobの具体的内容を表す表現が入ることから，オが入り，残る(3)にアが入って完成する。

【７】It is extremely important for Japan to promote mutual understanding through international exchange in various fields and public relations activities, and to establish friendly relationships with foreign countries based on mutual trust.

〈解説〉細かい枝葉の部分は後から処理することにして，まず，大きく見通しをつけることが大切である。「『わが国が，相互理解を増進し，友好関係を築くこと』が非常に重要である」という文の骨格を押さえれば，It…to構文を使って，It is [very important/crucial] for Japan to promote mutual understanding and to establish friendly [relations/relationships]. ができる。国際交流（international exchange），相互理解（mutual understanding），相互信頼（mutual trust）など，コミュニケーション分野と深く関連する定型表現は，確実に使いこなせるようになっておきたい。「分野」は，areasも可。「～することを通じて」のように，動詞句を使う場合は，by doingのようにbyが使えるが，名詞句を使って「手段」を表す場合は，throughが自然である。「相互理解を増進し」の部分は，promoteの代わりに，improve, increase, enhance, fosterなども使える。「～に基づいて」の部分は，on the basis ofとすることもできる。「友好関係を築く」の部分は，establishの他に，buildやdevelopも可能である。また，friendlyの代わりに，goodやcloseを選択することも考えられる。

【中学校】

【1】(1) ① 考え方　② 判断力　③ 心情　④ 生活
⑤ 言語　⑥ 尊重　⑦ 国際理解　⑧ 日本人

(2) ○実際に言語を使用して互いの気持ちや考えを伝え合うなどのコミュニケーションを図る活動を行うとともに，言語材料について理解したり練習したりする活動を行うようにすること。　○コミュニケーションを図る活動においては，具体的な場面や状況に合った適切な表現を自ら考えて言語活動ができるようにすること。　○言語活動を行うに当たり，言語の使用場面や言語の働きを取り上げるようにすること。

〈解説〉本問の(1)は，中学校学習指導要領p.97の「指導計画の作成と内容の取り扱い」の(2)で指摘されている（ア)～(ウ）の内容について出題されている。本問の(2)は，中学校学習指導要領p.92の「3学年間を通した全体的な配慮事項」について出題されている。ここで指摘されている（ア)～(ウ）の3点を答えればよい。

【2】(a)（例）・The presence of an ALT in a classroom gives the students a practical and immediate motive to use the language as a means of commuaication.　・Team-teaching provides good learning opportunities for a better understanding of cultural differences for both students and teachers.
・Interactive activities will be carried out more effectively when two teachers are present.　(b)（例）・The teacher should encourage all the members of the group to take part in talking.　・The topic should be easy and specific enough for students to talk about.　・The group size and members should be changed according to the content of the activity.

〈解説〉(a)　ティーム・ティーチングに関連する記述を高等学校学習指導要領で探すと，「また，ネイティブ・スピーカーなどの協力を得て行う授業を積極的に取り入れ，生徒のコミュニケーション能力を育成するとともに，国際理解を深めるようにすること（p.130. p.383)」とある。　(b)　高等学校学習指導要領には，「グループ・ワークなどを適宜取り入れたり（p.130. p.383」とある。いずれの点も，指定が緩やかなことは，地域の特性や現場の創意工夫に基づく「裁量」を比較的多く認めていることを示している。また，本問は，「英語」で書くことが指示されている点に目を向けると，英作文の能力を見ることに重点があると考えられる。どのような視点からの切り口が可能なのか模範解答を繰り返し音読し，参考にしよう。

【高等学校】

【1】① 考え方　② 判断力　③ 心情　④ 生活　⑤ 言語　⑥ 尊重　⑦ 国際理解　⑧ 日本人

〈解説〉本問は，第3款2　(1)（高等学校指導要領のp.129とp.382を参照のこと）の（ア）～（ウ）の内容について出題されている。

【2】○The teacher should encourage all the members of the group to take part in talking.　○The topic should be easy and specific for students to talk about.　○The group size and members should be changed according to the content of the activity.

〈解説〉高等学校学習指導要領には，「グループ・ワークなどを適宜取り入れたり（p.130. p.383」とあるだけで，具体的な指定はない。また，本問は，「英語」で書くことが指示されていることから，内容の当否以上に，英語の表現能力を重視していると考えられる。模範解答を参考にして，①メッセージが明確に伝わること，②（特に初歩的な）語法・文法的ミスを犯さないことを心がけて書こう。

【3】(A)（例）○英語を聞いてその内容を理解するととも，場面や目的に応じて適切に反応する。　○関心のあることについて相手に質問したり，相手の質問に答えたりする。　○情報や考えなどを，場面や目的に応じて適切に伝える。　○聞いたり読んだりして得た情報や自分の考えなどをまとめ，発表する。また，発表されたものを理解する。

（以上より3つ選ぶ）

(B)（例）○英語を聞いて，情報や話し手の意向などを理解したり，概要や要点をとらえたりする。　○英語を読んで，情報や書き手の意向などを理解したり，概要や要点をとらえたりする。　○聞いたり読んだりして得た情報や自分の考えなどについて，話し合ったり意見の交換をしたりする。　○聞いたり読んだりして得た情報や自分の考えなどについて，整理して書く。

（以上より3つ選ぶ）

〈解説〉本問の(A)は，高等学校学習指導要領p.119のオーラル・コミュニケーションIに関して，(1)の言語活動の内容について出題されている。具体的に4点指摘されているので，そのうちの任意の3つを解答すればよい。本問の(B)は，高等学校学習指導要領p.122の英語Iに関して，(1)の言語活動の内容について出題されている。具体的に，4点指摘されているので，そのうちの任意の3つを解答すればよい。

●書籍内容の訂正等について

弊社では教員採用試験対策シリーズ（参考書，過去問，全国まるごと過去問題集），公務員試験対策シリーズ，公立幼稚園・保育士試験対策シリーズ，会社別就職試験対策シリーズについて，正誤表をホームページ（https://www.kyodo-s.jp）に掲載いたします。内容に訂正等，疑問点がございましたら，まずホームページをご確認ください。もし，正誤表に掲載されていない訂正等，疑問点がございましたら，下記項目をご記入の上，以下の送付先までお送りいただくようお願いいたします。

① **書籍名，都道府県（学校）名，年度** （例：教員採用試験過去問シリーズ　小学校教諭 過去問　2025 年度版） ② **ページ数**（書籍に記載されているページ数をご記入ください。） ③ **訂正等，疑問点**（内容は具体的にご記入ください。） （例：問題文では“ア～オの中から選べ”とあるが，選択肢はエまでしかない）

〔ご注意〕

○ 電話での質問や相談等につきましては，受付けておりません。ご注意ください。

○ 正誤表の更新は適宜行います。

○ いただいた疑問点につきましては，当社編集制作部で検討の上，正誤表への反映を決定させていただきます（個別回答は，原則行いませんのであしからずご了承ください）。

●情報提供のお願い

協同教育研究会では，これから教員採用試験を受験される方々に，より正確な問題を，より多くご提供できるよう情報の収集を行っております。つきましては，教員採用試験に関する次の項目の情報を，以下の送付先までお送りいただけますと幸いでございます。お送りいただきました方には謝礼を差し上げます。

（情報量があまりに少ない場合は，謝礼をご用意できかねる場合があります）。

◆あなたの受験された面接試験，論作文試験の実施方法や質問内容

◆教員採用試験の受験体験記

送付先	
	○電子メール：edit@kyodo-s.jp ○FAX：03-3233-1233（協同出版株式会社　編集制作部 行） ○郵送：〒101-0054　東京都千代田区神田錦町2-5 協同出版株式会社　編集制作部 行 ○HP：https://kyodo-s.jp/provision（右記のQRコードからもアクセスできます）

※謝礼をお送りする関係から，いずれの方法でお送りいただく際にも，「お名前」「ご住所」は，必ず明記いただきますよう，よろしくお願い申し上げます。

教員採用試験「過去問」シリーズ

徳島県の
英語科 過去問

編　集　© 協同教育研究会
発　行　令和6年2月10日
発行者　小貫　輝雄
発行所　協同出版株式会社
〒101-0054　東京都千代田区神田錦町2－5
電話　03－3295－1341
振替　東京00190－4－94061
印刷所　協同出版・POD工場

落丁・乱丁はお取り替えいたします。